MW01534205

DIVORCE

The Best Resources To Help You Survive

Rich Wemhoff, Ph.D.
Editor

A Resource Pathways Guidebook

Seattle, Washington

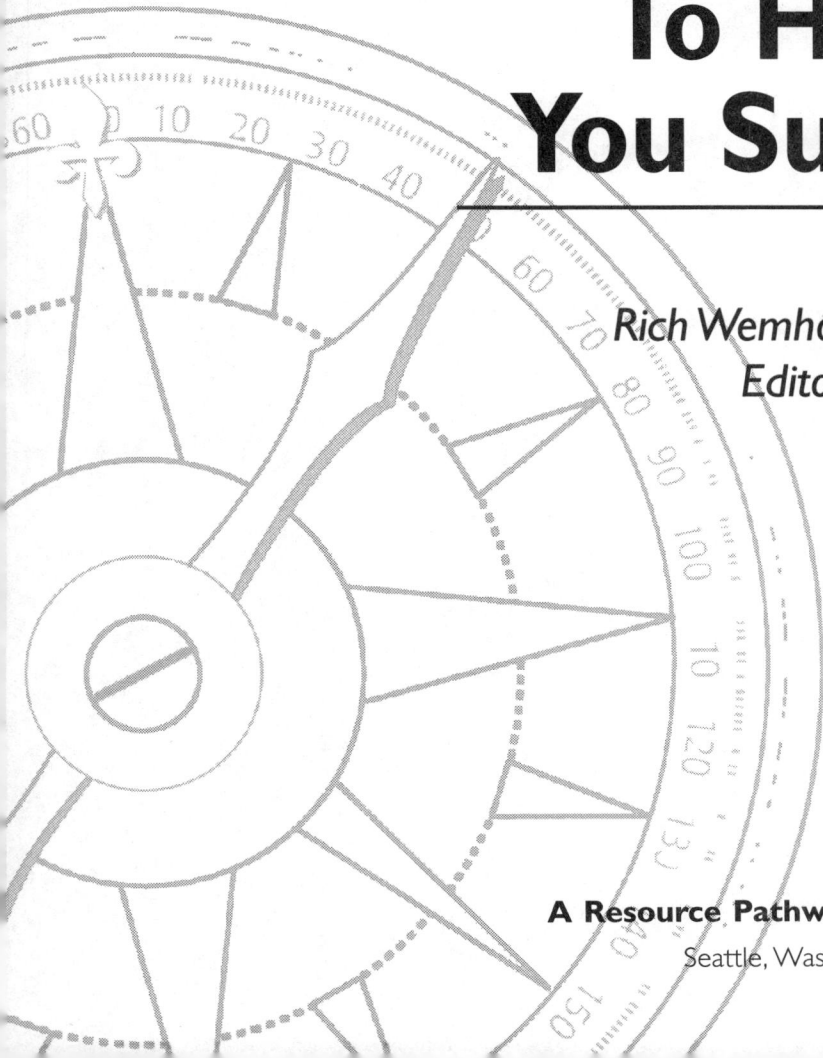

Copyright © 1997 by Resource Pathways, Inc. All rights reserved.

No part of this publication may be reproduced, stored in retrieval systems, or transmitted in any form or by any means, electronic, mechanical, photocopying, recording or otherwise, without the prior written permission of the publisher.

Published by Resource Pathways, Inc.
22525 S.E. 64th Place, Suite 253
Issaquah, WA 98027

Editor: Rich Wemhoff, Ph.D.

Associate Editors and Researchers:
        Mike Osborn, Lillias Bever, Sally Day, Jody Chatalas

Book Design and Production:
        Sandra Harner and Kelly Rush,
        Laing Communications Inc., Redmond, Washington

Printing: Maracle Press, Ltd., Oshawa, Ontario, Canada

Publisher's Cataloging-in-Publication

Wemhoff, Rich.
        Divorce : the best resources to help you survive / edited by
Rich Wemhoff.
        p. cm.
        Includes index.
        ISBN: 0-9653424-2-5

        1. Divorce--United States--Bibliography.   I. Title.

Z7164.M2W46 1998   016.3068'9
                               QBI97-40827

Printed in Canada.

CONTENTS

III. The Single Best Resource For Selected Divorce Topics — 57

INTRODUCTION

I

HOW TO USE THIS GUIDEBOOK

The Trauma Of Divorce

You've heard the statistics:

- Nearly 50% of marriages end in divorce

- The number of divorces annually now exceeds 1,000,000

- 40% of our children are children of a marriage that ended in divorce

Now, you think you're about to contribute to these statistics. You find yourself in the midst of an unanticipated trauma of unbelievable emotional intensity.

Divorce seems at first to be a challenge of overwhelming dimensions. The potential complexities of divorce, overlapping in their effect, in many cases involving unfamiliar legal and financial issues, and all having the potential for tremendous emotional impact, include:

- Negotiation of legal agreements covering the marriage dissolution, division of marital assets, and parenting and support responsibilities for children.

- Acquiring and managing professional resources, possibly including legal representation, financial advisors, and family therapists.

- Dealing with the reality of building a new life, frequently in unfamiliar surroundings.

Our message to you is one of hope and encouragement! This theme is neither naive nor unrealistic, because these challenges, even though seeming to be beyond your present ability to cope, are well within your ability to manage and control once you have learned what you need to know. You **can** make choices to **control** how you react to these challenges and to **influence** how they are ultimately resolved.

There is a growing body of evidence that suggests we've "turned the corner" in how we deal with divorce in our culture. Here are some examples:

- We've evolved from a society having **no** tolerance for divorce (75 years ago), to one of treating divorce as the best solution for

every marital problem (one or two decades ago), to beginning to realize in recent years that divorce is not the best solution in every case and should, if possible, be prevented.

- Virtually all professionals dealing with divorcing couples now talk about divorce being a **process**, a process with stages that both begin and **end**. As a process, divorce can be understood, managed, and survived; as a process, it can produce positive outcomes for the adults and children involved.

- Our treatment of the children of divorce has traveled along a continuum, from dismissing the effect of divorce on children as being unimportant (two decades ago), to today realizing that the effect of a divorce on children of any age is potentially catastrophic and must be fully understood, anticipated, and managed. Shepherding children safely through a divorce has now become the **primary** priority for responsible adults dissolving their marriage!

- In the last decade, mediated settlements (created in a constructive environment managed by a divorce mediator) have grown from being an unknown alternative to being an option virtually **every** divorcing couple should learn about.

Our purpose in creating this guidebook is twofold:

- To help you understand the breadth of issues that you might be facing during your divorce and provide you with the overview you will need to work your way through the various stages of this process called divorce.

- To provide you with a clear "pathway" to the **best** resources available to help you prepare for and manage your positive participation in resolving the issues you will encounter.

How This Book Is Organized

During the course of our ongoing research and analysis, we've identified the best resources to use to understand and cope with each of the principal issues encountered in divorce. We've grouped our recommendations together in Section II of this guidebook: "Divorce: The Best Resources To Help You Survive." Use this section to identify those resources which are best suited to help you understand and manage those elements of divorce that relate to your personal circumstances. We always recommend several resources that we believe can do the job well, so you'll have the freedom to choose resources that are convenient for you to find and that meet your specific requirements.

For those who want to learn about the single best resource we've found to deal with a **specific** topic typically encountered during a divorce, we've grouped a number of outstanding resources together in Section III: "The Single Best Resource For Selected Divorce Topics." Use this section if you've got limited time or a limited budget. In any case we'd encourage you to peruse the recommendations we make in Section II.

Finally, in Section IV we've provided descriptions of "Resources Of Interest To Specific Groups." The two subsets of focus that became apparent during our research were resources for "Women Only" and resources written from a "Christian Perspective." We've provided this separate section to create a "shortcut" to **all** the resources we've found with these areas of focus; we listed them in order of the Overall rating received. Again, we'd encourage you to take the time to learn about those resources we **recommend** in Section II.

This guidebook also contains a complete listing of all the resources we've reviewed, in a section titled "Resource Reviews." In this section, we've organized our full-page reviews by media type, so that those who might be interested in websites on the Internet, for example, can find reviews of all the websites that are focused on the topic of divorce. These reviews are ranked by Overall Star Rating (1-4 Stars) within each media section, so that the best resources are always listed first.

We've also provided a variety of indexes, which list all the resources reviewed in this guidebook alphabetically by title, author, publisher, and subject, so that those who might be interested in a title they've heard about can read our evaluation of that particular resource. Our subject index will be especially useful to those who want to learn about **all** the resources focused on a particular divorce topic.

Finally, let us know how we can improve this Guidebook—use the forms found at the end of this book to send us your ideas and suggestions!

Good luck to you. We know you're out there, struggling to learn and to cope. Take care of yourself and your loved ones, and find comfort in the fact that thousands have gone through this process before you and have created positive outcomes for **all** concerned.

MEET RESOURCE PATHWAYS

As consumers in the Information Age, we all want to take advantage of the many sources of information available to help us make important decisions or deal with major events we experience. Unfortunately, we don't always know where to find these sources of information. Often, we don't know very much about their quality, value, or relevance. In addition, we often don't know much about the issue we've encountered, and as a result don't really know where to begin our learning process.

Resource Pathways' guidebooks solve the problem of "information overload" faced by those who want to learn about a topic of critical importance in their life (like divorce). Consumers interested in doing such research typically:

- Don't know what resources are available, particularly those outside traditional print media.

- Don't know where to find most of those resources, particularly since most bookstores carry only a limited selection.

- Can't assess the quality or focus of those resources **before** spending time and money first finding, then evaluating, and perhaps buying them.

- Don't understand which resources will be particularly useful for each dimension of a multi-dimensional issue. For **each** aspect of the challenge we're trying to deal with, certain resources will be very helpful, while others will be pretty much worthless.

This guidebook, which is focused on the best resources for helping adults and children survive divorce, will help you overcome these hurdles. In this guidebook, you will find that:

- Virtually all available quality resources are reviewed, including those from "high-technology" media like the Internet or CD-ROMs.

- We make a reasoned judgment about the quality of each resource, and decide whether or not a resource should be recommended (only 25% are recommended).

- We define and explain the different issues that are typically encountered in dealing with a divorce, and classify each resource we review according to its primary focus. This helps ensure that you buy or access only the best resource for each aspect of divorce that might be encountered.

- Where to buy or how to access each resource is provided in each review, including ISBN numbers for obscure print media, direct order numbers for publishers, and URL "addresses" for sites on the Internet's World Wide Web.

After you have used this guidebook to learn which sources of information are best suited to help you deal with your particular set of circumstances, you can then acquire or access those resources knowing that your time and money will be well spent.

Our Quality Standards

Those who turn to Resource Pathways guidebooks find the best sources of information on critical issues having an important impact on their lives. To ensure that we merit the trust placed in our recommendations, we've developed a proven set of policies which help ensure that the highest quality standards are met:

- We are independent from the publishers of products we review; we do not accept advertising or compensation of any kind from those companies.

- We employ Advisory Councils of independent professionals with many years of experience in each subject area we cover. These professionals help ensure that we are kept abreast of developments in the field, and that our evaluations meet their standards for accuracy and relevance.

- We review new products and editions as they become available, so that our guidebooks include the most up-to-date information about products available in various media. We revisit websites on the Internet and the online services frequently, to keep up with changes in those offerings as they are introduced.

How We Develop Our Reviews And Recommendations

This guidebook includes our reviews of more than 100 resources that can help you deal with the issues you're likely to encounter in managing your own divorce.

Our Editors and Researchers have found virtually all available sources of information focused on divorce, including books, the Internet, software, CD-ROMs, commercial online services, etc.

We've created a concise, one-page review of each resource. Each review contains information about the resource (author, publisher, edition, etc.), describes the resource's content and focus, evaluates the quality, style, comprehensiveness, and effectiveness of the resource, and summarizes its findings in several ratings (a "1-4 Star" rating system is used). We expand these ratings with written evaluations explaining the rationale behind our ratings and providing guidance on how each source can be best applied. We also provide prices and "where to buy" information for each product.

We put a great deal of time and effort into reviewing and evaluating each resource carefully. Here's what that process includes:

- **Printed Guidebooks:** For these resources, we read the book from cover to cover, identify the particular focus taken by each author, and make a judgment about how the book's contents could be best applied. Our judgment about the relative quality of each source is based upon readability, organization, depth, and style. We make every effort to ensure that the latest editions of books are reviewed, and that no out-of-print resources are included.

- **Internet Websites & Online Services:** We review all websites and online services that have any significant amount of original material related to the subject of divorce. Our reviews include judgments about the site's graphic and navigation design, as well as the usefulness of material provided relative to that available in other media. We revisit sites frequently to stay abreast of changes and improvements.

- **CD-ROM & Software:** We carefully review each facet of each CD, including all branches and multimedia options, and thoroughly test software applications available on disk. Our reviews include judgments about the "cost/benefit" of multimedia additions, as well as the usefulness of the content provided relevant to the same offering in other media by the same publisher. We note technical problems in loading or using programs provided.

Because our mission is to help you find your way through this "forest" of information, we also provide you with our recommendations on which resources are best to help you each step of the way (only 25% of the resources we review are recommended). Our recommendations are based upon our judgment of value, not only relative to alternatives in the same media, but against all available sources regardless of media.

DIVORCE: THE BEST RESOURCES TO HELP YOU SURVIVE

II

INTRODUCTION

This section provides you with our recommendations for resources we think you will find particularly helpful as you learn about the process of divorce and begin to deal with different components of that process. During the course of our ongoing research and analysis, we've classified the resources we've encountered into **nine subject areas**, starting with resources which provide a useful overview of the divorce process, and ending with those resources which we think will be useful primarily to divorce counseling professionals. A particularly important subject area is resources focused on children of divorce; we've further divided those resources into those written for parents, and those written for children (in three age categories).

For each of these subject areas, our editor and researchers have picked the **best** 25% (roughly 1 in 4), and recommended those as resources you should use. Each subject area includes our introduction to the subject and an explanation of its importance. In making these recommendations, we have attempted to err on the side of providing too many choices rather than too few. In some cases we have recommended additional sources to broaden representation from different media. Take some time to read the full descriptions and evaluations for each recommended source carefully; we're certain that you will discover the right resources to best serve your needs.

Remember that we provide several other "views" of the resources we've reviewed. First, in Section III, we provide our recommendations for the single best resource dealing with one particular issue or question encountered during the divorce process; this section will be useful for those having limited time or limited budget, or for whom a single resource meets an urgent personal need. In Section IV, we've grouped all the resources we've found which encompass a **"Christian"** perspective and those which are focused on support for **women**; if either of these perspectives appeals to you, you should examine those resources closely (they are listed in order of Overall rating). Finally, we've created a number of helpful indexes at the back of this guidebook, by title, principal subject focus, author, and publisher—here, you can find a list of all resources we've reviewed.

I.

GAINING AN

UNDERSTANDING

OF DIVORCE

ISSUES IN

GENERAL

Every family experiences traumatic events; as members of a family we are all affected by them. In some families the traumatic events take the form of a major move, a financial crisis, members leaving the home, or wrestling with addictions. For all families, death—whether expected or not—is traumatic. The death of a marital relationship and the divorce which results has become an all-too-common traumatic event in our culture. But, unlike some other traumas, we know that divorce is an extended **process** which has far-reaching ramifications for all involved, whether they be adult or child.

If you are experiencing divorce for the first time (or even if this is a second or third divorce), and are in the initial stages of that divorce, you may well be feeling emotions of unimagined intensity. These feelings generally correspond to your role in the marital relationship which is ending. Each divorce generally has a "leaver" (one who is opting to leave the marriage) and one who is "left" (who wants the marital relationship to continue). For the "leaver," there are usually intense feelings of guilt, a burden which can only be worked through in pain and with constant reassurances from himself/herself and others that this major step is in the best interests of everyone. For the person who is "left," there is often more observable and longer lasting trauma than if the "leaver" had suddenly died, for the "leaver" is not only very much alive, but is often involved in another relationship.

So, you find yourself reaching out for help but feeling overwhelmed by the task of finding resources to help you understand the process of divorce and deal with the impact it is having and will have on you, your spouse, and your children. As the divorce rate has increased, self-help resources dedicated to helping you understand and cope with divorce have experienced similar growth. The principal benefit of this book is to help match your specific needs with the rich variety of resources that have been created to help you.

The resources recommended in this section have a predominant theme, the theme of **hope**. Not surprisingly, many of the creators of the resources available to you are themselves divorced and have "walked your walk." Along with helping you to realize that you can survive this trauma called divorce, these resources help you to realize that divorcing is a **process** that has identifiable stages. Although these stages may vary in name and number from resource to resource, they each portray three fundamental facts:

- Divorce involves a disintegration of the relationship as we have experienced it

- A breakup of the family unit will occur, with far-reaching consequences for both adults and children that must be understood and dealt with

• Recovery from that breakup and its aftereffects is possible, provided we take affirmative steps to heal ourselves and our children

What is important to remember is that these stages are **stages**, with a beginning and an end. As such, it is possible to move through them in a positive way. Conversely, you and/or your former spouse can become "stuck," with potentially destructive results for yourself and each other. You'll find that the resources we've recommended emphasize self-care (taking control of how you react to what happens to you) on all levels: emotional, physical, psychological, and spiritual.

Besides caring for yourself, many of the resources recommended in this section address the critical issue of how to care for your children as you go through the divorce process. Because there is so much attention being paid to this aspect of divorce, another section of this book also makes recommendations on resources which are specifically focused on this topic. Likewise, many of the resources recommended here can also help you begin thinking about the financial and legal aspects of divorce, with another section of this book identifying the best of those resources which address these topics in more depth.

The resources you'll read about in the following pages will help you:

• With your decision to divorce

• Manage the divorce process for you and your loved ones

• Heal yourself throughout the process

• Experience new beginnings

Take the time to read each full review so that you can identify the resources most suitable for you and your present needs.

Title:	**How To Survive The Loss Of A Love**
Overall Rating:	★★★★
Media Type:	Print
Author/Editor:	M. Colgrove Ph.D; H. Bloomfied M.D; P. McWilliams
Short Description:	A very popular self-help book, this book has four sections: "Understanding Loss," "Surviving," "Healing," "Growing." The latter three sections are divided into "days," each "day" having its own meditative thoughts and poetic words of self care.

Read The Full Review Of This Resource On Page 90.

Title:	**Growing Through Divorce**
Overall Rating:	★★★★
Media Type:	Print
Author/Editor:	Jim Smoke
Short Description:	This text focusing on getting through divorce, and reflects the author's Christian values and perspective. Text is presented in two parts, beginning with chapters focusing on the broader aspects of surviving divorce and ending with an intensive, 100 page workbook that may be used as a basis of discussion groups.

Read The Full Review Of This Resource On Page 98.

1. Gaining An Understanding Of Divorce Issues In General

Title:	**Crazy Time**
Subtitle:	Surviving Divorce & Building A New Life
Overall Rating:	★★★★
Media Type:	Print
Author/Editor:	Abigail Trafford
Short Description:	A popular text in its second edition, this book has three sections dealing with "Crisis" (stages leading to the divorce decision), "Crazy Time" (the divorce and its emotional aftermath), and the longest, "Recovery" (focused on emergence of self, sex, love, remarriage, etc.). Each chapter uses anecdotal experiences of couples to illustrate and the author's observations, insights, and suggestions.

Read The Full Review Of This Resource On Page 114.

Title:	**The Complete Divorce Recovery Handbook**
Overall Rating:	★★★
Media Type:	Print
Author/Editor:	John P. Splinter
Short Description:	This book contains a primarily Christian approach to handling divorce and recovery, divided into chapters outlining progressive stages of the divorce process; each chapter focuses on a particular psychological or spiritual issue, ending with questions, activities, and selected readings from the Bible to further understanding.

Read The Full Review Of This Resource On Page 138.

2

TAKING STEPS TO PREVENT DIVORCE

Some of the most dramatic changes in our American culture during the last three decades have been in our attitudes about, and our practice of divorce. In the beginning of this century, when our great grandparents or grandparents were marrying, divorce was just not an option. In the rare cases in which it took place, it was viewed either as a moral transgression or as the result of a sordid "fault" (adultery, abuse, or addiction).

Since that time, however, profound transformations affecting our society's attitudes have taken place. These changes included our industrial revolution, which took the husband and, in more recent years, the wife out of the home; the changing moral attitudes toward family dissolution; the perception that personal fulfillment must be one of the essential—if not the most essential—criteria for staying in a marriage. As a result, our divorce rate began to rise sharply (especially during the 1960s), and had doubled by 1975. Today, one half of us who marry can expect to be divorced and, if we enter into a second marriage, our "success" rate is even lower.

As we near the end of this century, however, many persons are concerned about this negative trend. Divorce, they say, is too easy in our society and is too readily chosen as the solution for one's unhappiness and/or lack of fulfillment. Also, they note, divorce is not just an event, but is a process whose effects continue throughout the lives of those who divorce and the lives of their children. Some of these professionals have created books reviewed in this section. They are primarily therapists and teachers whose work focuses on married and divorcing couples.

Many in these professions, especially the psychotherapeutic profession, are reflecting this more recent shift in our collective attitude towards divorce. Whereas divorce was quickly offered as the solution for marital discord in the recent past, today the literature of the profession resonates with encouragement for the therapist who helps troubled couples explore whether divorce is truly their **best** choice and fully understand its ramifications for themselves and their children before they proceed.

If you are wondering whether or not to divorce, or if you are looking for ways to strengthen a rocky marriage, you have numerous resources available to you. They are meant to help you to take a proactive role in saving your marriage. As you might expect, some of these resources have a Christian foundation, reflecting the Biblical attitude toward divorce. Common themes found throughout these resources encourage couples to:

- Develop skills for dealing with relationships problems (communication and conflict resolution skills)

2. Taking Steps To Prevent Divorce

- Identify issues at the core of the marriage conflict

- Define and practice methods for enhancing their relationship and improving their marriage

If divorcing is still just an option for you, or if you are looking for ways to strengthen your marriage, acquire and read (hopefully, both you and your spouse) one or more of the resources recommended on the following pages. Each of these resources can help you diagnose what's wrong and give you a helpful perspective on your marriage and relating to each other. Either way—choosing to remain married in a healthier way, or to divorce—are decisions which should not be taken lightly. You want to make the right choice for yourself and your family, and these resources can help you to make informed choices, find better ways of relating and, perhaps, even prevent your divorce.

2. Taking Steps To Prevent Divorce

Title:	**Divorce Busting**
Overall Rating:	★★★★
Media Type:	Print
Author/Editor:	Michele Weiner-Davis, M.S.W.
Short Description:	The purpose of this book is to help couples stay together in their marriage rather than to divorce. It consists of two major sections: the first offers a rationale for couples staying together and working things out; the second describes marriage-enriching, divorce preventing techniques that couples can use to improve their marriage.

Read The Full Review Of This Resource On Page 91.

Title:	**Fighting for Your Marriage**
Subtitle:	Positive Steps For Preventing Divorce and Preserving A Lasting Love
Overall Rating:	★★★★
Media Type:	Print
Author/Editor:	Howard Markman, Scott Stanley, Susan L. Blumberg
Short Description:	This book is for those who want to improve their relationship, and it is a proponent of the PREP (Prevention and Relationship Enhancement Program) approach. It covers a broad range of relationship issues and techniques for dealing with them; its three main sections are: Handling Conflict (techniques for managing disagreement), Core Issues (topics like expectations and commitment), and Enhancement (looks at the long term).

Read The Full Review Of This Resource On Page 106.

2. Taking Steps To Prevent Divorce

Title: **Saving Your Marriage Before It Starts**

Subtitle: Seven Questions To Ask Before (And After) You Marry

Overall Rating: ★★★★

Media Type: Print

Author/Editor: Dr. Les Parrott III and Dr. Leslie Parrott

Short Description: Written by Les and Leslie Parrott, a husband and wife team who are also co-directors of the Center for Relationship Development at Seattle Pacific University, this book introduces the "seven principles for happy marriages" with anecdotes, specific advice and techniques, and reflective exercises for each chapter. The authors believe that an awareness of these seven principles before (and after) couples marry can help create a healthy marriage.

Read The Full Review Of This Resource On Page 121.

Title: **Why Marriages Succeed Or Fail**

Subtitle: And How You Can Make Yours Last

Overall Rating: ★★★★

Media Type: Print

Author/Editor: John Gottman, PH.D. with Nan Silver

Short Description: This book is a compilation of anecdotal experiences and sound advice drawn from an extensive study of communication styles of couples. Three interaction patterns from successful relationships the author calls, "The Good, The Bad, and the Volatile" are presented with some surprising revelations. Healthy communication patterns are offered.

Read The Full Review Of This Resource On Page 122.

3.

UNDERSTANDING AND DEALING WITH THE IMPACT OF DIVORCE ON CHILDREN

Divorcing adults must deal with traumatic changes as they uncouple and begin their lives apart from each other. Many adults later report that they experienced new growth and personal healing which would not have been possible for them had they not decided to divorce. At the time, though, it was excruciatingly painful; if children were involved in the divorce, the effect of the divorce was felt by them too, with much the same severity.

Resources which have been developed to help you with your divorce invariably offer counsel and guidance on helping your children survive your divorce. Most of these sources offer advice focused on:

- How to tell your children about your plans to divorce

- How to prevent them from believing that they are the **cause** of the divorce

- How to provide them a safe and predictable environment following the separation.

Managing these three elements successfully will help your children make it through the various stages of your divorce with a better chance of minimizing its harmful long-term effects.

Just twenty ago, some published works fostered the message that children of divorce were **not** more likely to have emotional problems later in life than children whose parents had not divorced. In the past twenty years, however, the work of Wallenstein and others (most recently, the reported studies of Julia Lewis) has helped us understand more completely the long range effects of divorce on children. One conclusion of this research is sobering: for children, divorce is **not** a short term crisis; it has **long-term** effects. For many children of divorce, there are intense feelings of abandonment. Consequently, as adults, some find it difficult to commit to relationships, evidence a higher rate of divorce than the general population, have a higher rate of drug and alcohol abuse, and do less well academically. Even with these recent findings, the debate goes on: which is better for the child: to have divorced parents who are civil with each other, or to grow up in an unhappy home where the parents are staying married "for the sake of the children?"

Whatever the final answer to that question, it must be noted that not **every** child of divorce becomes a reclusive, underachieving person prone to drug and alcohol abuse. In fact, your child will have less chance of suffering negative long-term effects from your divorce, because of you and what you are doing right now to identify resources that will be helpful to you and your child. And, as you will learn, there are excellent resources to help you do the best for your child. If you select them wisely, they will be of invaluable assistance.

3. Understanding And Dealing With The Impact Of Divorce On Children

What immediately follows are the resources written for you as an **adult** in dealing with your child as he/she experiences the divorce with you. You should choose from that list the resource or resources most helpful to you.

Because children respond to divorce differently at different stages of their development, we also provide recommendations in this section for resources for children to read (or have read to them). We've divided our recommendations according to these age groupings: **preschool**, **ages 6-12**, and **children 13+**. Some of these resources are meant to be used by the child alone; others are meant to be used by the two of you together as interactive communications tools. What is extremely important for you to remember is that a preschooler's needs when experiencing divorce are quite different from a teenager's concerns. The resources reviewed will not only allow you to realize that, but will provide you and your children with appropriate and helpful tools.

3. Understanding And Dealing With The Impact Of Divorce On Children

Title:	**Helping Children Cope With Separation And Loss**
Overall Rating:	★★★★
Media Type:	Print
Author/Editor:	Claudia Jewett Jarratt
Short Description:	Written by a respected child and family therapist, this 232-page book serves as a guide for parents, therapists, and other caregivers who wish to help children move through the stages of grief and loss. Ways of identifying and dealing with children's grief reactions are found here, as well as creative methods to help children give voice to their feelings at all stages of the grief process.

Read The Full Review Of This Resource On Page 94.

Title:	**Helping Children Survive Divorce**
Subtitle:	What To Expect; How To Help
Overall Rating:	★★★★
Media Type:	Print
Author/Editor:	Archibald D. Hart, Ph.D.
Short Description:	Straightforward advice by a psychologist focusing on the effects of divorce on children including the parents' role in guiding their offspring through the process; emphasis on helping parents recognize the stresses on children and how the quality of their own recovery influences that of the entire family. A study guide explores ideas presented in the text.

Read The Full Review Of This Resource On Page 104.

3. Understanding And Dealing With The Impact Of Divorce On Children

Title:	**Parents Book About Divorce**
Overall Rating:	★★★★
Media Type:	Print
Author/Editor:	Richard A. Gardner
Short Description:	This is a thorough, psychologically-based exploration of children's issues in divorce written primarily for parents interested in more than "self-help," and useful also for professionals working in the field.

Read The Full Review Of This Resource On Page 110.

Title:	**Helping Children Cope With Divorce**
Overall Rating:	★★★★
Media Type:	Print
Author/Editor:	Edward Teyber
Short Description:	This is a guide for divorced parents who seek to understand their children's perspectives about divorce, and to develop effective parenting strategies. Issues discussed include children's anxieties and concerns, guidelines for parents on how to respond to those concerns, custody arrangements, cooperating with an ex-spouse, and child-rearing practices and discipline.

Read The Full Review Of This Resource On Page 119.

3. Understanding And Dealing With The Impact Of Divorce On Children

Title:	**Let's Talk About It: Divorce**
Overall Rating:	★★★
Media Type:	Print
Author/Editor:	Fred Rogers
Short Description:	Mr. Rogers' book encourages discussion between children and their parents. In its 30 pages, this book introduces topics and feelings brought about by divorce. The text provides easily understood statements to encourages discussion between parents and their preschool children. Each page includes a corresponding color photograph.

Read The Full Review Of This Resource On Page 137.

Title:	**Mom And Dad Don't Live Together Anymore**
Overall Rating:	★★★
Media Type:	Print
Author/Editor:	Kathy Stinson; Nancy Reynolds (Illustrator)
Short Description:	This storybook focuses on helping the child adjust to the period just after separation when the parents live in separate homes. It is a popular text in its tenth printing that is written with a focus on expression of feelings and opening lines of communication between parent and child.

Read The Full Review Of This Resource On Page 156.

3. Understanding And Dealing With The Impact Of Divorce On Children

Written For Children Ages 6-12

Title:	**Dinosaurs Divorce**
Subtitle:	A Guide For Changing Families
Overall Rating:	★★★★
Media Type:	Print
Author/Editor:	Laurene Krasny Brown and Marc Brown
Short Description:	An award winning, brightly illustrated description of divorce and its effects, written for children. The contents of this book include such items as "divorce words and what they mean," "why parents divorce," "living with one parent," "telling your friends," "meeting parents' new friends," and "having stepsisters and stepbrothers."

Read The Full Review Of This Resource On Page 92.

Title:	**Divorce Workbook**
Subtitle:	An Interactive Guide for Kids and Families
Overall Rating:	★★★★
Media Type:	Print
Author/Editor:	S. B. Ives, Ph.D.; D. Fassler, M.D.; & M. Lash, M.Ed., A.T.R.
Short Description:	An interactive workbook for young children that focuses on providing information about divorce and getting the child actively involved in the healing process. The child is invited to participate in group discussion, as well as, encouraged to write and draw on the pages of the workbook. A guide for parents, teachers and counselors.

Read The Full Review Of This Resource On Page 96.

3. Understanding And Dealing With The Impact Of Divorce On Children

Written For Children Ages 6-12

Title: **It's Not The End Of The World**

Overall Rating: ★★★★

Media Type: Print

Author/Editor: Judy Blume

Short Description: This is a short novel for teens telling the story of Karen Newman, a girl whose parents are getting a divorce. Karen tells of her trials and adventures, thoughts and feelings, as she chronicles the days leading up to and away from her parents' separation, and the beginning of a new, and very different, family life.

Read The Full Review Of This Resource On Page 97.

3. Understanding And Dealing With The Impact Of Divorce On Children

Written For Children Ages 13+

Title:	**When Divorce Hits Home**
Subtitle:	Keeping Yourself Together When Your Family Comes Apart
Overall Rating:	★★★★
Media Type:	Print
Author/Editor:	Beth Joselow and Thea Joselow
Short Description:	A 235-page book written for children of divorce from a teenager's perspective. Includes 50 short chapters about different feelings and situations a teenager may experience as a result of his/her parents' separation. Each chapter includes a summary of its main points and illustrative real-life accounts from teenagers.

Read The Full Review Of This Resource On Page 99.

Title:	**Blue Sky Butterfly**
Overall Rating:	★★★★
Media Type:	Print
Author/Editor:	Jean Van Leeuwen
Short Description:	In this novel, Twig, a middle school-aged girl, is experiencing the fallout of her parents' recent divorce. She is angry at her father, frustrated by her mother's behavior, and wants her family to return to "normal". Her grandmother visits and sparks the family into action. Twig's mom builds a garden which provides a backdrop for the personal growth the family experiences.

Read The Full Review Of This Resource On Page 107.

<table>
<tr><td>

**3. Understanding
And Dealing With
The Impact Of
Divorce On Children**

</td><td align="right">

Written For Children Ages 13+

</td></tr>
</table>

Title:	**How It Feels When Parents Divorce**
Overall Rating:	★★★★
Media Type:	Print
Author/Editor:	Jill Krementz
Short Description:	This 115-page book describes divorce as told through the stories of nineteen children ranging in age from 7-16, and as seen through the many photographs of these children, their homes and families, that accompany each story.

Read The Full Review Of This Resource On Page 113.

Title:	**How To Survive Your Parents' Divorce**
Overall Rating:	★★★
Media Type:	Print
Author/Editor:	Nancy O'Keefe Bolick
Short Description:	This is a unique book, directed at teenaged children, about how other young people have handled divorce. It is composed as a series of stories, each illustrating a particular issue raised by divorce, It ends with a brief chapter summing up the techniques and activities teenagers themselves have found most helpful.

Read The Full Review Of This Resource On Page 139.

4.

DEALING WITH CHILD CUSTODY ISSUES AND AGREEMENTS

When two parents divorce, their marriage ends but their parenting continues! Within the last several years, through research by experts in the field and observations of professionals working with children of divorce, we have come to know how important that statement is. While the **mode** of the parenting changes because both parents are no longer living together, parenting **must** continue in a different form.

Researchers have helped us to grow beyond the myth that children of divorce are "resilient" and will actually "do fine" once their conflicting parents are apart. Rather, divorcing parents **must** make informed judgments in the best interest of the child regarding where and with whom each child lives, and how they are to remain connected with **both** parents.

Unfortunately, emotionally-charged scenes can take place between divorcing parents, having potentially disastrous ramifications for the child both in childhood and in later life. These scenes generally contain one or more of the following elements:

- The child feels caught in the middle between two conflicting parents

- The child feels he/she is a burden to one or the other of the parents because many arguments seem to be about him/her

- The parenting plan is inflexible and does not take into account the changing needs of the child as he/she grows and matures

- Gradually, contact with one of the parents is lost (usually the father)

What both parents must realize is that "winning a battle" is **not** important. Rather, the best interests of the child must remain of paramount importance throughout the divorce process. Each child needs clarity, consistency, peace, and a feeling of being treasured by both parents. Decisions about custody need to reflect primarily those needs of the child, not those of the parents.

As the resources recommended on the following pages point out, the term "joint custody" can be a confusing term for parents. What the term means legally is that the parents have agreed to share in the major decisions affecting the child's life (education, living arrangements, health care, religious affiliation, etc.). A couple can have "joint" custody even with the child living almost exclusively in the home of the one parent and visiting the other parent. More recently, another term has come into usage: "joint physical custody;" this term refers to custody in which the child is physically living in two different homes (in most instances, time is not split 50/50 between the parents).

4. Dealing With Child Custody Issues And Agreements

From the research that has been done, an effective parenting and custody plan should include the following elements:

- The child's connection with both biological parents in his/her life should continue, and these relationships should be enhanced as much as possible

- The losses which occur for a child going through the divorce of parents should be minimized as much as possible (loss of home, neighborhood, friends, school, teachers, clubs, extended family members, baby-sitters, etc.)

- Any parenting and/or custody arrangement should recognize the developmental age of the child. If the plan for a four-year old is still in place when the child is fourteen, something is quite wrong.

In the pages that follow, we've recommended a number of resources to help you to establish a plan to best care for your child and his/her needs. Take time to carefully select the best resource for you. Share it with your former spouse, the parent of your child. Above all, remember: **the child's welfare is all-important; "winning" is not.**

4. Dealing With Child Custody Issues And Agreements

Title:	**Mom's House, Dad's House**
Subtitle:	Making Shared Custody Work
Overall Rating:	★★★★
Media Type:	Print
Author/Editor:	Isolina Ricci
Short Description:	Written by a "recognized pioneer in the field of counseling, mediation, and education for divorced families," this book focuses on the issue of child custody, providing advice and guidance for creating healthy, workable, "blended" families.

Read The Full Review Of This Resource On Page 102.

Title:	**Child Custody**
Subtitle:	Building Parenting Agreements that Work
Overall Rating:	★★★★
Media Type:	Print
Author/Editor:	Mimi E. Lyster
Short Description:	This book supports the creation of parenting agreements, arrangements for parenting separately and making child custody positive. These agreements include factors such as taking care of the children, making decisions on their behalf, and meeting their needs. A good portion of the book is devoted to formulating the agreement, and it has a 20-page skeleton to work from. Other topics include: negotiation, mediation and custody laws.

Read The Full Review Of This Resource On Page 108.

4. Dealing With Child Custody Issues And Agreements

Title:	**Children of Divorce**
Subtitle:	A Developmental Approach To Residence And Visitation
Overall Rating:	★★★★
Media Type:	Print
Author/Editor:	Mitchell Baris, Ph.D.; Carla Garrity, Ph.D.
Short Description:	Written by two psychologists who have functioned as custody mediators and as expert witnesses on behalf of children, the aim of the book is to help divorcing parents make informed choices concerning residence and visitation for their children. Specific guidelines are offered based on the age of the child.

Read The Full Review Of This Resource On Page 115.

5.

UNDERSTANDING THE FINANCIAL ASPECTS OF DIVORCE

Roughly half of our marriages end in divorce, some after many years together. When partners in a marriage make the decision to pursue a divorce, the single largest impact is an emotional one, felt immediately and the focus of a sustained healing effort for years to come.

Why make that healing process more difficult by having an unfair or unnecessarily complex legal and financial separation? Clearly, being able to focus on potentially complex legal and financial issues is **most** difficult when the emotionally shattering decision to divorce has just been made. Nonetheless, agreeing to dissolve a marriage sets in motion a process that has a potentially profound impact on each spouse's subsequent financial well-being. There is no luxury of time when these issues are being decided; each spouse must take the initiative to understand and take control of the issues that seem routine to the lawyers, accountants, and judges who deal with them day-to-day. Coming to grips with these issues simply **must** be done, if one is to stay in control of one's divorce and its financial aftereffects.

Clearly, when coming to grips with the financial aspects of divorce, the size of the challenge facing us depends somewhat on:

- How much involvement each spouse has had in the couple's financial affairs; the less involvement, the more important it is to get informed, quickly, in order to protect your interests in the negotiations that will follow.

- How sizable the marital assets are and how those assets are currently held; the more assets there are, the more complex the potential pitfalls.

- Whether children are involved; if there are children, then their future well-being must be protected.

- To what degree the divorce will be amicable versus contentious; the higher the antagonism between partners, the higher becomes the potential for one partner not dealing fairly with the other and the more important it becomes to be able to negotiate knowledgeably.

The financial issues that divorcing partners may have to deal with include:

- Disposition of joints accounts, to protect assets and limit one's exposure to joint liabilities (debts).

- Compiling necessary records and understanding the nature of the marital assets.

- Projecting and funding cash flow requirements for two separate households, including alimony and child support.

**5. Understanding
The Financial
Aspects Of Divorce**

- Funding a plan for future financial commitments (college educations for children, medical and life insurance, etc.), including disposition of retirement benefits.

- Minimizing and balancing immediate and future tax liabilities between the partners; these liabilities can be sizable, unanticipated, and unfairly burdensome to one or the other partner if not identified and dealt with in advance.

- For those couples owning a home (possibly their principal asset), wrestling with the difficult decision of keeping or selling the home (sometimes necessary to fund a settlement).

- Assessing and dividing business and personal assets and liabilities (debts).

- In the case of a contentious divorce, defining negotiation and settlement objectives and strategies in advance of formal legal proceedings.

Overwhelming? Seems like it, particularly for adults who've not been focused on household financial issues in the past. Fortunately, there are some really helpful resources available to help divorcing adults both **understand** and **gain control** of these and other financial aspects of divorce. In some cases, these resources may be all a couple needs to construct the most important elements of a fair settlement agreement. In other cases, where settlement of property and assets are likely to be negotiated, these same resources can serve to help a spouse make informed decisions that protect his or her best interests.

We've recommended several resources in the pages that follow. Some of these resources provide objective instructions without regard to gender, while others are somewhat more focused on the woman's perspective. Most are written by experienced lawyers, tax attorneys, or financial planners who have specialized in helping couples work their way through the financial consequences of divorce. We've worked hard to select those most accessible to the typical adult wrestling with these issues for the first time.

Read the full-page reviews for each of these recommended resources to discover which are best suited in tone and focus to your particular needs and circumstances.

5. Understanding The Financial Aspects Of Divorce

Title:	**Divorce & Money**
Subtitle:	How To Make The Best Financial Decisions During Divorce
Overall Rating:	★★★★
Media Type:	Print
Author/Editor:	V. Woodhouse, J.D., CFP and V. F. Collins, Ph.D., CFP
Short Description:	This is a detailed financial resource book outlining money management decisions/process, from separation to divorce. Its focus is on viewing divorce as a business process and equitable sharing of assets as the result of careful planning. In its third edition, this text covers such divorce-related topics as dividing debts and obtaining a fair settlement, to planning financially for your future.

Read The Full Review Of This Resource On Page 109.

Title:	**Survival Manual For Women In Divorce**
Subtitle:	182 Questions and Answers
Overall Rating:	★★★
Media Type:	Print
Author/Editor:	Carol Ann Wilson & Edwin Schilling III
Short Description:	This book, written by an attorney and financial consultant, provides answers to many of the most often asked questions women have when separating or divorcing. Some of the many topics discussed include finding an attorney, court processes, child custody, property division, and tax responsibilities.

Read The Full Review Of This Resource On Page 147.

5. Understanding The Financial Aspects Of Divorce

Title:	**Resolving Divorce Issues**
Subtitle:	Heed "Warning Signals" And The Misdeeds Of Spouse
Overall Rating:	★★
Media Type:	Print
Author/Editor:	Holmes F. Crouch
Short Description:	This is a guide to tax issues in divorce, complete with chapter summaries, charts, and diagrams, intended to be read by divorcing taxpayers for advice in such issues as avoiding hidden tax traps in child support, alimony, and property settlement, and the advantages and disadvantages to filing separately and jointly.

Read The Full Review Of This Resource On Page 165.

6.

UNDERSTANDING THE LEGAL ASPECTS OF DIVORCE

For many adults, making the decision to seek a divorce will involve them in significant legal proceedings for the first time in their life. Unfortunately, the months or years leading to a decision to dissolve a marriage are at best full of stress and at worst an overwhelming emotional catastrophe—not the best time to begin a forced "seminar" on legal agreements, lawyers, negotiations, and the like!

Our advice to you is to slow down a bit, if you can. **There is time** to learn what you need to know about the spectrum of potential legal issues that might be encountered during divorce. There is time to consider mediation (see our next chapter) or negotiate the necessary agreements amicably (most divorce agreements are negotiated, not litigated in court). There is time, if the right decision for you is to engage an attorney, to carefully evaluate alternatives before settling on one to work with. There is adequate time to learn about the financial aspects of divorce, and to understand how property settlements fit into the array of legal issues you'll encounter (see our previous chapter).

A number of legal agreements (each governed by state law) addressing one or more of these issues might be necessary during the process of completing a divorce:

- Legal separation, intended primarily to govern the actions and protect the interests of the parties to the divorce. The agreement may also specify financial support to be paid during the period of separation or child visitation rights.

- Division of marital property and debts acquired during the marriage. Non-marital property (brought into the marriage and maintained separately) is typically not included. Some states simplify the division of marital property through provisions for a 50/50 or otherwise "equitable" distribution.

- In many marriages, the family home is the principal financial asset and agreement must be reached on which partner, if any, will continue to live in the home, and if the home is to be sold, when and how proceeds and accompanying tax liability will be divided. Family-owned businesses can be the focus of even more complex agreements.

- Alimony (payments from one spouse to another) are awarded on the basis of spousal need and the ability of the other spouse to pay, and can be of several types and duration (temporary, permanent, lump-sum, etc.).

- Financial support for children, with a starting point typically set by state guidelines (specifying a percentage of the supporting party's income to be paid). Support for college education may be part of this agreement.

- Sole or joint child custody, which specifies visitation rights, the right to make major decisions about the child or children, and other rights and duties.

This list of issues is clearly intimidating to the average adult unfamiliar with working with lawyers and with the negotiation process! While the dissolution of some marriages can proceed quickly (little marital property, no-fault state, no children), some marriages, particularly where minor children or significant marital property are involved, can require complex agreements and seemingly endless negotiations over tedious details.

Take the time to acquire and read carefully one or more of the resources we recommend on the following pages. Each of these resources can help you gain an understanding of the general legal issues involved in your divorce; each can help you prepare to resolve those issues successfully. Most provide advice on how to select an attorney. Some provide more emphasis on one or more of these issues.

Most important, take the time to read the full reviews of each recommended resource before you spend time or money to acquire it (many are available from libraries); that way, you'll be assured that you're using the resource that **best** matches up with your particular set of circumstances.

Title:	**American Bar Association Guide To Family Law**
Subtitle:	The Complete And Easy Guide To The Laws Of Marriage, Parenthood, Separation And Divorce
Overall Rating:	★★★★
Media Type:	Print
Author/Editor:	Jeff Atkinson
Short Description:	This 179-page book gives its reader an overview of the laws which affect the family, from marriage to parenthood to divorce. It has sections on division of property, custody and visitation, and the legal process. Other subjects addressed include divorce in general, the stresses of divorce, steps marriage counselors uses to improve marriage, prenuptial agreements, alimony, and child support.

Read The Full Review Of This Resource On Page 100.

Title:	**The Divorce Sourcebook**
Overall Rating:	★★★
Media Type:	Print
Author/Editor:	Dawn Bradley Berry, J.D.
Short Description:	This text draws on the author's legal expertise and the wisdom of other experts in the field to offer information and advice in understanding and making correct choices on legal, emotional, financial, and ethical issues that arise during any divorce. An extensive listing of additional resources is contained in the Appendix.

Read The Full Review Of This Resource On Page 126.

6. Understanding The Legal Aspects Of Divorce

Title:	**Almost Painless Divorce**
Subtitle:	What Your Lawyer Won't Tell You
Overall Rating:	★★★
Media Type:	Print
Author/Editor:	Jenny Garden
Short Description:	The focus of this book is the legal aspects of divorce: how to look for and choose a lawyer; how to speed up the legal process, thereby cutting the costs; how to pursue other legal alternatives besides hiring a lawyer; and consideration of mediation (the "almost painless divorce") as a preferable choice for divorcing couples.

Read The Full Review Of This Resource On Page 128.

7.

EXPLORING

THE OPTION

OF MEDIATION

A startling fact to many adults learning about the process of divorce is that most (90%+) divorces are **not** litigated (not argued in a court before a judge by opposing attorneys). Most divorce agreements, in fact, are negotiated between the divorcing parties using the services of separate attorneys for advice and drafting the agreements ultimately submitted to a court for approval. Nonetheless, both these paths (using attorneys) have the potential to lead to contentious deliberations and high legal fees.

An alternative is mediation, now more than a decade old and growing in popularity. What is mediation? It's a process by which a trained mediator (paid hourly) creates a process, atmosphere, and dialog within which the divorcing parties decide **for themselves** the questions and issues encountered in negotiating their divorce settlement. This leaves control of the decision-making in their hands, and maintains their freedom to ultimately agree or not agree. For couples who can manage it, this alternative can be an excellent way to work through the process of communicating needs and wants, and making the compromises necessary to create an agreement that works for the best interests of **both** parties, without extended court proceedings or additional attorney's fees generated by potentially antagonistic and protracted negotiations, conducted through the lawyers as third parties.

Those who practice mediation professionally generally feel that mediation can work for virtually any marital situation, even those with complex financial issues, child custody situations, or high levels of emotional negativism from one or both parties. Situations which most mediators will choose **not** to take on, however, includes divorces where one or both parties is being dishonest about finances, or is subject to severe drug abuse or mental illness, or is involved in a continuing case of domestic violence.

Does choosing a mediator mean that no lawyers can be involved? Not at all! In a growing number of cases, lawyers specializing in family law are turning to careers in mediation as a way to create non-litigated agreements for divorcing couples. Recommended practices vary among mediators, but many encourage parties to a divorce to have their own legal representation apart from the mediation process. This approach can be particularly useful in situations where a "weaker" spouse is concerned that the "stronger" spouse may somehow manipulate their negotiations; with independent legal representation, both spouses can separately have their lawyers review tentative agreements being generated by the mediation process.

While mediation is growing in popularity, it is still a relatively new vehicle for negotiating divorce settlements, and not all states have created certification requirements for divorce mediators. The importance of doing your homework to select a competent and

7. Exploring The Option Of Mediation

experienced mediator cannot be overemphasized. In states without certification requirements, virtually anyone can advertise himself as a mediator. Even in states that license mediators, the standards to be met do not approach the education and training necessary for a lawyer to pass a bar exam. Several of the resources we recommend on the following pages include chapters on how to go about the process of evaluating, selecting, and working with the mediator that is right for you; we **strongly** recommend you read them carefully and follow their suggestions. For more information, or for a referral to mediators in your area, you can call the Academy of Family Mediators (their national association) in Lexington, Massachusetts at 800-292-4236.

There are other alternatives to litigation as well: a couple using a single lawyer together to create an agreement (similar to mediation), self-representation, and arbitration. While we've not found resources which deal exclusively with these options, several of the resources recommended on mediation also describe and evaluate these choices as well; read the full-page reviews of the resources recommended on the following pages for more information.

7. Exploring The Option Of Mediation

Title:	**Getting Divorced Without Ruining Your Life**
Subtitle:	A . . . Guide To . . . Negotiating A Divorce Settlement
Overall Rating:	★★★★
Media Type:	Print
Author/Editor:	Sam Margulies
Short Description:	Written by an experienced divorce litigator and mediator, this is a 318-page guide to the emotional, legal, and financial issues of divorce settlement, including advice about how to successfully negotiate with your spouse on such issues as alimony, property division, and a successful parenting agreement for your children. The book aims to help you gain knowledge so you can take control of the divorce process.

Read The Full Review Of This Resource On Page 103.

Title:	**Choosing A Divorce Mediator**
Subtitle:	A Guide To Help Divorcing Couples Find A Competent Mediator
Overall Rating:	★★★★
Media Type:	Print
Author/Editor:	Diane Neumann
Short Description:	This book is a 204-page, information-based resource for those considering mediation to reach a divorce settlement, containing an overview of the mediation process as well as guidelines about how to choose a competent mediator.

Read The Full Review Of This Resource On Page 111.

**7. Exploring The
Option Of Mediation**

Title:	**Almost Painless Divorce**
Subtitle:	What Your Lawyer Won't Tell You
Overall Rating:	★★★
Media Type:	Print
Author/Editor:	Jenny Garden
Short Description:	The focus of this book is the legal aspects of divorce: how to look for and choose a lawyer; how to speed up the legal process, thereby cutting the costs; how to pursue other legal alternatives besides hiring a lawyer; and consideration of mediation (the "almost painless divorce") as a preferable choice for divorcing couples.

Read The Full Review Of This Resource On Page 128.

8.

CREATING A NEW LIFE AFTER DIVORCE

Divorce is one of the most profound transitions we can experience in our lifetime. For the more than 1 million men **and** 1 million women in the United States who divorce every year, it is a journey, a "passing over" which must be completed alone. Some set out on the road willingly, others with great trepidation. Regardless of one's mindset when beginning this journey, most who have completed a transition to a their new life tell us that the road they traveled had curves they never imagined and hills and valleys they could not anticipate. But, for all, there **is** life after divorce.

What the quality of that life becomes, however, depends to some extent on how the individual has been able to make his or her transition from being married to being divorced. Some are able to speak, at the end of their journey, of having arrived in a place worth the work it took to arrive; others speak of becoming stuck in potholes along the way. There are, of course, many factors which distinguish one journey from another, but an essential factor which is the implicit focus of the resources reviewed in this section is how divorce as a transition **is perceived by the traveler.**

For some, divorce is an event which is meant to be passed through as quickly as possible. For people like this, divorce is a transition which must be rushed through so that they can get on with their life. This kind of hurried transition, fed by the "quick fix" mentality we have cultivated in our society, often leads to disaster further down the road. These "wrecks" might well take the form of a second marriage which is entered into too soon, or continuing to suffer the effects of unresolved feelings of dependency, guilt, obsession, or anger.

For others, divorce is a process which takes some time to complete. As a transition, it begins with an ending—the ending of a marriage—which does not take place overnight. It usually involves a period of time when an individual may feel that nothing is happening and that progress is not being made. But this is a very important time, for it is a time of "internal work" during which the negative feelings accompanying any divorce are more completely understood and dealt with. This is the time for counseling, receiving support from fellow travelers, and spiritual growth and healing. Then, this transition can end with a new beginning.

Wherever you are in your transition, know that the road **does** lead somewhere, and know that it **can** lead to a new and better place. But, travel slowly. Pick up helpful companions. Take time to stop at the rest areas you find along the way, to check your compass, to ask others about the road ahead, to reassure yourself that you are on the correct road, headed in the right direction.

8. Creating A New Life After Divorce

The resources presented to you in this section will help you do that. Take time to select one or two that seem right for you. You will pass this way only once, and the wisdom contained in these works will comfort and guide you.

8. Creating A New Life After Divorce

Title:	**Life Lessons**
Subtitle:	50 Things I Learned From My Divorce
Overall Rating:	★★★★
Media Type:	Print
Author/Editor:	Beth Joselow
Short Description:	A guide broadly focusing on lessons gleaned from many women who have experienced divorce and how to apply them. Text is presented in fifty chapters each with its own "life lesson" that pairs the author's comments with other's anecdotal experiences. At each chapter's conclusion, its three main points are highlighted for the reader.

Read The Full Review Of This Resource On Page 105.

Title:	**Life After Divorce**
Subtitle:	Create A New Beginning
Overall Rating:	★★★
Media Type:	Print
Author/Editor:	Sharon Wegscheider-Cruse
Short Description:	This work traces the process of "life after divorce" by examining the dynamics of the dissolving marriage, the hurt and pain experienced by all involved and the ingredients of recovery. Each chapter begins with antecdotal experiences of four different individuals who are experiencing divorce from their unique perspectives.

Read The Full Review Of This Resource On Page 123.

8. Creating A New Life After Divorce

Title:	**Divorce & New Beginnings**
Subtitle:	Guide To Recovery And Growth, Solo Parenting, And Stepfamilies
Overall Rating:	★★★
Media Type:	Print
Author/Editor:	Genevieve Clapp, Ph. D
Short Description:	This is an intensively researched and very readable guide for adults working through divorce crises. All aspects of divorce survival are discussed focusing on the needs of today's couples, including planning for healthy relationships by learning from past mistakes.

Read The Full Review Of This Resource On Page 133.

9.

RESOURCES OF INTEREST TO COUNSELING PROFESSIONALS

Twenty five years ago, divorce was viewed as failure and avoided by most. During the seventies and eighties, it became much more common and was often seen as an essential element in the quest for personal fulfillment. More recently, we are becoming more aware of the losses (both personal and societal) created by divorce, and we are now trying to "work it out" more often than not.

The catalyst for this change has been the research conducted on this phenomenon in the past three decades, and the findings this research has produced. We have included this section to increase awareness of this research and its findings (which the better self-help resources have drawn upon). It contains reviews of resources (directed to professionals and/or the serious lay reader) which provide a sample of where we are and, in several instances, where we are going.

Where we are now in our understanding of divorce and its effects includes these elements:

- Divorce has become a stable part of our American culture

- For men and women, there are sharp differences in how divorce is experienced and responded to

- Many of us are recognizing that children of divorce are frequently a causal factor in second marriages

- Mediation, rather than litigation, has become more commonplace as a means of ending the marriage

- Financial stability of the custodial parent (usually the mother) and a low level of conflict between the divorced parents are essential ingredients for maintaining the well being of children of divorce

Where we are going in our understanding of divorce and its effects includes a growing awareness of these issues:

- The economic and moral constraints which kept marriages together in the past have changed so profoundly that we no longer expect the divorce rate to return to pre-1965 levels

- We are paying more attention to the custodial parent (usually the mother), and are attempting to discern ways we can help and support that parent (though no real solutions have emerged)

- We are aware that ongoing conflict between divorcing adults has been shown to have disastrous effects on their children, and we are working hard to remind them of that

- There is a growing sentiment that maintaining a tie between the child and the non-custodial parent is important

9. Resources Of Interest To Counseling Professionals

• We expect continued societal changes in our attitudes towards child support, workplace reforms, custody, litigation, mediation, child support, and other critical issues surrounding divorce

The resources that follow can provide some insights into these developments. All are written by university professors and researchers. These resources are only a representative sample, not an exhaustive compendium. But they can offer you, as a professional or serious lay reader, examples of the work which is being accomplished. They also pay tribute to the dedicated researchers in the field who help us to make informed, caring choices that affect all of us.

9. Resources Of Interest To Counseling Professionals

Title:	**The Good Divorce**
Subtitle:	Keeping Your Family Together When Your Marriage Comes Apart
Overall Rating:	★★★★
Media Type:	Print
Author/Editor:	Constance Ahrons, Ph.D.
Short Description:	This book presents the conclusions of the author's life work on the subject of divorce, experienced first hand, through the eyes of countless couples in 25 years as a therapist, and based on a long-term study of divorce and its aftereffects on nearly 100 couples. The author's conclusion, and the consistent theme of this book, is that a "good divorce" is not only achieveable, but is actually the normative outcome in a majority of cases.

Read The Full Review Of This Resource On Page 95.

Read The Full Review Of This Resource On Page 95.

Title:	**Surviving The Breakup**
Overall Rating:	★★★★
Media Type:	Print
Author/Editor:	Judith S. Wallerstein & Joan B. Kelly
Short Description:	This book is based on the Children of Divorce Project, a recognized landmark study of sixty families during the first five years after divorce. As such it reports on the the short term and long term effects of family dissolution on children. It is regarded as a classic in the field.

Read The Full Review Of This Resource On Page 116.

9. Resources Of Interest To Counseling Professionals

Title:	**Second Chances**
Subtitle:	Men, Women And Children A Decade After Divorce
Overall Rating:	★★★★
Media Type:	Print
Author/Editor:	Judith S. Wallerstein & Sandra Blakeslee

Short Description: This book is based on the author's continued study of sixty families ten and more years following their divorce. As such, it provides a comprehensive account of the long-term emotional, economic, and psychological effects of divorce on adults and, most especially, on children.

Read The Full Review Of This Resource On Page 117.

Title:	**Joint Custody & Shared Parenting**
Overall Rating:	★★★
Media Type:	Print
Author/Editor:	Jay Folberg, Editor

Short Description: This second edition, updated text written by many experts in the field of social services and law, focuses on joint custody. Four sections cover joint custody in historical perspective, what makes it the right choice for some divorcing couples, current case study research, and latest law.

Read The Full Review Of This Resource On Page 148.

9. Resources Of Interest To Counseling Professionals

Title:	**Custody Revolution**
Subtitle:	The Father Factor And The Motherhood Mystique
Overall Rating:	★★★
Media Type:	Print
Author/Editor:	Richard A. Warshak, Ph.D.
Short Description:	This extensively researched book examines the effects of mother-custody and father-custody families to make the argument that fathers make equally good caretakers of their children as mothers. This book is intended to be read by those in the child custody field (judges, psychologists, lawyers) as well as by parents considering custody plans for their children.

Read The Full Review Of This Resource On Page 151.

Title:	**Women And Divorce, Men And Divorce**
Subtitle:	Gender Differences In Separation, Divorce, And Remarriage
Overall Rating:	★★★
Media Type:	Print
Author/Editor:	Sandra S. Volgy, Ph.D.
Short Description:	This book is a collection of twelve research articles which are arranged under three headings: "Comparison of Gender Differences," "Men and Divorce," and "Women and Divorce."

Read The Full Review Of This Resource On Page 154.

THE SINGLE BEST RESOURCE FOR SELECTED DIVORCE TOPICS

III

INTRODUCTION

As we've developed this directory, we've chosen a few resources that are the single best choice we've found for helping with one particular aspect of the divorce process. We've provided this "short list" on the pages that follow for those readers who:

- Might be interested in a shortcut to the best resource to answer a specific question

- Are on a limited budget and can purchase or acquire only a few resources to support their research (don't forget that many recommended resources are available for free at your local library)

- Are pressed for time

Listed below are a number of resources that we've found to be particularly useful in gaining an understanding of one (or more) aspects of the typical divorce process, or in helping a loved one deal with the effects of divorce. In this section, we've provided for each topic we've selected:

- The resource and author name

- Its overall rating and media type

- A short description of its contents

While you'll find this list of outstanding resources helpful in every case, we want to emphasize that the breadth of issues encountered in most divorces will generally require that more than one resource be used. Be sure to read the complete, one-page review of any resource of interest, to help ensure that you gain a full understanding of its content, focus, style, and quality **before** you purchase or acquire the resource!

Best Resource For:	Adults needing reassurance and perspective as they enter the divorce process
Title:	**Crazy Time**
Subtitle:	Surviving Divorce & Building A New Life
Overall Rating:	★★★★
Media Type:	Print
Author/Editor:	Abigail Trafford
Short Description:	A popular text in its second edition, this book has three sections dealing with "Crisis" (stages leading to the divorce decision), "Crazy Time" (the divorce and its emotional aftermath), and the longest, "Recovery" (focused on emergence of self, sex, love, remarriage, etc.). Each chapter uses anecdotal experiences of couples to illustrate and the author's observations, insights, and suggestions.

Read The Full Review Of This Resource On Page 114.

Best Resource For:	Christian adults looking for guidance during divorce and recovery
Title:	**The Complete Divorce Recovery Handbook**
Overall Rating:	★★★
Media Type:	Print
Author/Editor:	John P. Splinter
Short Description:	This book contains a primarily Christian approach to handling divorce and recovery, divided into chapters outlining progressive stages of the divorce process; each chapter focuses on a particular psychological or spiritual issue, ending with questions, activities, and selected readings from the Bible to further understanding.

Read The Full Review Of This Resource On Page 138.

Best **Resource For:**	**Those concerned about divorce or wishing to enrich their marriage**
Title:	**Divorce Busting**
Overall Rating:	★★★★
Media Type:	Print
Author/Editor:	Michele Weiner-Davis, M.S.W.
Short Description:	The purpose of this book is to help couples stay together in their marriage rather than to divorce. It consists of two major sections: the first offers a rationale for couples staying together and working things out; the second describes marriage-enriching, divorce preventing techniques that couples can use to improve their marriage.

Read The Full Review Of This Resource On Page 91. |

Best **Resource For:**	**Understanding the psychological issues impacting children of divorce**
Title:	**Growing Up With Divorce**
Subtitle:	Helping Your Child Avoid Immediate And Later Emotional Problems
Overall Rating:	★★★★
Media Type:	Print
Author/Editor:	Neil Kalter, Ph.D.
Short Description:	This book aims to help parents understand the stresses and challenges that divorce presents to their children. It outlines three stages of divorce and how they apply to each phase of a child's development. The book includes chapters about the five development phases of children, plus chapters about helping children of each age group cope with divorce. Several case studies throughout the book illustrate the experiences of divorced families.

Read The Full Review Of This Resource On Page 93. |

Best Resource For:	**Adult caregivers who seek to help children through recovery from loss**
Title:	**Helping Children Cope With Separation And Loss**
Overall Rating:	★★★★
Media Type:	Print
Author/Editor:	Claudia Jewett Jarratt
Short Description:	Written by a respected child and family therapist, this 232-page book serves as a guide for parents, therapists, and other caregivers who wish to help children move through the stages of grief and loss. Ways of identifying and dealing with children's grief reactions are found here, as well as creative methods to help children give voice to their feelings at all stages of the grief process.

Read The Full Review Of This Resource On Page 94. |

Best Resource For:	**Parents who need to introduce and discuss the subject of divorce with their preschoolers**
Title:	**Mom And Dad Don't Live Together Anymore**
Overall Rating:	★★★
Media Type:	Print
Author/Editor:	Kathy Stinson; Nancy Reynolds (Illustrator)
Short Description:	This storybook focuses on helping the child adjust to the period just after separation when the parents live in separate homes. It is a popular text in its tenth printing that is written with a focus on expression of feelings and opening lines of communication between parent and child.

Read The Full Review Of This Resource On Page 156. |

Best **Resource For:**	**Preteens who can benefit from a gentle novel about divorce's emotional impact**
Title:	**It's Not The End Of The World**
Overall Rating:	★★★★
Media Type:	Print
Author/Editor:	Judy Blume
Short Description:	This is a short novel for teens telling the story of Karen Newman, a girl whose parents are getting a divorce. Karen tells of her trials and adventures, thoughts and feelings, as she chronicles the days leading up to and away from her parents' separation, and the beginning of a new, and very different, family life.

Read The Full Review Of This Resource On Page 97.

Best **Resource For:**	**Teens seeking to learn more about the emotions of divorce**
Title:	**How It Feels When Parents Divorce**
Overall Rating:	★★★★
Media Type:	Print
Author/Editor:	Jill Krementz
Short Description:	This 115-page book describes divorce as told through the stories of nineteen children ranging in age from 7-16, and as seen through the many photographs of these children, their homes and families, that accompany each story.

Read The Full Review Of This Resource On Page 113.

Best Resource For:	**Parents who want to develop a detailed parenting agreement on their own**
Title:	**Child Custody**
Subtitle:	Building Parenting Agreements that Work
Overall Rating:	★★★★
Media Type:	Print
Author/Editor:	Mimi E. Lyster
Short Description:	This book supports the creation of parenting agreements, arrangements for parenting separately and making child custody positive. These agreements include factors such as taking care of the children, making decisions on their behalf, and meeting their needs. A good portion of the book is devoted to formulating the agreement, and it has a 20-page skeleton to work from. Other topics include: negotiation, mediation and custody laws.

Read The Full Review Of This Resource On Page 108.

Best Resource For:	**Understanding, acting upon, and managing the financial aspects of divorce**
Title:	**Divorce & Money**
Subtitle:	How To Make The Best Financial Decisions During Divorce
Overall Rating:	★★★★
Media Type:	Print
Author/Editor:	V. Woodhouse, J.D., CFP and V. F. Collins, Ph.D., CFP
Short Description:	This is a detailed financial resource book outlining money management decisions/process, from separation to divorce. Its focus is on viewing divorce as a business process and equitable sharing of assets as the result of careful planning. In its third edition, this text covers such divorce-related topics as dividing debts and obtaining a fair settlement, to planning financially for your future.

Read The Full Review Of This Resource On Page 109.

Best Resource For:	**Those seeking an understanding of the legal issues encountered in a divorce**
Title:	**American Bar Association Guide To Family Law**
Subtitle:	The Complete And Easy Guide To The Laws Of Marriage, Parenthood, Separation And Divorce
Overall Rating:	★★★★
Media Type:	Print
Author/Editor:	Jeff Atkinson
Short Description:	This 179-page book gives its reader an overview of the laws which affect the family, from marriage to parenthood to divorce. It has sections on division of property, custody and visitation, and the legal process. Other subjects addressed include divorce in general, the stresses of divorce, steps marriage counselors uses to improve marriage, prenuptial agreements, alimony, and child support.

Read The Full Review Of This Resource On Page 100.

Best Resource For:	**Information on and resources for mediation as an alternative**
Title:	**Choosing A Divorce Mediator**
Subtitle:	A Guide To Help Divorcing Couples Find A Competent Mediator
Overall Rating:	★★★★
Media Type:	Print
Author/Editor:	Diane Neumann
Short Description:	This book is a 204-page, information-based resource for those considering mediation to reach a divorce settlement, containing an overview of the mediation process as well as guidelines about how to choose a competent mediator.

Read The Full Review Of This Resource On Page 111.

Best Resource For:	Adults needing the knowledge to negotiate a mutually satisfying divorce settlement
Title:	**Getting Divorced Without Ruining Your Life**
Subtitle:	A . . . Guide To . . . Negotiating A Divorce Settlement
Overall Rating:	★★★★
Media Type:	Print
Author/Editor:	Sam Margulies
Short Description:	Written by an experienced divorce litigator and mediator, this is a 318-page guide to the emotional, legal, and financial issues of divorce settlement, including advice about how to successfully negotiate with your spouse on such issues as alimony, property division, and a successful parenting agreement for your children. The book aims to help you gain knowledge so you can take control of the divorce process.

Read The Full Review Of This Resource On Page 103.

Best Resource For:	Women wanting to learn from other women's divorce/post-divorce experiences
Title:	**Life Lessons**
Subtitle:	50 Things I Learned From My Divorce
Overall Rating:	★★★★
Media Type:	Print
Author/Editor:	Beth Joselow
Short Description:	A guide broadly focusing on lessons gleaned from many women who have experienced divorce and how to apply them. Text is presented in fifty chapters each with its own "life lesson" that pairs the author's comments with other's anecdotal experiences. At each chapter's conclusion, its three main points are highlighted for the reader.

Read The Full Review Of This Resource On Page 105.

RESOURCES OF INTEREST TO SPECIFIC GROUPS

IV

INTRODUCTION

During the process of researching and evaluating resources on the subject of divorce, we've encountered two subsets of these resources that will be of interest to those having a particular interest in two unique perspectives on the subject of divorce. In the pages that follow we've provided a separate listing of these resources, ranked by their Overall rating and grouped within the topics shown below. Some of these resources have also been **recommended** for use for one or more topics of divorce, and will be found in those separate listings as well (see Section II: The Best Resources To Help You Survive). The listings that follow include **all** resources that reflect particular emphasis on the topics shown below, regardless of how we've rated them.

Resources For Women Only   72

These are resources that reflect the author's priority of providing advice and counsel directed solely or predominantly towards **women** experiencing divorce. They vary in tone from a caring, empathetic woman's point of view of the issues many women encounter during their divorce, to combative, "take no prisoners" advice to women on how to maximize their gain from a divorce. The full reviews of these resources should be read before deciding to acquire a particular resource with this focus.

Resources Written With A Christian Perspective   79

For the many adults who are active Christians, resources which reflect an author's Christian training and beliefs may provide counsel of particular value. These resources tend to draw upon Biblical passages for fundamental guidance to adults in resolving issues encountered during marriage and, when unavoidable, divorce. The resources we've included in our listing vary in intensity from those which are decidedly "mainstream," with the added benefit of providing a God-centered foundation for decision-making during divorce, to those which are dominated by strict adherence to Biblical guidance on marriage and the marriage relationship between man and woman. Again, we suggest that you read the full reviews of each of these resources to gain a full understanding of their tone and approach, before deciding to acquire a particular resource with this focus.

**Resources For
Women Only**

Title:	**Life Lessons**
Subtitle:	50 Things I Learned From My Divorce
Overall Rating:	★★★★
Media Type:	Print
Author/Editor:	Beth Joselow
Short Description:	A guide broadly focusing on lessons gleaned from many women who have experienced divorce and how to apply them. Text is presented in fifty chapters each with its own "life lesson" that pairs the author's comments with other's anecdotal experiences. At each chapter's conclusion, its three main points are highlighted for the reader.

Read The Full Review Of This Resource On Page 105.

Title:	**Learning To Leave**
Subtitle:	A Woman's Guide
Overall Rating:	★★★★
Media Type:	Print
Author/Editor:	Lynette Triere with Richard Peacock
Short Description:	This text focuses on helping women survive divorce and is a revised edition of a version that came out in the early 1980s. With a slant toward viewing women as equal partners with men in life, ideas are presented that guide women, as they work their way through divorce, towards that means; includes discussions on realities of divorce and survival techniques.

Read The Full Review Of This Resource On Page 118.

Resources For Women Only

Title:	**Our Turn**
Subtitle:	Women Who Triumph In The Face Of Divorce
Overall Rating:	★★★
Media Type:	Print
Author/Editor:	C. L. Hayes, Ph.D., Deborah Anderson, Melinda Blau
Short Description:	Based on a survey of divorced women, this book provides a view of women who have experienced divorce in midlife and how they have dealt with its aftereffects. Results from the survey ("Divorce After 40") paint a sometimes surprising picture of women in the 90's and compares that picture with cultural expectations.

Read The Full Review Of This Resource On Page 130.

Title:	**Survival Manual For Women In Divorce**
Subtitle:	182 Questions and Answers
Overall Rating:	★★★
Media Type:	Print
Author/Editor:	Carol Ann Wilson & Edwin Schilling III
Short Description:	This book, written by an attorney and financial consultant, provides answers to many of the most often asked questions women have when separating or divorcing. Some of the many topics discussed include finding an attorney, court processes, child custody, property division, and tax responsibilities.

Read The Full Review Of This Resource On Page 147.

**Resources For
Women Only**

Title:	**Don't Settle For Less**
Subtitle:	A Woman's Guide To Getting A Fair Divorce
Overall Rating:	★★★
Media Type:	Print
Author/Editor:	Beverly Pekala
Short Description:	This 272-page book aims to help women understand how to create successful divorce settlements with their husbands, and through knowledge of divorce law and its hidden pitfalls, give them "an advantage in a system that isn't always fair." A wide variety of strategies, suggestions, and advice is given so that women can learn to take action and make choices that will benefit them as they encounter each stage of the legal process of divorce.

Read The Full Review Of This Resource On Page 152.

Title:	**Dear Client**
Subtitle:	A Complete Handbook For Understanding And Surviving Your Legal Divorce Process
Overall Rating:	★★★
Media Type:	Print
Author/Editor:	Ellen D. Ostman
Short Description:	This 525-page resource offers an in-depth look at the legal side of divorce for women, combining anecdotes from the author's clients, questionnaires to help you compile essential personal and financial information, transcripts from actual court trials, as well as discussion of such issues as child custody, alimony, property division, various litigation procedures, and how to prepare for a court trial.

Read The Full Review Of This Resource On Page 158.

Resources For Women Only

Title:	**Money-Smart Divorce**
Subtitle:	What Women Need To Know About Money And Divorce
Overall Rating:	★★
Media Type:	Print
Author/Editor:	Esther M. Berger
Short Description:	Written by an expert and speaker on women's finances, this 236-page book is intended to be read by women about to undergo divorce, to help them gain knowledge and control over their own finances before, during, and after divorce. It includes advice on negotiating finances during a divorce settlement with your spouse, and investing for the future.

Read The Full Review Of This Resource On Page 166.

Title:	**The Best Is Yet to Come**
Subtitle:	Coping With Divorce And Enjoying Life Again
Overall Rating:	★
Media Type:	Print
Author/Editor:	Ivana Trump
Short Description:	The personal context for this book, written primarily for women, is the author's own divorce experience and her personal recovery. Based on this experience, the author gives advice on recognizing the "beginning of the end," surviving the breakup, and beginning a new and productive life.

Read The Full Review Of This Resource On Page 180.

Resources For Women Only

Title:	**Breaking Up**
Subtitle:	From Heartache To Happiness In 48 Pages
Overall Rating:	★
Media Type:	Print
Author/Editor:	Yolanda Nave
Short Description:	This is a small, "pocket-sized" comic book written for women, illustrating in a humorous fashion how to recover from being left by a spouse, and the road from loneliness to freedom.

Read The Full Review Of This Resource On Page 181.

Title:	**Living & Loving After Divorce**
Overall Rating:	★
Media Type:	Print
Author/Editor:	Catherine Napolitane & Victoria Pellegrino
Short Description:	This is a 241-page book that discusses a wide range of post-divorce issues for women, based on the anecdotes and experiences of women in the Nexus support network group. Issues explored include bringing up children on your own, dealing with your ex-husband, dating, sex, personal finances and the job world.

Read The Full Review Of This Resource On Page 184.

Resources For Women Only

Title:	**Divorce**
Subtitle:	A Woman's Guide to Getting a Fair Share
Overall Rating:	★
Media Type:	Print
Author/Editor:	Patricia Phillips and George Mair
Short Description:	This is a 243-page book intended to help women gain understanding and control of the divorce process, and ultimately get a "fair share" in divorce settlements. Issues explored include choosing and working with a lawyer, gathering essential information about yourself and your spouse for use in settlement and custody hearings, depositions, and court trials.

Read The Full Review Of This Resource On Page 185.

Title:	**There's Hope After Divorce**
Overall Rating:	★
Media Type:	Print
Author/Editor:	Jeenie Gordon
Short Description:	This book was written by a family therapist and divorce survivor, and looks at a variety of issues in divorce and its aftermath as opportunities for positive change. There is a Christian touch throughout, and a bias towards the woman's perspective.

Read The Full Review Of This Resource On Page 186.

Resources For Women Only

Title:	**Divorce War!**
Subtitle:	50 Strategies Every Woman Needs To Know To Win
Overall Rating:	★
Media Type:	Print
Author/Editor:	Bradley A. Pistotnik
Short Description:	"50 Strategies Every Woman Needs to Know to Win" are clearly outlined in this 224-page book, which takes the view that women should not hesitate to use every effective tactic against their husbands in order to win successful settlements, and get what they deserve: "a larger share of the divorce pie."

Read The Full Review Of This Resource On Page 187.

Resources Written With A Christian Perspective

Title:	**Growing Through Divorce**
Overall Rating:	★★★★
Media Type:	Print
Author/Editor:	Jim Smoke

Short Description: This text focusing on getting through divorce, and reflects the author's Christian values and perspective. Text is presented in two parts, beginning with chapters focusing on the broader aspects of surviving divorce and ending with an intensive, 100 page workbook that may be used as a basis of discussion groups.

Read The Full Review Of This Resource On Page 98.

Title:	**Helping Children Survive Divorce**
Subtitle:	What To Expect; How To Help
Overall Rating:	★★★★
Media Type:	Print
Author/Editor:	Dr. Archibald D. Hart

Short Description: Straightforward advice by a psychologist focusing on the effects of divorce on children including the parents' role in guiding their offspring through the process; emphasis on helping parents recognize the stresses on children and how the quality of their own recovery influences that of the entire family. A study guide explores ideas presented in the text.

Read The Full Review Of This Resource On Page 104.

Resources Written With A Christian Perspective

Title:	**Marriage Savers**
Subtitle:	Helping Your Friends and Family Avoid Divorce
Overall Rating:	★★★★
Media Type:	Print
Author/Editor:	Michael J. McManus
Short Description:	Extensively researched text focusing on preparing for and maintaining a healthy marriage. How parents and schools can help children develop character attributes vital to a sound marriage is presented. Mentoring and educational programs are covered in detail.

Read The Full Review Of This Resource On Page 112.

Title:	**Saving Your Marriage Before It Starts**
Subtitle:	Seven Questions To Ask Before (And After) You Marry
Overall Rating:	★★★★
Media Type:	Print
Author/Editor:	Dr. Les Parrott III and Dr. Leslie Parrott
Short Description:	Written by Les and Leslie Parrott, a husband and wife team who are also co-directors of the Center for Relationship Development at Seattle Pacific University, this book introduces the "seven principles for happy marriages" with anecdotes, specific advice and techniques, and reflective exercises for each chapter. The authors believe that an awareness of these seven principles before (and after) couples marry can help create a healthy marriage.

Read The Full Review Of This Resource On Page 121.

**Resources Written
With A Christian
Perspective**

Title:	**Fresh Start Divorce Recovery Workbook**
Overall Rating:	★★★
Media Type:	Print
Author/Editor:	Bob Burns & Tom Whiteman
Short Description:	Developed as a workbook for the "Fresh Start" seminar program, this book can be used individually or in groups. It is task intensive and relies on commitment of the reader to work through the steps in recovery from divorce. Its focus is on learning and practicing the characteristics of healthy relationships.

Read The Full Review Of This Resource On Page 132.

Title:	**Insuring Marriage**
Subtitle:	25 Proven Ways to Prevent Divorce
Overall Rating:	★★★
Media Type:	Print
Author/Editor:	Michael J. McManus
Short Description:	This small book, Christian in focus, promotes the theme that divorce can be prevented, and offers ways to best prepare for and improve upon marriage. It wants its readers to become Marriage Savers, those who preserve their own marriage or help to save others. The book includes 25 short chapters ranging from premarital relations to support for divorced couples.

Read The Full Review Of This Resource On Page 136.

Resources Written With A Christian Perspective

Title:	**The Complete Divorce Recovery Handbook**
Overall Rating:	★★★
Media Type:	Print
Author/Editor:	John P. Splinter
Short Description:	This book contains a primarily Christian approach to handling divorce and recovery, divided into chapters outlining progressive stages of the divorce process; each chapter focuses on a particular psychological or spiritual issue, ending with questions, activities, and selected readings from the Bible to further understanding.

Read The Full Review Of This Resource On Page 138.

Title:	**Divorce And Remarriage**
Subtitle:	A Perspective For Counseling
Overall Rating:	★★★
Media Type:	Print
Author/Editor:	John R. Martin
Short Description:	This counseling guidebook for pastors has two major sections. Part One provides historical background and "Counseling Perspectives" relating to divorce and remarriage. Part Two provides counselors with specific procedures in dealing with clients experiencing these major life events. The book reflects the author's strong Christian orientation.

Read The Full Review Of This Resource On Page 141.

Resources Written With A Christian Perspective

Title:	**Children Of Divorce**
Subtitle:	Helping Kids When Their Parents Are Apart
Overall Rating:	★★★
Media Type:	Print
Author/Editor:	Debbie Barr
Short Description:	This book is a short guide to helping children cope with the trauma of divorce. It includes insights from many researchers, and case histories of children caught up in divorce revealed in their own words. A "village" approach to helping children cope is foremost among the author's suggestions.

Read The Full Review Of This Resource On Page 142.

Title:	**Divorce Recovery**
Subtitle:	Putting Yourself Back Together Again
Overall Rating:	★★
Media Type:	Print
Author/Editor:	Randy Reynolds & David Lynn
Short Description:	This is a divorce recovery pamphlet written from a Christian perspective, intended mainly for use by divorce recovery groups and workshops. It consists of 11 chapters, each dealing with one set of issues and including suggested Bible readings, focus questions, and goal-setting activities.

Read The Full Review Of This Resource On Page 164.

Resources Written With A Christian Perspective

Title:	**Our Family Is Divorcing**
Subtitle:	A Read-Aloud Book For Families Experiencing Divorce
Overall Rating:	★★
Media Type:	Print
Author/Editor:	Patricia Polin Johnson and Donna Reilly Williams
Short Description:	This slim storybook is meant to be read to children by, or in the company of, a parent or other care giver. The story tells of one young girl's experience with separating parents, and its effects on herself and other members of her family. The book contains an advice section for adults about how best to use this story to open up lines of communication with a child about such painful issues as divorce.

Read The Full Review Of This Resource On Page 173.

Title:	**Adult Child of Divorce**
Subtitle:	A Recovery Handbook
Overall Rating:	★★
Media Type:	Audiotape
Author/Editor:	Bob Burns and Michael J. Brissett, Jr., Ph.D.
Short Description:	This resource consists of a set of two audiotapes which deal with the issues facing adult children of divorce. The tapes begin with a general discussion of functional vs. dysfunctional families, and the unique problems that children of such families face as they grow to adulthood. The discussion centers on positive ways to overcome unhealthy patterns of coping and "break the cycle" of dysfunction. Includes some perspectives from a Christian standpoint.

Read The Full Review Of This Resource On Page 199.

Resources Written With A Christian Perspective

Title:	**I Only See My Dad On Weekends**
Subtitle:	Kids Tell Their Stories About Divorce
Overall Rating:	★
Media Type:	Print
Author/Editor:	Beth Matthews and Andrew Adams with Karen Dockrey
Short Description:	"I Only See My Dad on Weekends" is a slim, 42-page book with a Christian focus, written by children for other children experiencing divorce or living in "blended" families; composed as a series of imaginary "discussions" about the various issues children must face. Each chapter closes with focus questions.

Read The Full Review Of This Resource On Page 182.

Title:	**There's Hope After Divorce**
Overall Rating:	★
Media Type:	Print
Author/Editor:	Jeenie Gordon
Short Description:	This book was written by a family therapist and divorce survivor, and looks at a variety of issues in divorce and its aftermath as opportunities for positive change. There is a Christian touch throughout, and a bias towards the woman's perspective.

Read The Full Review Of This Resource On Page 186.

RESOURCE
REVIEWS

V

INTRODUCTION

In this section you'll find our full-page reviews of all the resources we've encountered in our research into, and analysis of the best information available on the subject of divorce. These reviews are organized by media type, and within each media type, by our overall "Star" rating (1-4 Stars).

Print Resources   90

These reviews are focused primarily on printed self-help books. Some of these books are hundreds of pages long; some just dozens of pages. We work hard to ensure that we've reviewed the latest edition of books. The edition date included in each review shows when the most recent edition was published, or the latest copyright date. We don't review books that are no longer in print or not readily available from bookstores, since we want our recommendations to be readily available to those who want to acquire them.

Internet Website Resources   189

These reviews include Internet websites we've been able to find that are focused on divorce topics. Our criteria for selecting a website for review include these requirements:

- A substantial portion of its content must be focused on divorce

- It must be substantially complete, not substantially under construction.

- Commercial sites that have products or services for sale to visitors are reviewed, provided they also contain some relevant, free content.

- We don't review sites which have as their primary focus simply providing links to other sites, particularly since most of those linked sites will be included in our reviews.

Commercial Online Service Resources

These reviews include forums or special interest areas containing proprietary or sponsored content focused on divorce. Content offered by the commercial online services through their linked or proprietary websites are reviewed in the Internet section.

Videotape Resources

Audiotape Resources

HOW TO SURVIVE THE LOSS OF A LOVE

★★★★

Media Type:
Print

Price:
$5.95

Principal Subject:
All-Inclusive

Written For:
Adults

ISBN:
0931580439

Author/Editor:
M. Colgrove Ph.D;
H. Bloomfied M.D;
P. McWilliams

Edition Reviewed:
1993

About The Author:
(From Cover Notes)

M. Colgrove is an author and consultant;
H. Bloomfield is a best selling author and clinician;
P. McWilliams is a best selling author and poet.

Publisher:
Prelude Press

Internet URL:
N/A

"Christian" Orientation?:
N/A

Focused On Issues For:
N/A

1-4 Stars

Overall Rating   ★★★★   An experiential guide to survival of any significant loss

Design, Ease Of Use   ★★★★   Very simple, creative, insightful writing style

---

Recommended For:
All-Inclusive

Description:
This self-help book is meant to be read by a person suffering a significant loss of any kind, but it is especially relevant for those who are experiencing the loss of a love which has occurred through divorce or death. The authors introduce the process of healing in their preliminary section entitled "Understanding Loss." If reader is in need of emotional "first aid," however, they direct him/her to skip this more cognitive section and to return to it later. Following this introduction they lead the reader through ninety-four "days" of "survival," "healing" and "growing." Each "day" consists of practical advice to the reader on self care issues and techniques necessary to move through the process of recovery. In addition to this process, the reader is given a relevant, short poetic meditative thought for each day. This work is meant to be read and re-read slowly, contemplatively.

Evaluation:
This particular work is a beautiful work and is one of the most helpful written for those suffering the loss of a love. Consequently, it is one of the ten most recommended books by clinical psychologists to their clients (over two million copies of this work have been printed). The authors gently lead the reader through the stages of recovery from loss: from shock/denial to fear/anger to understanding/acceptance. This leading is done with a respect and sensitivity for the reader who is in pain, mourning his/her loss. But, most importantly, this work is a work of hope, encouraging the reader to continue to move through the pain, to survive it and to grow from it. This book, then, is an "experience" and has found a widespread acceptance, regardless of where the reader is in his/her process of healing. Its pages are meant to be returned to more than once by the reader who wishes to use this resource as an indispensable tool for survival and growth. Highly recommended.

Where To Find/Buy:
Bookstores and libraries.

1-4 Stars		
Overall Rating	★★★★	Straightforward, effective advice
Design, Ease Of Use	★★★	Clear, easy to read style

DIVORCE BUSTING

★★★★

Media Type:
Print

Price:
$11.00

Principal Subject:
Preventing Divorce

Written For:
Adults

ISBN:
0671797255

Author/Editor:
Michele Weiner-Davis, M.S.W.

Edition Reviewed:
1993

About The Author:
(From Cover Notes)
The author is a therapist in private practice specializing in Solution-Oriented Brief Therapy. She is married and has two children.

Publisher:
Simon & Shuster (Fireside Book)

Internet URL:
N/A

"Christian" Orientation?:
N/A

Focused On Issues For:
N/A

Best Resource For:
Those concerned about divorce or wishing to enrich their marriage

Recommended For:
Preventing Divorce

Description:
This book is written by a marriage and family therapist who has made a major shift in her therapeutic work: from agreeing with distressed couples that divorce was probably their answer, to instead offering them a rationale for keeping their marriage together (and giving them the tools needed to accomplish this). This book is an enthusiastic endorsement for couples in trouble to rid themselves of such statements as "divorce is the answer," "our problems can't be solved," "it's too late," etc. The book consists of two parts: the "why to" and the "how to." The "why to" offers a rationale for couples to stay together and to work things out. The "how to" are the techniques which are necessary for the changes to take place and for the marriage to continue in a functional, satisfying way. The book is based on and further develops techniques of Solution-Orientated Brief Therapy (SBT). These techniques are solution focused. They can be used in marital therapy or at home, with or without one's spouse.

Evaluation:
For married persons who have any question about whether or not divorce is the answer for their marital difficulties, this book is a "must read." Contemporary research is showing again and again that, although one out of two American couples end their marriage with a divorce, divorce is not always the best solution. The author does an excellent job of explaining how so many couples' reasons for divorcing are actually illusions and need to be perceived as such. She then explains the techniques of Solution-Orientated Brief Therapy in a way that the lay-person can easily understand. This understanding can then be applied to a therapy session with a therapist who would be using those techniques, or to a home environment either by the couple together or by one spouse individually. This book is a book of hope for couples who are hopelessly moving toward divorce. Best of all, it is not filled with "generic" marriage-saving advice, but provides a practical, step-by-step approach to getting unstuck and making the marriage loving.

Where To Find/Buy:
Bookstores and libraries.

DINOSAURS DIVORCE
A Guide For Changing Families

★★★★

Media Type:
Print

Price:
$6.95

Principal Subject:
Children Of Divorce

Written For:
Children 6-12

ISBN:
0316109967

Author/Editor:
Laurene Krasny Brown and Marc Brown

Edition Reviewed:
1988

About The Author:
(From Cover Notes)
No information provided.

Publisher:
Little, Brown and Co.

Internet URL:
N/A

"Christian" Orientation?:
N/A

Focused On Issues For:
N/A

1-4 Stars

Overall Rating	★★★★	A sensitive exploration of children's experience of divorce
Design, Ease Of Use	★★★★	Very colorful, attractive; dinosaur characters easy for the child to relate to

Recommended For:
Children Of Divorce

Description:
This 32-page, illustrated description of "Mr. and Mrs. Dinosaur" getting divorced allows the child to explore for himself/herself what divorce is all about. In a very sensitive way, the child's feelings are acknowledged and validated. The first question the book addresses is the "why"—"why do parents divorce?" The second question asked is "what about you?" "After the Divorce" is the third section of this book and describes how the divorce can bring good changes, how the child is not to be placed in the middle between feuding parents, and how they are not to be message carriers between one parent and the other. The fourth section is "Living with One Parent." The possibility of having less money, the need to be more independent, and missing the other parent are issues alluded to in this section. The remainder of the book approaches the following topics in like fashion: visiting your parent, having two homes, celebrating holidays, telling your friends, and living with stepfamilies.

Evaluation:
In a very creative and sensitive way, this book helps the younger child address the many changes of any divorcing family, completely outside his/her control: parents no longer living together, intense negative feelings, living with one parent and visiting the other, becoming a member of another marital relationship and/or family. This book is an excellent tool for the child to use individually. It enables her/him to realize that the feelings being experienced are normal and natural. It can be a "security blanket" guide through a process that is often intensely painful and bewildering. Second, it can be an excellent "conversation starter" between a parent and the child, providing as it does a fairly complete scenario of the divorce process through its dinosaur characters. Also, the "Divorce Words and What They Mean" glossary can help parents explain legal jargon in the language of the child.

Where To Find/Buy:
Bookstores and libraries.

1-4 Stars

Overall Rating	★★★★	Comprehensive coverage of the stages of divorce and phases of child development
Design, Ease Of Use	★★★	Easy-to-follow format; lots of text filling over 400 pages

Best Resource For:
Understanding the psychological issues impacting children of divorce

Description:
Growing Up With Divorce focuses on how to help parents identify and deal with the challenges their children encounter as a result of divorce. This book describes three stages of divorce—the immediate crisis stage, the short-term adjustment stage, and the long-range aftermath—and how each stage affects children in different phases of their development. Each of the five age phases of child development rates a chapter (infancy, preschool, early elementary school, later elementary school, and adolescence), including discussion of a child's typical divorce experiences during each phase. Each chapter about an age group is followed by a related chapter on how to best help the child cope with his/her divorce issues. Dr. Kalter uses several examples of families from his research to further illustrate and relate situations that children and parents going through a divorce may face. Among other topics covered in these 400 pages are communicating with children, recognizing distress in children, the psychological defenses a child may engage in, and the effects of parents' dating on children.

Evaluation:
This resource thoroughly covers the subject of helping kids through the stages of divorce. The author possesses a strong knowledge of child psychology and applies it within the context of divorce and its effects on children. Despite the book's clinical subject matter, it is well-written and understandable, presenting information in an easy-to-follow, sequential manner. The case studies and analysis are helpful and realistic; the children mentioned are not emotionally disturbed, but are typical of children in their age group. Although lengthy (400 pages, small type, no figures or illustrations), the book can be easily accessed by the reader—one may go straight to the age group that applies and find helpful tips and background. This book has a good chapter on communicating with children, including how to use the technique of displacement communication. The sections on how children adapt to the presence of a significant other or step-parent should be helpful to parents making this adjustment. Overall, an excellent guide for adults seeking to understand the impacts divorce may have on children of various ages.

Where To Find/Buy:
Bookstores and libraries.

GROWING UP WITH DIVORCE
Helping Your Child Avoid Immediate And Later Emotional Problems

★★★★

Media Type:
Print

Price:
$12.95

Principal Subject:
Children Of Divorce

Written For:
Adults

ISBN:
0449905632

Author/Editor:
Neil Kalter, Ph.D.

Edition Reviewed:
2nd (1991)

About The Author:
(From Cover Notes)
The author is Director of the Center for the Child and Family at the University of Michigan, and Associate Professor of Psychology and Psychiatry at the University of Michigan.

Publisher:
Fawcett Columbine (Ballantine Books)

Internet URL:
N/A

"Christian" Orientation?:
N/A

Focused On Issues For:
N/A

HELPING CHILDREN COPE WITH SEPARATION AND LOSS

★★★★

Media Type:
Print

Price:
$12.95

Principal Subject:
Children Of Divorce

Written For:
Adults

ISBN:
1558320512

Author/Editor:
Claudia Jewett Jarratt

Edition Reviewed:
1994

About The Author:
(From Cover Notes)

The author is a child and family therapist and the author of another book about children, *Adopting the Older Child.*

Publisher:
Harvard Common Press

Internet URL:
N/A

"Christian" Orientation?:
N/A

Focused On Issues For:
N/A

	1-4 Stars	
Overall Rating	★★★★	A creative, sensitive, and insightful guide to helping children cope with grief and loss
Design, Ease Of Use	★★★★	Eloquent and readable

Best Resource For:
Adult caregivers who seek to help children through recovery from loss

Recommended For:
Children Of Divorce

Description:
This 232-page book is intended to be read by parents and other primary caregivers, as well as "helping" adults such as therapists, school counselors, and teachers who wish to help a child work through the stages of recovery from loss. Various types of experiences are explored here, from the death of a parent, to special issues of adoption and foster care, to grief caused by parental divorce or separation. The book begins with a discussion about how to tell a child about a loss, and then moves in progressive chapters to the specific losses a child may face. Successive chapters trace the progressive stages of the grieving process, and typical and atypical reactions by children. Specific ways to help children work through these stages are also discussed, including creative games and discussions to help them understand their own feelings, and deal with problems of self-esteem, self-blame, and anxiety. The final chapter focuses on the grief process over time: the need to "revisit and readdress grief experiences" and the changing feelings of children as they themselves learn and grow.

Evaluation:
This is an sensitive and perceptive book about children's unique ways of coping with grief, written by a respected child and family therapist. Although its focus is not solely on children of divorce, this book is very useful reading for parents or therapists working with such children, as they too must undergo a grieving process—the "death of the family" and the loss of normal expectations of what a family should be. The best parts of this book include those which discuss how children perceive the world at various ages, which can determine how adults should speak to them about loss (such as the "magical thinking" stage until age 7, during which a child tends to believe that his or her thoughts and feelings directly affect the people around them). The book provides a number of lively, creative exercises designed to help a child identify and give voice to his/her feelings. This book, in contrast to many other books about children, looks at them from the inside-out, with empathy, intelligence, and feeling, and would be of help to any parent/caregiver who seeks to help a child through separation, divorce, or other trauma.

Where To Find/Buy:
Bookstores and libraries.

THE GOOD DIVORCE
Keeping Your Family Together When Your Marriage Comes Apart

★★★★

Media Type:
Print

Price:
$13.00

Principal Subject:
All-Inclusive

Written For:
Adults

ISBN:
0060926341

Author/Editor:
Constance Ahrons, Ph.D.

Edition Reviewed:
1995

About The Author:
(From Cover Notes)
The author "is a professor of sociology and associate director of the Marriage and Family Therapy Program at the University of Southern California. Dr. Ahrons maintains a private practice in Santa Monica, California."

Publisher:
HarperPerennial

Internet URL:
N/A

"Christian" Orientation?:
N/A

Focused On Issues For:
N/A

1-4 Stars

Overall Rating	★★★★	A comprehensive case for getting through divorce in a healthful way
Design, Ease Of Use	★★★	Very well written, some helpful anecdotes; generally, a "heavy" read

Recommended For:
Professionals Only

Description:
This 300 page book is based on the author's study of 98 bi-nuclear families over six years (including 91 new partners who later joined as stepparents). The author used this study, as well as her experience as a divorced parent and therapist, to form conclusions about the process and effects of divorce on the average family. Her conclusions are communicated through a long introduction ("What's Good In Divorce") and end with a summary of "Pathways To A Good Divorce." In between lie six chapters, focusing on understanding the traditional myths of divorce, forming a new vision of what divorce can be, examining the emotional stages of divorce, the bi-nuclear family, staying in control of the legal process of divorce to help ensure a healthy outcome, and examining the consequences of expanding families following divorce. The theme of approaching these issues with the objective of controlling their impact positively is consistently applied. An epilogue, centered around the author's daughter, provides closure. Then follow 50+ pages of study methodology, acknowledgements, chapter notes, and a comprehensive index.

Evaluation:
A good divorce, according to the author, is "one in which both the adults and children emerge at least as emotionally well as they were before the divorce." This, we'd argue, should the primary objective of all self-help books on the subject of divorce: to get through the process in a constructive, positive, and forward-looking manner. The author critically examines traditional thinking about divorce, tearing down the negativism that tends to fight for dominance in our thinking, and replacing it with thoughtful discourse on how divorce should be dealt with by thinking adults concerned about their long term health and that of their families. The author's "greatest hope is that [this book] will be a powerful antidote . . . to the negativity of society about divorce." We'd argue she's done this job well. A good divorce, she argues, has only three goals: "Keeping your family a family, Minimizing negative effects on your children, and Integrating your divorce in your life in a healthy way." While a "heavy" read, we'd recommend this book to any divorcing (or divorced) adult who needs the emotional and intellectual ammunition to achieve these goals.

Where To Find/Buy:
Bookstores and libraries.

DIVORCE WORKBOOK
An Interactive Guide for Kids and Families

★★★★

Media Type:
Print

Price:
$12.95

Principal Subject:
Children Of Divorce

Written For:
Children 6-12

ISBN:
0914525050

Author/Editor:
S. B. Ives, Ph.D,
D. Fassler, M.D., and
M. Lash, M.Ed., A.T.R.

Edition Reviewed:
1996

About The Author:
(From Cover Notes)

Sally Blakeslee Ives "is a child psychologist practicing in Burlington, Vermont." David Fassler "is a child psychiatrist practicing in Burlington." Michele Lash has a M.Ed. in expressive art therapies and is a registered art therapist.

Publisher:
Waterfront Books

Internet URL:
N/A

"Christian" Orientation?:
N/A

Focused On Issues For:
N/A

1-4 Stars

Overall Rating ★★★★ Empowering, participative workbook for children surviving divorce

Design, Ease Of Use ★★★★ Inviting, attractive writing style for children

---

Recommended For:
Children Of Divorce

Description:
This 145-page book (in its tenth printing) is an interactive workbook for children to use in exploring feelings about divorce. The author's open with advice for parents, teachers, counselors, and librarians on how to assist the child in using the book to their best advantage. Text is presented in six chapters that cover the topics of marriage, separation, divorce, "Legal Stuff", feelings, and "Helping Yourself". The authors have provided a mix of text that includes discussion-provoking ideas and questions in a classroom presentation style, with answers and illustrations by children themselves. Space is provided for children to draw in the book such things as their idea of a family or a picture of divorce. "Legal Stuff" helps to de-mystify court proceedings that might seem scary to a child who may have to appear in court to resolve custody issues. The book finishes with some ideas the child can use to help themselves survive divorce.

Evaluation:
Compared to other books for children and divorce this one encourages the child to become more directly involved in solving some of their challenges. It helps empower the child who may feel absolutely powerless in the divorce situation and in so doing, acknowledges their ability to come up with ways they can help. One page tells children, "Kids have lots of good ideas that could help." When used as the basis for a group discussion, children can help each other by bringing up ideas on how they adjusted to their parents divorce, or different ways of safely expressing feelings. Being invited to color or write in the book helps children more freely express themselves. Short discussion sections are interspersed with children's drawings and spaces for readers to draw or fill in their own ideas. Used as part of a school program to teach children about divorce, this book could help children understand and cope with a life event that happens all too often. A recommended resource for parent-child processing, for individual and group therapy, and for classroom instruction.

Where To Find/Buy:
Bookstores and libraries.

	1-4 Stars	
Overall Rating	★★★★	A lively, sensitive, and consoling story about divorce for young people
Design, Ease Of Use	★★★★	Entertaining and believable

Best Resource For:
Preteens who can benefit from a gentle novel about divorce's emotional impact

Recommended For:
Children Of Divorce

Description:
This book is one in a series of the author's novels (written for young people) that explore some of the difficult and painful passages in children's lives in fictional form. Here we follow the story of Karen Newman, a young girl whose parents are on the verge of divorcing, and the troubles and crises she goes through at home and school as she experiences first-hand the emotional turbulence that accompanies the splitting up of a family. The book follows Karen's life from the time she learns of her parents' separation to the struggles she goes through adapting to a single-parent family, and visiting her father in a separate apartment. The reverberations of divorce are also described through Karen's observations of her mother, father, siblings, grandparents, and friends all reacting to the phenomenon of divorce.

Evaluation:
Any young person who has grown up in America from the '70s on will have read or heard of the popular Judy Blume books. She manages to explore the most sensitive issues that young people face in an engaging and lively manner. Kids can strongly identify with the characters she presents, learning something about similar issues in their own lives while being reassured that these problems (menstruation, obesity, unpopularity, divorce) happen to others as well. For young people, there is no better way to explore painful subjects than through the healing power of fiction that has the ability to entertain even as itconsoles. In this short novel, the author captures the confusion and mild mood swings of adolescence, and the quiet, inward ways in which young people react to pain. Her "Karen" is funny, alert, and intelligent, and able to generate a positive response to the grim reality of divorce. Parents looking for a book that will introduce their children to some of the issues inherent in divorce could do no better than this novel, which treats this potentially destructive time in a child's life as an opportunity for self-growth and change.

Where To Find/Buy:
Bookstores and libraries.

★★★

Media Type
Print

Price:
$4.50

Principal Subject:
Children Of Divorce

Written For:
Children 6-12

ISBN:
0440441587

Author/Editor:
Judy Blume

Edition Reviewed:
1972

About The Author:
(From Cover Notes)
Judy Blume is an author of many books for young people, including the popular *Are You There God? It's Me, Margaret*, *Tales of a Fourth Grade Nothing*, and *Otherwise Known as Sheila the Great*. She lives in New York City.

Publisher:
Bantam Doubleday Dell

Internet URL:
N/A

"Christian" Orientation?:
N/A

Focused On Issues For:
N/A

IT'S NOT THE END OF THE WORLD

1-4 Stars

★★★★ Great workbook for groups with valuable focus on healing

★★★★ Excellent organization with easily readable writing style

1565073223

Author/Editor:
Jim Smoke

Edition Reviewed:
1995

About The Author:
(From Cover Notes)
Jim Smoke has been a nationally recognized pioneer in the divorce recovery field for over 20 years. He travels throughout North America conducting seminars, conferences, and retreats and is the author of nine books on life issues.

Publisher:
Harvest House Publishers

Internet URL:
N/A

"Christian" Orientation?:
Yes

Focused On Issues For:
N/A

Description:

This 260+ page is the revised, updated edition of the author's earlier work on the topic of surviving divorce. It begins with a one page, ten point strategy entitled "How to Survive a Divorce" that is also available in video form, with the author presenting. Fifteen chapters, each capped with "Personal Growth and Discussion Questions" precede a very extensive working guide. This book can be used either by the reader alone or as a reference text and workbook for weekly discussion groups. Chapter topics deal with a couple's struggles with the many emotions and progressions of the divorce process, such as facing the reality of divorce or establishing a new family environment. A single chapter dealing with the author's "Twenty Years of the Most Frequently Asked Question About Divorce" provides insight by answering specific questions the reader might have. The book's focus is on the individual's responsibility to work through the divorce and develop goals leading to a satisfying future. The accompanying "Working Guide", focuses on the author's wish to help the reader "grow through divorce".

Evaluation:

The reader will quickly recognize a strong Christian perspective as the author places great value on the healing value associated with committed biblical belief. The author's approach to guiding couples experiencing the trauma of divorce is based upon these beliefs. Compared to other such books, this is an excellent resource that recognizes human failing and presents its biblical teaching in a manner that non-Christians will find both useful and non-intrusive. The author places himself in the role of gentle task master—a role lending itself well for use by structured weekly discussion groups. This book does not merely provide advice as other texts on this topic might. There is strong emphasis on accepting responsibility for behavior towards oneself, one's children and one's ex-spouse. Particularly valuable is the chapter entitled "Get a Life . . . Yours!" that goes beyond divorce into healing and discusses establishing healthy relational, vocational and personal goals. The workbook guide is an excellent self-help guide for individuals and groups.

Where To Find/Buy:

Bookstores and libraries.

WHEN DIVORCE HITS HOME
Keeping Yourself Together When Your Family Comes Apart

★★★★

	1-4 Stars	
Overall Rating	★★★★	A valuable resource for teenagers and their parents regarding divorce
Design, Ease Of Use	★★★	Very easy reading in a well-organized, attractive package

Recommended For:
Children Of Divorce

Description:
Written for children with divorced parents, this book provides tips, anecdotes, and real-life accounts. It examines the various aspects of divorce from a teenager's perspective, and discusses some of the feelings he/she may encounter during this oft-traumatic time. Though the focus is children of divorce, the authors encourage divorced parents, teachers and other adults to read this book for insight on a child's mind set. The book is comprised of 50 chapters, all roughly four pages long. Each chapter presents a self-explanatory topic (for example, "It's Not Your Fault," "Don't Be Afraid to Ask Questions," "Holidays Will Be Strange," "Most Divorces Cause Money Problems"). Chapters conclude with a three point summary of its content, as well as a few first-hand accounts from teenagers relating their experiences. Each chapter begins with a reflective quote (from the likes of Thurber and TS Eliot).

Evaluation:
Books aimed at helping children of divorce grapple with their feelings are of critical importance, and this book is a good attempt at helping teenagers come to grips with their tumult. The focus of the authors is to provide empathetic insights rather than a psychological treatise, and it does present some realistic feelings and situations that kids can relate to. Written from the teenager's point of view, it provides a sensible approach toward feeling better about one's self and one's parents. The book should be helpful for most teenagers in turmoil over their parents' split and its ramifications. It is well organized, appealing in appearance, written with a light touch, and poses nothing too grave or "psychological" for its intended audience. A recommended resource for teenagers, parents, counselors and teachers.

Where To Find/Buy:
Bookstores and libraries.

Media Type:
Print

Price:
$11.00

Principal Subject:
Children Of Divorce

Written For:
Children 13+

ISBN:
0380779579

Author/Editor:
Beth Joselow and Thea Joselow

Edition Reviewed:
1st (1996)

About The Author:
(From Cover Notes)
This mother/daughter team experienced the effects of divorce in their own household. Beth Joselow is an assistant professor at The Corcoran School of Art in Washington DC. Thea Joselow was a student at Oberlin College when she wrote this book.

Publisher:
Avon Books (Heart Corporation)

Internet URL:
N/A

"Christian" Orientation?:
N/A

Focused On Issues For:
N/A

AMERICAN BAR ASSOCIATION GUIDE TO FAMILY LAW

The Complete And Easy Guide To The Laws Of Marriage, Parenthood, Separation And Divorce

★★★★

Media Type:
Print

Price:
$12.00

Principal Subject:
Legal Issues

Written For:
Adults

ISBN:
0812927915

Author/Editor:
Jeff Atkinson

Edition Reviewed:
1st (1996)

About The Author:
(From Cover Notes)

Jeff Atkinson is an adjunct professor at Depaul University College of Law. He trains Illinois judges in family law and legal ethics, and is a former chair of the ABA's Child Custody Committee.

Publisher:
Times Books (Random House)

Internet URL:
N/A

"Christian" Orientation?:
N/A

Focused On Issues For:
N/A

1-4 Stars

Overall Rating	★★★★	Covers all phases of family law in a well-written and helpful overview
Design, Ease Of Use	★★★★	Clear, concise and easy to follow; well organized chapters, extensive index

Best Resource For:
Those seeking an understanding of the legal issues encountered in a divorce

Recommended For:
Legal Issues

Description:
This legal guide encompasses the wide-ranging area of family law, from marriage to parenthood to divorce. It provides an interpretation of the laws and how they may apply to situations one may encounter. The book uses examples and simple definitions in efforts to better explain some of the "legalese." Particular emphasis is placed upon the subject of divorce and its intricacies. Among the divorce issues covered in depth are property, alimony, child support, custody, and visitation. The chapter on division of property has tips on how to make it easier and how to avoid involving a judge. A chapter providing an overview of divorce includes an outline of the steps marriage counselors use to improve a marriage; this chapter talks about the stresses of divorce and the subjects that must be addressed upon considering splitting up. The book also has sections on marital and premarital situations, including prenuptial agreements and the rights of those living together. Also included are chapters on working with lawyers and other alternatives such as mediation.

Evaluation:
This book is a useful resource for those who need to gain an overview of the laws governing marriage and divorce. Legal topics can often be confusing, but this book helps to clarify them in a straightforward manner. Its coverage is broad: prenuptial agreements, marital and non-marital property, child support, and visitation. The chapter on division of property helps define "what belongs to whom." Child support, custody and visitation, and other complicated issues, are described in easy-to-understand terms. The author maintains an objective tone throughout; there's no bias expressed, just a plain presentation of the applicable law and how it applies to various situations typically encountered in a divorce. One caveat: although the author provides numerous lists delineating various facets of marriage and family law state by state, the reader is advised to further research the law as it applies in his/her particular state.

Where To Find/Buy:
Bookstores and libraries.

DOES WEDNESDAY MEAN MOM'S HOUSE OR DAD'S?
Parenting Together While Living Apart

★★★★

Media Type:
Print

Price:
$14.95

Principal Subject:
Child Custody

Written For:
Adults

ISBN:
0471130486

Author/Editor:
Marc J. Ackerman, Ph.D.

Edition Reviewed:
1st (1997)

About The Author:
(From Cover Notes)
Marc J. Ackerman is a clinical psychologist who has worked with thousands of divorcing families and written three books on the subject of child custody. He has a counseling and consulting practice in Milwaukee.

Publisher:
John Wiley & Sons

Internet URL:
N/A

"Christian" Orientation?:
N/A

Focused On Issues For:
N/A

	1-4 Stars	
Overall Rating	★★★★	An abundance of relevant custody information in an easy to understand style
Design, Ease Of Use	★★★	Lots of chapters and subsections; sometimes tough to find an exact subject quickly

Description:
This book walks a couple through the entire process of raising a child while experiencing divorce. It aims to help parents make divorce and custody issues as comfortable as possible for their child. The book makes it clear that the child is to be the primary concern; the statement "winning is never more important than the well-being of your children" is repeated often throughout the text. In its 10 chapters, this book covers several topics. The first chapter provides facts about divorce and lets the reader know of the complexities they will face. Other chapters address how to tell the children about the divorce, custody options, and the legal process, including many nuances of placement and custody. Another chapter addresses the facets of "How to Parent Apart," including making visits better, sleeping arrangements, and the issue of cooperation. A resource section is included, referring the reader to professionals, organizations, and books which may lend further help.

Evaluation:
This book is obviously written by a psychologist who has extensive experiential knowledge regarding child custody. He is also widely read in the field and is a good communicator. He writes with the best interest of the child in mind, in a simple, explanatory tone, and does a good job interpreting this sometimes complex subject matter. An overture that emerges over and over again in this book is that divorce adversely affects children and that it is parents who determine the extent of that affect. His lists of "Custody Do's" and "Custody Don'ts" in the latter part of the book summarize the current wisdom in the field. Parents in the throes of divorce would be well advised to xerox those lists, sign them, and place them on their seperate bulletin boards. Then they could read the rest of the book. Also, of particular note are: the useful overview of divorce facts; the legal section, covering the legal issues likely to be encountered; and the practicalities of custody and parenting apart.

Where To Find/Buy:
Bookstores and libraries.

MOM'S HOUSE, DAD'S HOUSE

Making Shared Custody Work

★★★★

Media Type:
Print

Price:
$10.00

Principal Subject:
Child Custody

Written For:
Adults

ISBN:
0020777108

Author/Editor:
Isolina Ricci

Edition Reviewed:
1st (1982)

About The Author:
(From Cover Notes)
Isolina Ricci, Ph.D., is a family counselor and mediator, as well as a researcher at Stanford University, and the Executive Director of the New Family Center in Palo Alto, CA.

Publisher:
Collier Books (Macmillan)

Internet URL:
N/A

"Christian" Orientation?:
N/A

Focused On Issues For:
N/A

1-4 Stars

Overall Rating	★★★★	A highly insightful and practical guide to child custody
Design, Ease Of Use	★★	Very small text and very crowded pages, but excellent writing throughout

Recommended For:
Child Custody

Description:
The focus of this 270-page book is on how to make shared custody a workable reality, by creating a cooperative relationship with your ex-spouse and two healthy homes for your children. The first four chapters consist of a history and overview of the 2-home concept and how it redefines our notion of a "family," including a self-survey to help you assess your own situation. Chapter 5, "Watch Your Language," deals with our choice of words for describing situations of divorce and custody and its effect upon children. Chapters 7-9 discuss the emotional effects of divorce, as well as how to build a new "working" relationship with your ex-spouse. Chapter 10, "Mom's House, Dad's House," includes advice on how to make each house into a comfortable home and advice on how to divide time between two homes. Chapters 11-12 discuss how to negotiate the practical and legal aspects of custody: child expenses and support, and a division of parental rights and responsibilities. The last chapter, "After Two Years," confronts the kinds of negative "flashbacks" that can occur when family dynamics change again (especially with remarriages and second divorces). This book includes 6 appendixes with guidelines for special issues such as "The Holidays."

Evaluation:
This is a densely-packed but informative book that seeks (and largely succeeds) to cover the issues pertaining to shared child custody after divorce. Written in 1980, now over seventeen years ago, it goes over territory which at the time was relatively new and unorthodox, but which now may seem familiar to some readers. However, because divorce and "two-home" families have persisted as realities, most of the advice offered here still has value. The book is well-written, although some readers may have difficulty with the small print and crowded pages. The best sections of this book are those that deal with how to create a healthy two-home family that children can live comfortably and happily with. The advice offered is practical, sound, and sensitive, especially when discussing the emotions and needs of children. Although the tone of this book is serious, its message is overall a positive one: that "when marriage ends, the family does not break, does not magically disappear. It can instead . . . divide and multiply into separate, healthy organisms."

Where To Find/Buy:
Bookstores and libraries.

1-4 Stars

Overall Rating	★★★★	An excellent, informed resource on how to successfully negotiate a divorce settlement
Design, Ease Of Use	★★★★	Clear structure and a lucid writing style

Best Resource For:

Adults needing the knowledge to negotiate a mutually satisfying divorce settlement

Recommended For:

Mediation

Description:

This is a 318-page guide to negotiating a divorce settlement, taking you step-by-step through the emotional, legal, and financial dimensions of the process, using anecdotes and advice from the author's own experience as both a lawyer and a mediator. The first section of the book "informs, equips, and empowers you" to negotiate a divorce settlement, addressing the emotional and economic territories of divorce and taking a detailed look a divorce law, including the "three routes to settlement:" litigation by lawyers, negotiation by lawyers, and mediation. Part Two introduces you to the actual process of negotiating an agreement, including creating a parenting agreement, preparing a budget and ascertaining your financial needs, negotiating child support and alimony, and dividing marital property and assets. This section also includes worksheets for figuring out your monthly budget and expenses, dividing children's time between their parents, and a sample division of marital property.

Evaluation:

This is an enormously helpful resource for those considering a divorce settlement. The author is a lawyer, a mediator and a social scientist. His book is written for the average middle-class divorcing couple who seeks to spend as little money as possible while still achieving a reasonable, fair settlement. The author's take on the adversarial legal process is that litigation is basically an inefficient, outmoded, and harmful means of handling divorce. The author believes that the more responsibility and control divorcing couples can take in pursuit of a fair settlement (using mediation), the better they will be to emerge healthy and intact and ready to go on with their lives. This book equips the reader with the know-how and tools to necessary to create such a settlement, from successfully navigating the emotional waters of divorce to the nitty-gritty of negotiating child support, alimony, and property division. A strongly recommended resource.

Where To Find/Buy:

Bookstores and libraries.

GETTING DIVORCED WITHOUT RUINING YOUR LIFE
A . . . Guide To . . . Negotiating A Divorce Settlement

★★★★

Media Type:
Print

Price:
$12.00

Principal Subject:
Mediation

Written For:
Adults

ISBN:
0671728261

Author/Editor:
Sam Margulies

Edition Reviewed:
1992

About The Author:
(From Cover Notes)
Sam Margulies, Ph.D., J.D., is experienced in divorce litigation, negotiation, and mediation. He currently runs a private practice, and is co-director of the Institute for Dispute Resolution of the Seton Hall University Law School.

Publisher:
Fireside (Simon & Schuster)

Internet URL:
N/A

"Christian" Orientation?:
N/A

Focused On Issues For:
N/A

HELPING CHILDREN SURVIVE DIVORCE

What To Expect; How To Help

★★★★

Media Type:
Print

Price:
$12.99

Principal Subject:
Children Of Divorce

Written For:
Adults

ISBN:
0849939496

Author/Editor:
Dr. Archibald D. Hart

Edition Reviewed:
1996

About The Author:
(From Cover Notes)

The author "is professor of psychology and former dean of the Graduate School of Psychology at Fuller Theological Seminary in Pasadena, California. He is the author of eighteen books including *Stress and Your Child* and *Overcoming Anxiety*."

Publisher:
Word Publishing

Internet URL:
N/A

"Christian" Orientation?:
Yes

Focused On Issues For:
N/A

1-4 Stars

Overall Rating	★★★★	Valuable, in-depth guide on divorce with a strong focus on the child
Design, Ease Of Use	★★★★	Accessible writing style in an easy to use format

Recommended For:
Children Of Divorce

Description:
This revised and updated version of a book originally entitled *Children & Divorce* provides 200+ pages of straightforward advice on surviving divorce. Written by a psychologist who, as a child, experienced firsthand the trauma of his own parent's divorce, this book seeks to help parents help their children. A tone-setting introduction provides a brief look into the author's childhood experiences in a disintegrating family. Subsequent chapters progress through topics relating to the effects of divorce on the child and what parents, relatives, and friends can do to help. These chapters discuss in great detail those specific feelings children going through divorce may experience, such as anger, resentment, and anxiety and how these feelings can be manifested in different behaviors. Final chapters deal with re-establishing and strengthening family bonds whether within a single parent family or within combined families after remarriage. Material is derived from the author's experience working in the mental health field, and his writing reflects a Christian emphasis (scriptural references, using faith/prayer to work on problems, etc.)

Evaluation:
Knowing that children understand and pick up on what's going on around them more than we tend to think, especially while experiencing divorce, the author writes about children at a level that demonstrates deep concern for, and sensitivity to this issue. Chapters that deal in great depth with the emotional aftereffects of divorce (anxiety, anger, and depression) attest to this concern. Responsibility is placed upon parents to make mature choices. Such choices allow them to gain sufficient perspective on the divorce situation to be able to understand and respond to the destructive processes impacting their children. Chapter 3, "Healing Your Resentment" highlights some of the hostile, revengeful feelings parents, especially the one left behind, may experience. How these feelings are dealt with directly affects how the children cope. This book intelligently challenges parents to see divorce through the eyes of their children and consider the importance of their own actions in shaping their child's recovery. The Christian perspective brought by the author is helpful food for thought, and not "off-putting" to non-Christians.

Where To Find/Buy:
Bookstores and libraries.

LIFE LESSONS
50 Things I Learned From My Divorce

★★★★

Media Type:
Print

Price:
$10.00

Principal Subject:
Life After Divorce

Written For:
Adults

ISBN:
0380774941

Author/Editor:
Beth Joselow

Edition Reviewed:
1994

About The Author:
(From Cover Notes)
Beth Joselow is a divorced mother of three children. She is a poet, playwright, and assistant professor of academic studies at The Corcoran School of Art, Washington, D.C.

Publisher:
Avon Books

Internet URL:
N/A

"Christian" Orientation?:
N/A

Focused On Issues For:
Women

1-4 Stars

Overall Rating ★★★★ Insightful guide, intelligently presenting unique, useful material on surviving divorce

Design, Ease Of Use ★★★★ Very accessible writing style with illustrative anecdotes throughout

Best Resource For:
Women wanting to learn from other women's divorce/post-divorce experiences

Recommended For:
Life After Divorce

Description:
In this 150-page book, the author's experience with her own divorce and how she found ways to cope—the basis for the advice she presents—are revealed in a thoughtful introduction. The author offers the reader the same comfort and advice she found from turning to other women while she was experiencing her own separation. With hope of it helping as much as a "support group", the author provides anecdotal examples throughout her text from many women of all adult ages who have gone though divorce. Each of the 50 brief chapters bears a title of a life lesson, such as "Make the most of being alone", or "Look before you leap into new commitments." Chapter contents (always prefaced with interesting quotes by well known women) are initially presented broadly, then followed by a listing of the three most important points or tasks for the reader to think about. The author presents many aspects of coping with divorce and its aftermath not anticipated by most readers.

Evaluation:
Men, and more lately women, have known the beneficial power of mentoring as a problem solving tool. Even though a book such as this cannot expect to replace that real-life experience, it definitely does provide a look at the beneficial power of sharing life's hardships with others who have experienced it. The author's insightful text focuses not only on surviving divorce, but on survival beyond divorce in the most healthy way possible. Reading the different anecdotal comments by women who have survived, tucked into the close of each chapter, allows the reader to stand back and see her own experience more clearly, or with new insights. The book's contents go beyond the usual broad-based advice by thoughtfully presenting ideas the reader would probably not think of when dealing with divorce (for example: health concerns, or planning for a fulfilling life after divorce). Perhaps the author's best advice is found in her introduction: get together, frequently, with your best women friends; they'll help you in ways you can neither anticipate nor live without. Highly recommended.

Where To Find/Buy:
Bookstores and libraries.

FIGHTING FOR YOUR MARRIAGE
Positive Steps For Preventing Divorce and Preserving A Lasting Love

★★★★

Media Type:
Print

Price:
$14.00

Principal Subject:
Preventing Divorce

Written For:
Adults

ISBN:
0787902802

Author/Editor:
Howard Markman, Scott Stanley, Susan L. Blumberg

Edition Reviewed:
1st (1994)

About The Author:
(From Cover Notes)

Howard Markman, PhD, is co-director of the Center for Marital Studies at the University of Denver. Scott Stanley, PhD, is a professor of family therapy at Fuller Theological Seminary. Susan L. Blumberg, PhD, is a psychologist who works with families and couples.

Publisher:
Jossey-Bass, Inc.

Internet URL:
N/A

"Christian" Orientation?:
N/A

Focused On Issues For:
N/A

1-4 Stars		
Overall Rating	★★★★	Great book with focus on communication, conflict management and relationship issues
Design, Ease Of Use	★★★★	Easy to follow, well laid out, and attractive; requires commitment to get through

Recommended For:

Preventing Divorce

Description:

The thrust of this book is that couples who handle conflict and disagreement in an appropriate manner stand the best chance of having a successful marriage. Along those lines, this book offers the PREP (Prevention and Relationship Enhancement Program) approach. The authors claim that PREP is the most researched program ever developed for couples. It was originally based upon premarital counseling, but research showed that it was also effective for couples in troubled relationships. The book is divided into three sections, which also are the three fundamentals of PREP. Part 1, communication and conflict management, focuses on developing skills for dealing with relationship problems. Part 2, Core Issues, examines the attitudes of strong relationships and how you can adopt them yourself. Part 3, Enhancement, focuses on the relationship over the long term. The book has a resource section for finding a counselor if needed. At the end of each chapter, a variety of exercises are provided for couples to experiment with.

Evaluation:

This book is truly dedicated to making relationships work, and its approach is sensible, realistic and humanistic. The book speaks matter-of-factly about the components of relationships and their common problem areas. The chapters flow well from one to another, and the topics are always interesting. The section on communication and problem solving lay out typical patterns of conflict, and teaches the reader how to use the speaker/listener technique to work through troubles. It also offers ground rules for helping couples manage disagreements better. The section on core issues really delves into the heart of relationships, concentrating on topics like expectations, commitment, forgiveness, and hidden issues. There is a chapter in this section about discerning between issues and events that surely will hit home for most couples. The entire book does a good job describing different situations, and it uses examples to further illustrate them. Amusing cartoons, relating what's being discussed in the book, bring levity to the serious subjects at hand. In summary, the PREP approach is worthwhile and valid.

Where To Find/Buy:

Bookstores and libraries. The book is also available in audiotape or videotape, call 800-366-0166 for information and to place an order.

BLUE SKY BUTTERFLY

★★★★

Media Type:
Print

Price:
$14.99

Principal Subject:
Children Of Divorce

Written For:
Children 13+

ISBN:
0803719728

Author/Editor:
Jean Van Leeuwen

Edition Reviewed:
1st (1996)

About The Author:
(From Cover Notes)
Jean Van Leeuwen is the author of books for children and young adults. Included among her award-winning novels are: Bound for Oregon; The Great Summer Camp Catastrophe; and Dear Mom, You're Ruining My Life.

Publisher:
Dial Books for Young Readers (Penguin USA)

Internet URL:
N/A

"Christian" Orientation?:
N/A

Focused On Issues For:
N/A

	1-4 Stars	
Overall Rating	★★★★	Fictional story with realistic accounts of how kids see divorce and its components
Design, Ease Of Use	★★★	Hardcover novel, nicely produced, a gentle read

Recommended For:
Children Of Divorce

Description:
This novel tells the story of Twig, a middle school-aged girl whose parents have recently gone through a divorce. She harbors resentment toward her Dad, is baffled by her Mother's apathetic behavior, and wants her family life to return to its former state. She is confused about her many feelings, and she gets frustrated trying to take on her Mother's chores. Eventually, after a visit from busy-body grandma Ruthie, Twig's Mother begins to get active again and creates a garden in the back yard. This garden provides a backdrop for the growth that Twig, her brother Nathan, and her other undergo through these difficult early stages of the divorce. Among the many situations brought up in this book are misguided anger at parents, involvement of extended family and friends, the importance of communication, and working together for the good of the family. In the end, Twig realizes a family can still be normal and happy amid the chaos of divorce.

Evaluation:
This is an excellent fictional story that gives a realistic account of a child's views of divorce. This book covers some typical situations and feelings that younger children encounter during a separation and divorce: animosity toward the father, feelings of alienation and insecurity, and an unwillingness to let others know that this is difficult. The book portrays Twig as a normal girl whose life is turned upside down by the departure of her Father. Her older brother Nathan helps the story by providing a level-headed conscience. The book does a wonderful job explaining Twig's feelings, but it also describes her transformation as she sees the family interact, learns more, and becomes more open minded. For example, at first she dreads grandma Ruthie's involvement; but after grandma Ruthie's visit, Twig's eyes are opened to a new attitude. This steady progression of growth what children of divorce must strive for and hope to achieve, and this book does a fine job portraying one young girl's successful journey.

Where To Find/Buy:
Bookstores and libraries.

CHILD CUSTODY
Building Parenting Agreements that Work

★★★★

Media Type:
Print

Price:
$24.95

Principal Subject:
Child Custody

Written For:
Adults

ISBN:
0873373456

Author/Editor:
Mimi E. Lyster

Edition Reviewed:
2nd (1996)

About The Author:
(From Cover Notes)
Mimi Lyster is a professional mediator with over 12 years of experience specializing in family and child custody issues; she serves on the Board of the California Dispute Resolution Council.

Publisher:
Nolo Press

Internet URL:
N/A

"Christian" Orientation?:
N/A

Focused On Issues For:
N/A

1-4 Stars

Overall Rating ★★★★ Packed with helpful information for creating/negotiating a parenting agreement

Design, Ease Of Use ★★★★ Attractive, easy-to-follow style; cross-referenced worksheets and forms

Best Resource For:
Parents who want to develop a detailed parenting agreement on their own

Recommended For:
Child Custody

Description:
This book focuses on helping divorced parents deal with child custody issues through the creation of parenting agreements. These agreements address factors such as taking care of the children, making decisions on their behalf, assuring they spend time with both parents, and meeting their needs (medical, psychological, educational, social, etc.). The book devotes a sizable chunk to the actual formulation of a parenting agreement—preparation, negotiation, and drafting. Building the agreement takes into consideration 42 issues, ranging from medical care and education to surname and religion. The appendix contains a 20-page agreement for the parents to follow when they do their own, and there are some other worksheets to help. Another subject given attention is an explanation of mediation—this chapter shows how that process can be a viable option for settling agreement issues. Among the other topics discussed are: understanding children's needs, dealing with change, state and federal custody laws, and other sources of reference.

Evaluation:
This is an excellent resource for those addressing custody issues, as it lays the foundation for building a successful parenting agreement. It shows that, if done with careful planning, custody can be a positive experience between parents and children. It places a priority on the best interest of the children, but it also seeks to make it easier on the parents by determining in advance how everything will be handled. The book is well-written and is presented in an easy-to-follow outline style with sidebars and cross references. The chapters walk you step-by-step through designing the agreement and includes a detailed sample agreement in the Appendix. The author is an experienced mediator, so it is no surprise that she gives that topic ample attention; she praises the virtues of mediation as a preferred method for settling sticky issues. There is a fine chapter on negotiation techniques and how to apply them. Strongly recommended.

Where To Find/Buy:
Bookstores and libraries, or direct from the publisher by calling 800-992-6656.

DIVORCE & MONEY
How To Make The Best Financial Decisions During Divorce

★★★★

Media Type:
Print

Price:
$24.95

Principal Subject:
Financial Issues

Written For:
Adults

ISBN:
0873373421

Author/Editor:
V. Woodhouse, J.D., CFP and V. F. Collins, Ph.D., CFP

Edition Reviewed:
1996

About The Author:
(From Cover Notes)
Violet Woodhouse is an attorney and Certified Financial Planner, Victoria F. Collins is a Certified Financial Planner with a Ph.D. in Psychology. Both specialize in divorce and property settlement issues.

Publisher:
Nolo Press

Internet URL:
N/A

"Christian" Orientation?:
N/A

Focused On Issues For:
N/A

		1-4 Stars
Overall Rating	★★★★	Detailed financial planner for those considering divorce
Design, Ease Of Use	★★★★	Easy to read writing style with time saving chapter format

Best Resource For:
Understanding, acting upon, and managing the financial aspects of divorce

Recommended For:
Financial Issues

Description:
This is a financial guide for those considering divorce (in its third edition), focusing on equitable sharing of property and other assets. Written by Certified Financial Planners, this 330+ page text offers advice on many topics relating to the financial aspects of divorce, including selling the house, to child support and alimony, to dividing debts. Chapters topics are built upon a progression through the divorce process, starting with separation and ending with final dissolution. Opening topics relating to seeing the divorce process in a different light include, "Lessons in Legal Reality" and "Developing a Financially Focused Mental Attitude". Chapters that follow get down to business with substantial financial advice; they include include worksheets for the reader to complete on evaluating assets and planning details of a settlement. The text ends with advice on future planning, as well as an extensive Appendix on "Resources Beyond the Book."

Evaluation:
This is an up-to-date financial resource guide that could be of use to anyone involved in divorce, from those with a great deal of assets to those with very little. Thoroughly covering financial matters, including retirement, investing, and personal goal setting, this book can be helpful to both novices and those more sophisticated in financial matters. Its emphasis on seeing the marriage contract as a business proposition may be a jolt to some, but is well grounded by many examples provided by the authors. This book is an easy-to-use resource, with chapter headings clearly defining contents for quick reference. Its early chapters help focus divorcing adults on the financial issues they MUST come to grips with, no matter how unpleasant; the latter chapters provide detailed analyses and recommendations on all financial issues likely to be encountered. Also helpful are icons used to alert the reader to situations needing immediate action or referral to an attorney. Chapter 7, "Getting Help: Whom Can I Turn To?", is especially useful in defining the roles of professional services the reader might want to consider, including accountants and credit counselors.

Where To Find/Buy:
Bookstores and libraries.

PARENTS BOOK ABOUT DIVORCE

★★★★

Media Type:
Print

Price:
$6.50

Principal Subject:
Children Of Divorce

Written For:
Adults

ISBN:
0553286323

Author/Editor:
Richard A. Gardner

Edition Reviewed:
2nd (1991)

About The Author:
(From Cover Notes)
Richard A. Gardner, M.D., is a Clinical Professor of Child Psychiatry at Columbia University, and has published a number of works on divorce. He currently runs a practice in New Jersey, working with divorced parents and their children.

Publisher:
Bantam Books (Bantam Doubleday Dell Publishing Group, Inc.)

Internet URL:
N/A

"Christian" Orientation?:
N/A

Focused On Issues For:
N/A

1-4 Stars

Overall Rating	★★★★	An intelligent, informed exploration of children's psychological issues in divorce
Design, Ease Of Use	★★	Well-written but dense, crowded text

Recommended For:
Children Of Divorce

Description:
This 393-page book concentrates on psychological issues faced by children of divorce, and was written by an expert in the field of child psychiatry (also the author of other books on divorce, including The Boys and Girls Book About Divorce). This edition, first published in 1977 and revised in 1991, reflects some changes in viewpoint as well as new insights on mediation and custody issues. The book is organized into seven major sections, dealing in a chronological fashion with the stages of divorce. The first section discusses early issues (counseling, the advantages of mediation over litigation, choosing a lawyer, and pros and cons of "staying together for the children's sake"). Part 2 discusses how and when to tell children about an impending separation. Advice about telling friends, neighbors, and teachers about divorce is included in Part 3, as well as a discussion about how children may adjust to parents' new homes. Parts 4-6 deal with the stages children may go through when faced with divorce; "grown-up" issues of alimony, visitation rights, and custody laws; and how a new "extended family" can affect children.

Evaluation:
This densely-packed book, written by a leading child psychiatrist, reflects his extensive knowledge of the psychological impact of divorce upon children. Readers should probably be forewarned that this is not a "light" read: the language used is at times technical and knotty, and there is little breathing space between pages of text. It differs also from the standard "popular" books on divorce in that it does not include the usual focus questions, self-evaluation checklists, and exercises: this is less a "self-help" book than an informative exploration of children's issues in divorce. Although this makes for tough going, the benefits of this approach are that the author never tries to simplify the problems inherent in divorce—because the problems themselves are so complex, simple solutions simply will not work for long. What is offered here is specific, practical advice from an expert in the field, and the quality of that advice is extremely high. Professionals and parents who are interested in the psychology of children and who are not seeking a "quick fix" will find this book well worth their while.

Where To Find/Buy:
Bookstores and libraries.

1-4 Stars

Overall Rating	★★★★	An excellent, informative resource to the advantages of mediation
Design, Ease Of Use	★★★★	Well laid-out format and crisp, clear writing style

Best Resource For:
Information on and resources for mediation as an alternative

Recommended For:
Mediation

Description:
This 204-page book was written by an experienced, certified divorce mediator and attorney; it begins with a history of the field and a description of the mediation process. Chapters 2-4 deal with pre-mediation issues such as who may or may not be appropriate candidates for mediation, how to get an unwilling spouse to try mediation, and a list of qualifications that a good mediator should have. Chapters 5-6 include information on how/where to find names of potential mediators, as well as a list of questions to help you ascertain the mediator's competency, procedures, experience, training, and fees. Chapter 7 considers the possible effects of a mediator's gender (and possible biases). Chapter 8 discusses the use of a lawyer in conjunction with mediation, and the last chapter provides a summary of the most crucial factors in choosing a mediator. This book contains three appendices: a "Sample Information Packet" and "Contract" from the author's own mediation practice; the Academy of Family Mediators' "Standards of Practice," and a state-by-state list of Practitioner Members of the Academy; a list of other helpful books on the subject; and an index.

Evaluation:
This is an excellent, professional, and sympathetic introduction to the field of divorce mediation: its values and benefits as well as an honest look at its limits; and an indispensable guide to the choosing and obtaining of a competent, qualified divorce mediator. The book is well-written and structured: a potential maze of information is presented smoothly and succinctly, so that by the end any reader will feel able to go out and obtain the services of a good mediator. Divorce mediation, as the author points out, is a field very much still in its infancy: requirements and standards for practice are almost non-existent, although a few states now provide for the certification of mediators. Thus, if you are considering using the services of a mediator, this book is an invaluable resource: it not only serves as an introduction to the process but tells you, in a straightforward fashion, how to get the most out of it by finding the right mediator for your needs. Highly recommended.

Where To Find/Buy:
Bookstores and libraries.

CHOOSING A DIVORCE MEDIATOR
A Guide To Help Divorcing Couples Find A Competent Mediator

★★★★

Media Type:
Print

Price:
$16.95

Principal Subject:
Mediation

Written For:
Adults

ISBN:
080504762

Author/Editor:
Diane Neumann

Edition Reviewed:
1996

About The Author:
(From Cover Notes)
Diane Neumann is a certified divorce mediator, and a past president of the Academy of Family Mediators. She practices also as an attorney, has worked as a couples therapist, and is the author of *Divorce Mediation*.

Publisher:
Owl Books (Henry Holt & Company, Inc.)

Internet URL:
N/A

"Christian" Orientation?:
N/A

Focused On Issues For:
N/A

MARRIAGE SAVERS

Helping Your Friends and Family Avoid Divorce

★★★★

Media Type:
Print

Price:
$14.99

Principal Subject:
Preventing Divorce

Written For:
Adults

ISBN:
0310386616

Author/Editor:
Michael J. McManus

Edition Reviewed:
1995

About The Author:
(From Cover Notes)

Michael McManus writes a syndicated newspaper column, 'Ethics and Religion,' and co-directs marriage preparation with his wife, Harriet, at Fourth Presbyterian Church in Bethesda, Maryland.

Publisher:
Zondervan Publishing House

Internet URL:
N/A

"Christian" Orientation?:
Yes

Focused On Issues For:
N/A

1-4 Stars		
Overall Rating	★★★★	Focused on preparing for and maintaining a healthy marriage
Design, Ease Of Use	★★★	Well organized. Though heavily documented, easy to read and use

Description:

This is a 346 page text focusing on prevention of divorce that presents a values-based Christian approach to helping marriage relationships work. This heavily researched text presents data from many resources ranging from sex education teachers, to marriage counselors, to church pastors. The book's focus has a framework built upon ideas showing that strong values, such as respect for one another, saving sexual intimacies until marriage, and lifelong commitment are important for a strong marriage partnership. The author begins with three chapters that discuss the growing divorce problem in our society and the lack of effective and extensive (in many churches) pre-marriage counseling. The chapter "Help for the Seriously Dating Couple" discusses a plan ("Prepare") that churches can use to help couples get ready for marriage. Subsequent chapters cover marriage expectations, different strategies for healing troubled marriages, and the need for divorce and marriage law reform.

Evaluation:

Marriage in the church is taken seriously as a life-long commitment made by two people. In light of this, the author has taken a preventative approach with ideas and teaching plans based on a strict interpretation of Christian values. Heavily researched and presenting data on the rise in teen pregnancies and single parent families (with no turnaround in sight), the author suggests a return to old fashioned family values. He concludes that sex education in schools is only an effective tool if it is coupled with a strong values system taught at home by parents or through an ongoing association with one's church. The author suggests a strong commitment by parents to involve themselves in teaching family values to children, by schools to adopt a "proper" approach to sex education (teaching respect and delay of gratification), and by churches to help prepare premarital couples using extensive counseling and workshops. This is not a text that one reads in one sitting, but demands careful attention. Especially recommended for pastors and church ministers.

Where To Find/Buy:

Bookstores and libraries.

HOW IT FEELS WHEN PARENTS DIVORCE

★★★★

Media Type:
Print

Price:
$15.00

Principal Subject:
Children Of Divorce

Written For:
Children 13+

ISBN:
0394758552

Author/Editor:
Jill Krementz

Edition Reviewed:
1996

About The Author:
(From Cover Notes)
The author works as a journalist, photographer, and portraitist, and has written many other books for children. In 1984 she was awarded the Washington Post/Children's Book Guild Nonfiction Award. She lives in New York City.

Publisher:
Knopf

Internet URL:
N/A

"Christian" Orientation?:
N/A

Focused On Issues For:
N/A

	1-4 Stars	
Overall Rating	★★★★	A compelling and intimate look at divorce through the eyes of a child
Design, Ease Of Use	★★★★	Lovely photographs accompany the children's sensitive and revealing accounts

Best Resource For:
Teens seeking to learn more about the emotions of divorce

Recommended For:
Children Of Divorce

Description:
This book is filled with the stories and photographs of nineteen children (ages 7-16) who have experienced divorce. The children narrate their own histories: describing each family's unique situation, what they remember of the divorce itself, and the different ways in which they and their families have tried to put themselves back together again. Each story is illustrated with portraits of the child and his/her parents and extended family.

Evaluation:
The author's books have always been popular with children due to her way of "telling the story" of young people's lives through her unadorned and revealing photographs. This book, as well, succeeds largely through the quality of the "portraits" of these children—we get a real glimpse into their homes and lives—as well as through the sensitive text that accompanies them. The method of having children tell their own stories about divorce is a very powerful way to help other children explore their own experiences: there is no "didactic force" at work telling them what they should or should not feel or think, just the voices and pictures of other children talking about their own lives. The stories these children tell about divorce are very different, ranging from stories of near-painless divorces and successful shared parenting arrangements to stories of very painful separations and abandonment. Throughout, these children stress the powerful effect their parents' actions can have upon them, for good and for ill. This is an honest look at the reality of divorce through a child's eyes—though not all the outcomes they describe are perfectly happy, most are, at least, graced by their insights and wisdom.

Where To Find/Buy:
Bookstores and libraries.

CRAZY TIME
Surviving Divorce & Building A New Life

★★★★

Media Type:
Print

Price:
$13.00

Principal Subject:
All-Inclusive

Written For:
Adults

ISBN:
0060923091

Author/Editor:
Abigail Trafford

Edition Reviewed:
2nd (1992)

About The Author:
(From Cover Notes)

The author "is a health editor of the Washington Post, and is a former assistant managing editor of U.S. News & World Report. An award-winning journalist, she has contributed articles to Time, the Boston Globe, and many other publications."

Publisher:
HarperPerennial
(HarperCollins)

Internet URL:
N/A

"Christian" Orientation?:
N/A

Focused On Issues For:
N/A

1-4 Stars

Overall Rating ★★★★ An anecdotal and insightful guide to surviving divorce and its aftermath

Design, Ease Of Use ★★★★ A simple, easily understood chapter progression, very accessible writing style

---

Best Resource For:
Adults needing reassurance and perspective as they enter the divorce process

Recommended For:
All-Inclusive

Description:
This 275+ page book starts with a thoughtful prologue, written by the author about her own divorce and her reasons for writing this book. The book has three major sections, "Crisis", "Crazy Time", and "Recovery"; these sections deal with what the author defines as the three stages of divorce: a countdown to crisis (up to a year or more), the divorce and its aftermath (1-2 years), and the recovery period (3 to 5 years). Each section has several chapters, and each chapter uses stories from couples the author has interviewed to help readers understand (and relate to) each stage of divorce. Throughout, the author provides observation, analysis, lessons learned, and suggestions. "Crisis" describes deadlock, confrontation, and separation. "Crazy Time" includes chapters on relief/disbelief, shock, anger, and depression. "Recovery", the longest section, deals with the emergence of self, sex, love, dealing with the "public" aspects of divorce, remarriage, and others. A bibliography and index are included.

Evaluation:
The cover of this book notes that 250,000+ copies are in print; that makes it a best-seller in this field. We can easily see why. It's not preachy (yet has obviously benefited from professional input), it's based on the author's (and countless others') real experiences, it's a gentle mix of anecdote, observation, and guidance; in short, it's both real and accessible. The prologue is a great overview of how the book came about; its themes (carried throughout the book) are positive, focusing on the crisis of divorce as a positive agent for individual change necessary for building a new life. The focus of the book is not really on prevention, though a careful reading of the "Crisis" section could help couples understand the cracks in their own marriage. The fundamental impact of this work will be to help those about to divorce understand and deal with what they are about to experience. In this focus is found its principal value, which is to reassure individuals that they are not alone, that the emotions they're being battered with are not unique, are survivable, and will (if used to fuel positive change) lead to happier times. Highly recommended.

Where To Find/Buy:
Bookstores and libraries.

CHILDREN OF DIVORCE
A Developmental Approach To Residence And Visitation

★★★★

Media Type:
Print

Price:
$14.95

Principal Subject:
Child Custody

Written For:
Adults

ISBN:
0940929066

Author/Editor:
Mitchell Baris, Ph.D.;
Carla Garrity, Ph.D.

Edition Reviewed:
1988

About The Author:
(From Cover Notes)

Mitch Baris, Ph.D. and Carla Garrity, Ph.D. practice psychology in Denver, Colorado. A part of their work has been in helping families resolve residence and visitation issues.

Publisher:
Blue Ridge

Internet URL:
N/A

"Christian" Orientation?:
N/A

Focused On Issues For:
N/A

1-4 Stars

Overall Rating ★★★★ A clear, concise, well informed work

Design, Ease Of Use ★★★★ Very readable; well organized

Recommended For:
Child Custody

Description:
This relatively short book developed out of the authors' interest in finding a means to help families resolve residence and visitation issues outside the courtroom. It is written for parents who are bonded to their children, who possess competent parenting skills, and who are available and willing to co-parent. In terms of enabling parents to make the best decisions for their children's residence and/or visitation, the authors follow three basic guidelines: minimize the loss; maximize the relationship with each parent; allow the successful mastery of age-appropriate developmental tasks. Following these principles, the authors present five chapters in the first half of the book, each of which addresses a different developmental age from infancy to adolescence. Each chapter outlines the residence and visitation recommendations appropriate for that age as well as the risks and specific circumstances involved. The second half of the book is a compendium of questions the authors have been asked by parents and the authors' responses.

Evaluation:
It is a common observation among marriage/family therapists that, in the divorce process, the child's needs are oftentimes overlooked by parents whose focus is on their own trauma. The authors of this book certainly share that concern. According to them, what is of paramount importance is the realization by parents that divorce affects children differently depending upon their developmental stage. The authors address this quite well through the use of graphs, chapters on the developmental stages, and questions and answers in the second half of the book. There are many other positives about this work: 1) it is clearly written; 2) it is based upon solid scientific knowledge and experiential knowledge of professionals actively involved in the field; 3) it is extremely practical with concrete directives for the parent who wants the best for his/her child. And, as the authors state, it is not recommended for everyone, especially for parents who must win at all costs or for those who cannot put their own needs aside to allow their children to be the "winners."

Where To Find/Buy:
Bookstores and libraries.

SURVIVING THE BREAKUP

★★★★

Media Type:
Print

Price:
$14.50

Principal Subject:
Children Of Divorce

Written For:
Adults

ISBN:
0465083455

Author/Editor:
Judith S. Wallerstein &
Joan B. Kelly

Edition Reviewed:
1979

About The Author:
(From Cover Notes)

Judith S. Wallerstein is
principal investigator of the
Children of Divorce Project;
Joan Kelly co-directed that
project until 1980. They are
internationally recognized.

Publisher:
Harper Collins (Basic
Books)

Internet URL:
N/A

**"Christian"
Orientation?:**
N/A

Focused On Issues For:
N/A

1-4 Stars

Overall Rating	★★★★	A classic in the field; well researched and written
Design, Ease Of Use	★★★	Well organized; technical language style

Recommended For:
Professionals Only

Description:
This 300+ work consists of four parts which chronicle children and parents over a five year period following the dissolution of the marriage. Part 1 concerns the actual separation. As the four chapters in this section describe, this period is profoundly stressful for the children and adolescents as well as many of the parents. Feelings ran high, conflicts escalated and unhappiness was widespread. Part 2 describes the parents and children after the separation, especially in terms of the changes which take place in the parent-child relationship. Part 3 is entitled "Transition" and it reports the findings of the Project eighteen months after the separation. This time is marked by many external changes in social, economic and family circumstances, as well as changes in the family. Part 4 consists of six chapters and describes the families five years beyond the separation. By this time the families were diverse and ranged from stable, happy new homes to being stuck in unhappiness.

Evaluation:
Wallerstein's name and "children of divorce" have become synonymous because of her work in the field over the past decades. Like any pioneer, her work has been praised and criticized. Critics frequently point out that her sixty families are a sample without a comparison group of intact families. Consequently, all of the problems which emerged in the children and parents in the sixty families are blamed on the divorce without comparison to intact families. Also, her "sample" is composed of volunteer families who had come to the clinic for counseling; many parents of these families had extensive psychiatric histories. Social scientists will probably continue to debate the study's limitations; nonetheless, Wallerstein's work clearly captured the turmoil, negative feelings, and pain which impact children of divorce. She has helped sensitize us to divorce's effects on the children, and books written later by children themselves have helped substantiate her findings. This book is not an easy read for the non-professional, but for the parent and/or the professional who wishes to enter into the world of children affected by divorce, it is a convincing treatise.

Where To Find/Buy:
Bookstores and libraries.

SECOND CHANCES
Men, Women And Children A Decade After Divorce

★★★★

Media Type:
Print

Price:
$12.95

Principal Subject:
Children Of Divorce

Written For:
Adults

ISBN:
0395735335

Author/Editor:
Judith S. Wallerstein &
Sandra Blakeslee

Edition Reviewed:
1996

About The Author:
(From Cover Notes)
Judith S. Wallerstein is considered the world's foremost authority on the effects of divorce. She is the founder of the Center for the Family in Transition. Sandra Blakeslee is an award-winning freelance science and medical writer.

Publisher:
Houghton Mifflin

Internet URL:
N/A

"Christian" Orientation?:
N/A

Focused On Issues For:
N/A

1-4 Stars

Overall Rating	★★★★	A landmark book
Design, Ease Of Use	★★★★	Language is narrative and engaging

Recommended For:
Professionals Only

Description:
This book follows five years after her first book, Surviving the Breakup, which reported her findings on sixty divorced families five years after their breakup. Second Chances takes a look at some of those families ten years later (some of the children in Second Chances are now parents themselves). The book consists of five parts. Part I describe divorce from the author's point of view and her getting back in touch with her divorced families ten years later. The next three parts of the book take an in-depth look at three of the families (both parents and children) and also contain chapters on the legacy of violence, the overburdened child, and joint custody. The book concludes with Part V which addresses the "danger and opportunity" relative to divorce today, including the psychological tasks that must be accomplished in any divorce, and the "state of the union" concerning how our society is handling divorce through its attitudes and institutions.

Evaluation:
This book, as well as all that Judith Wallerstein has authored, is the result of diligent research. It is research that has been accomplished by rubbing shoulders with persons of divorce as they have walked through that process over the years, either as adults or as children. This book shows how she has come to know and love families like the Moores, the Burrelles, and the Catalanos. The reader who is contemplating or experiencing the beginnings of a divorce is thus able to vicariously project what challenges his/her family will experience in the years ahead if the divorce continues to progress. What we are learning from Wallerstein's work is also found in the better self-help books: that divorce is a process, not an event; that it is a wrenching experience for almost all children; that the effects of divorce are often long-lasting; that almost all children of divorce regard their childhood and adolescence as having taken place in the shadow of divorce. This is a great book and a " must read" for anyone who feels that an intact family is worth fighting for.

Where To Find/Buy:
Bookstores and libraries.

LEARNING TO LEAVE
A Woman's Guide

★★★★

Media Type:
Print

Price:
$13.99

Principal Subject:
All-Inclusive

Written For:
Adults

ISBN:
0446394831

Author/Editor:
Lynette Triere with
Richard Peacock

Edition Reviewed:
1993

About The Author:
(From Cover Notes)

Lynette Triere "is a lecturer,
workshop leader, and a
nationally recognized
divorce expert." Richard
Peacock "is an Associate
Professor of Cinema,
teaching screen writing at
Palomar College, San
Marcos, CA and has
authored numerous articles
on human relationships."

Publisher:
Warner Books

Internet URL:
N/A

**"Christian"
Orientation?:**
N/A

Focused On Issues For:
Women

1-4 Stars

Overall Rating	★★★★	Forward thinking guide with survival techniques for women facing divorce
Design, Ease Of Use	★★★	Easy to read, well organized; small font size is a burden

Description:

This revised edition of an early 1980's text of the same title offers 370 pages of advice to women considering leaving an unhappy marriage. The text opens with an Introduction that speaks about the first edition and its introduction at a time when cultural views were more strongly against divorce and the women who chose that route. Chapter One, "The Reality of Divorce" is an explanation on how our society views divorcing women and how parents, friends and economic considerations enter into the picture. Included in this chapter is the author's own story of her painstaking choice to divorce after a nineteen year marriage and some of the extremely hard decisions she had to make at that time. The eight chapters that follow cover such topics as "Indecision", "Emotional Problems" and "Necessary Strategies". The major focus of this text is in helping women survive divorce, financially and emotionally, with a slant on feminist ideas.

Evaluation:

The authors have chosen an interesting and helpful focus in this book, one that cultivates the feminist ideals of independence, equality, safety, and respect for all women. This book is different from others in that it focuses on some of the unique ways divorce can be different for women than for men. Highlighted are some of the different issues women face when divorcing compared to men, including making sure the woman is safe as she leaves her marriage. The most helpful aspect of the authors' writing is the fine detail applied to their suggestions; for example, a chapter on "Husbands—And Leaving Them" describes what motivates men's views of marriage and divorce, how they might react to a divorce in different ways, outlines possible indicators of how they might react, and makes specific suggestions on how a wife should tell a husband that she wants a divorce. Legal advice, though offered sparingly in this text, includes getting restraining orders and divorce proceedings in general. The book closes with a lengthy annotated section of reference books applicable to each of nine chapters as well as a "Helpful Organizations" referral section.

Where To Find/Buy:

Bookstores and libraries.

1-4 Stars

Overall Rating	★★★★	A knowledgeable guide to understanding and dealing with your child after divorce
Design, Ease Of Use	★★★	Well-ordered structure; somewhat "academic" language

Recommended For:
Children Of Divorce

Description:
Composed of four major parts, this 221-page book teaches divorced parents how to help their children cope successfully with divorce and its aftermath. The author states that he will act as "your child's advocate" to let parents know what their children may be thinking and feeling throughout the various stages of divorce. Each chapter concentrates on a specific issue and then gives guidelines and advice to help you respond effectively to your child's needs and concerns. It is the author's opinion that "children do not have to suffer long-term negative consequences of divorce" if parents are aware of their children's thoughts and feelings, and act upon the guidelines suggested in this book. The first part provides an overview of divorce and its effects upon children. Part Two discusses children's separation anxieties, the wish to reunite their parents, and feeling responsible for the break-up. Part Three explains how to cooperate with an ex-spouse, the importance of each parent's contact with the children, and custody arrangements. Part Four presents an in-depth look at child-rearing issues and practices.

Evaluation:
This book provides a knowledgeable look at how children typically react to and deal with the divorce of their parents. The author has presented these issues from the children's viewpoint, so that parents will become aware of their unique needs and concerns, and learn to deal with them effectively. This viewpoint will provide many revelations for parents baffled by their children's behavior after divorce. Just as children may misinterpret their parents' divorce (e.g. thinking it was their fault), so do parents misinterpret their children's actions after a divorce (e.g. flunking out of school). This book will help to clear up many of these mutual "mysteries." There are some particularly useful sections on how to effectively discipline a child, and the importance of "validating" a child's natural sadness. The section on step-families is also helpful. Readers should receive a plethora of insights about their children's feelings and behavior after divorce, and sensitive, effective parenting strategies to deal effectively with these reactions.

Where To Find/Buy:
Bookstores and libraries.

HELPING CHILDREN COPE WITH DIVORCE

★★★★

Media Type:
Print

Price:
$14.00

Principal Subject:
Children Of Divorce

Written For:
Adults

ISBN:
0669270687

Author/Editor:
Edward Teyber

Edition Reviewed:
1992

About The Author:
(From Cover Notes)
The author is a child-clinical psychologist, professor of psychology, and director of the Community Counselor Center at California State University, San Bernardino. He has written many articles related to children and the family.

Publisher:
Jossey-Bass Publishers

Internet URL:
N/A

"Christian" Orientation?:
N/A

Focused On Issues For:
N/A

101 WAYS TO BE A LONG-DISTANCE SUPER DAD . . . OR MOM, TOO!

★★★★

Media Type:
Print

Price:
$9.95

Principal Subject:
Children Of Divorce

Written For:
Adults

ISBN:
1568751885

Author/Editor:
George Newman

Edition Reviewed:
2nd (1996)

About The Author:
(From Cover Notes)

The author is a writer living in Tucson, Arizona. He received his MS degree in psychology from the University of Wisconsin-Milwaukee in 1973 and has spent a great portion of his professional life as a reporter.

Publisher:
R & E Publishers

Internet URL:
N/A

"Christian" Orientation?:
N/A

Focused On Issues For:
N/A

1-4 Stars

Overall Rating	★★★★	Useful guide for non-custodial parents to stay involved with their children
Design, Ease Of Use	★★★	Easy to ready style and straightforward presentation

Description:

This 121-page book provides exactly what its title promises—101 ways to stay in touch with your children when you are not the custodial parent or are away from your children through a job or military service. It is the second revised edition of an earlier book by the author entitled, "101 Ways to be a Long-Distance Super-Dad," It has been rewritten to include advice for Moms experiencing separation from their children. Chapters, one for each suggested activity, are one to two pages long and simply illustrated. Individual chapters focus on some of the many ways parents can stay in touch with their children. These include both in-person contact with the child, such as sharing vacations and spending special occasions together, as well as the less direct, staying in touch by telephone, mail, fax, and e-mail. Activities range from purely fun to those with a focus on learning that involve sharing of cultural and educational experiences.

Evaluation:

The main focus of this book is on ways parents can provide a sense of stability for children of divorced families and to demonstrate by their involvement that they will always love and be there for their children. Suggestions provided in this book will facilitate parental involvement in the child's life in many ways. Chapter 61, "A Child's Own Room", speaks to the child's needs for stability, for example, by suggesting that non-custodial parents create a permanent space in their home for their child. The author makes the possibilities for involvement in the child's school, hobbies, and sports activities by long distance methods seem easier than might be the case in real life. Although some suggestions for parents involve spending money (long distance phone calls, purchasing science kits, private lessons, or magazine subscriptions), some require very little expenditure. The fact that the author includes such a variety of suggestions makes it easier for readers to find and use more than a few of the gems from its pages.

Where To Find/Buy:

Bookstores and libraries.

SAVING YOUR MARRIAGE BEFORE IT STARTS
Seven Questions To Ask Before (And After) You Marry

★★★★

Media Type:
Print

Price:
$16.00

Principal Subject:
Preventing Divorce

Written For:
Adults

ISBN:
0310492408

Author/Editor:
Dr. Les Parrott III and Dr. Leslie Parrott

Edition Reviewed:
1995

About The Author:
(From Cover Notes)
The Parrott husband and wife team are co-directors of the Center for Relationship Development at Seattle Pacific University, where Les is a professor of clinical psychology and Leslie is a marriage and family therapist.

Publisher:
Zondervan Publishing House

Internet URL:
N/A

"Christian" Orientation?:
Yes

Focused On Issues For:
N/A

1-4 Stars

Overall Rating	★★★★	A sensitive, down-to-earth look at the make-up of a healthy marriage
Design, Ease Of Use	★★★	Highly readable and personable writing style

Recommended For:
Preventing Divorce

Description:
The Parrotts wrote this book out of their own experiences with married life, and the experiences of the "hundreds of married couples" they've counseled as a psychologist and a marriage/family therapist. This book is intended to be read by young couples before marriage in order to prepare them for a healthy, lifelong commitment, although it can also be used by older couples and those already married. The book is based on the seven principles of happily married couples (such as "healthy expectations of marriage," "a realistic conception of love," "the ability to communicate feelings," and "a common spiritual foundation and goal"), and follows these principles chapter by chapter. Each chapter includes anecdotes and reflective exercises, as well as an in-depth discussion of the issues. Some treatment of the issues reflects the authors' Christian perspective (especially towards the end), although this treatment is light and does not overwhelm the book's focus.

Evaluation:
This book offers much in the way of good, practical, and insightful advice on building and maintaining a successful marriage. The writing is warm and personable, and one gets a comforting sense of authors' benevolent presence all the way through, speaking intimately from personal and professional experience. This makes for a nice change from the rather cooler, distanced tone of some self-help books. The seven chapters, focussed on the seven principles of a happy marriage, are highly readable—one of this book's chief virtues is that it never lectures or condescends. All the chapters provide helpful advice and thoughtful exercises; the weakest, however, being the chapter entitled "Have You Bridged the Gender Gap?," which presents stereotypes of male and female characteristics instead of the real complexity of "the gender gap." This book reflects the Christian orientation of its authors, but this is couched in a wider sense of "spirituality" within marriage, and so is unlikely to discourage those readers of different religious persuasions. Overall, readers will find this a sensible, intelligent guide to creating a happy, healthy marrige.

Where To Find/Buy:
Bookstores and libraries.

WHY MARRIAGES SUCCEED OR FAIL

And How You Can Make Yours Last

★★★★

Media Type:
Print

Price:
$12.00

Principal Subject:
Preventing Divorce

Written For:
Adults

ISBN:
0684802414

Author/Editor:
John Gottman, PH.D. with Nan Silver

Edition Reviewed:
1994

About The Author:
(From Cover Notes)
The author "is a professor in the Department of Psychology at the University of Washington in Seattle."

Publisher:
Simon & Schuster

Internet URL:
N/A

"Christian" Orientation?:
N/A

Focused On Issues For:
N/A

	1-4 Stars		
Overall Rating	★★★★	A relationship strengthening, research based guide
Design, Ease Of Use	★★★	Well organized; although based on a scientific study, easy to read.

Recommended For:
Preventing Divorce

Description:
This 234-page book is the culmination of twenty years of research by the author involving couples with a focus on what keeps them together and what tears them apart. In bringing couples into a laboratory setting the author was able to examine their responses directly by using video cameras and electrodes, by noting raises in heart rate, changes in expressions, and through noting body movements. Chapter One, "What Makes Marriage Work?", begins with an introduction covering the authors research and similar projects by others in the field of psychology. This chapter also introduces the topics of conflict resolution and communication techniques useful in a healthy relationship. Chapters Two through Five provide insight into the causes of marital unhappiness and offer self tests to discover trouble spots. "Diagnostic Checklist", Chapter Six presents a test you and your partner can complete and discusses methods to use as remedies for communication problems. Chapter Seven, "The Four Keys To Improving Your Marriage", suggests ways to communicate more effectively.

Evaluation:
The author of this book strongly believes that habits can be changed with a little effort and that it is the responsibility of each person in a relationship to make it work. With this in mind, and armed with knowledge of three different styles of problem solving practiced in successful marriages, the reader is presented with ways to make major changes in communication patterns. This text serves as a useful guide for those who are serious about working towards a better relationship by effectively pointing out problem areas and strategies for making changes. The information presented here differs from that presented in other divorce prevention workbooks by the sheer weight of its body of research drawn directly from an analysis of relationships gathered over many years. In the presentation of these findings one discovers that arguments are necessary for a good relationship and a willingness to occasionally defer to the other person is a good decision. The final chapter, "Strengthening Your Foundations," particularly, presents ideas for positively changing our own patterns of relating to our spouse.

Where To Find/Buy:
Bookstores and libraries.

1-4 Stars

Overall Rating	★★★	Insightful guide to understanding and coping with divorce
Design, Ease Of Use	★★★	Readable style

Recommended For:
Life After Divorce

Description:
The audience for this work is intended to the be person experiencing divorce. It has grown out of the author's therapeutic work with couples and families, an interview process which she devised for her study of two hundred divorced couples as well as her personal experience of her own divorce. She examines the dynamics of how the marriage came to dissolve, the pain of both the "leaver" and the one "left" and the feelings which need to be felt by anyone experiencing divorce. An essential part of the process of divorce, according to this author, is recovery. In support of this, her book contains suggestions for: self care, perceiving divorce as a positive force, helping children cope with divorce and, in general, creating a new life. Along with the primary text of the book are informative illustrations and the antecdotal stories of four individuals who experienced the trauma of divorce.

Evaluation:
Sharon Wegscheider-Cruse has distinguished herself primarily through her writings on addictions, co-dependency and recovery. Her written work is always quite readable, practical, and grounded in her therapeutic work with her clients. This book is no exception. It is not only easy to read, but the reader has the distinct impression that she/he is reading the words of someone who has already "walked the walk" and has not only survived her own personal divorce, but has seen it as a positive force in her life and the lives of others. The personal experiences of the author, then, are definitely a strength of this book. But, as such, it tends to be experiential and often lacks a research base that other similar works contain. It also appears to have been quickly written, incorporating large segments from earlier works and addresses some topics with a certain superficiality. Her discussion concerning legal guidelines of divorce does not even mention mediation, for example, which is widely used today by many couples.

Where To Find/Buy:
Libraries and bookstores.

LIFE AFTER DIVORCE
Create A New Beginning

★★★

Media Type:
Print

Price:
$8.95

Principal Subject:
Life After Divorce

Written For:
Adults

ISBN:
1558742824

Author/Editor:
Sharon Wegscheider-Cruse

Edition Reviewed:
1994

About The Author:
(From Cover Notes)
The author is president of ONSITE Training and Consulting, Rapid City, S.D. She is a popular presenter and has authored a number of self help books.

Publisher:
Health Communications, Inc.

Internet URL:
N/A

"Christian" Orientation?:
N/A

Focused On Issues For:
N/A

GROWING UP DIVORCED

How to Help Your Child Cope With Every Stage

★★★

Media Type:
Print

Price:
$5.99

Principal Subject:
Children Of Divorce

Written For:
Adults

ISBN:
0449205703

Author/Editor:
Linda Bird Francke

Edition Reviewed:
1990

About The Author:
(From Cover Notes)
Linda Bird Francke is a journalist and an editor. She has written and edited for several prominent newspapers and magazines. She's a divorced mother of three.

Publisher:
Ballantine Books

Internet URL:
N/A

"Christian" Orientation?:
N/A

Focused On Issues For:
N/A

1-4 Stars

Overall Rating	★★★	Excellent descriptions of stages of child's life; outdated statistics
Design, Ease Of Use	★★★	Engaging writing style; small print is hard to read

Description:

This book begins with a very poignant description of the author's former husband sharing with their children that he would be moving out of the house that day and that divorce was imminent. On the surface, the children seemed to handle this news and the divorce quite well and it was only later as the author began to interview them for an article she was preparing did she realize how traumatized her own children were by her divorce. As a result she began to two year project of interviewing children of divorce as well as top specialists in the divorce field. This book is the result of that research. The heart of the book are the chapters addressing divorce through the eyes of the child. Developmental stages of the child are explained with particular emphasis on the feelings associated with that age relative to the divorce of the parents. Each chapter concludes with helpful suggestions concerning how the parent can deal with the feelings of the child at each developmental age.

Evaluation:

Previous reviewers have used words like "sensible," "warm," "heart-wrenching" to describe this work; we would agree. The primary message of this work is that divorce is painful, not only for adults, but especially for children. Long after the decree has been signed, children may have problems the adults have not imagined. The author pleads with the adult parent to reach out in understanding to the child and to directly address the needs of each child affected by the divorce. Her writing is enriched by innumerable antedotes and quotations from children she interviewed. Consequently, the reader cannot help but gain a perspective on the divorce experience, the life of the stepfamily, the interventions of the courts, and so forth, through the eyes of the child. One disappointment: all statistical references are now dated, since this edition is now 13 years' old.

Where To Find/Buy:

Bookstores and libraries.

DIVIDED FAMILIES
What Happens to Children When Parents Part

★★★

Media Type:
Print

Price:
$12.50

Principal Subject:
Professionals Only

Written For:
Adults

ISBN:
067465577X

Author/Editor:
Frank F. Furstenberg, Jr.;
Andrew J. Cherlin

Edition Reviewed:
1994

About The Author:
(From Cover Notes)
Frank F. Furstenberg, Jr., is Professor or Sociology at the University of Pennsylvania; Andrew J. Cherlin is Professor of Sociology at John Hopkins University.

Publisher:
Harvard University Press

Internet URL:
N/A

"Christian" Orientation?:
N/A

Focused On Issues For:
N/A

	1-4 Stars	
Overall Rating	★★★	Summary of research; a "self-help" book solely in terms of information
Design, Ease Of Use	★★★	Very well organized, clear; restricted audience

Description:

This is a short book (119+ pages). It consists of six relatively brief chapters which summarize the findings of social scientists, focused on divorces which take place primarily in the United States. The focus of the first three chapters are expressed in the subtitle of the book, "what happens to children when parents part." The principal message from the research which the authors discuss in these chapters is that, after parental separation, most children adapt successfully as long as their mother does well both psychologically and financially, and conflict between the former spouses is low. What is alarming about divorce and children, they note, is that the relationship between father and children oftentimes weakens after the divorce. The final two chapters discuss the children's well being in remarriage. Also discussed in the final chapters is the topic of divorce as influenced by law/public policy.

Evaluation:

This book is quite readable, and the reader is well aware that every word is backed by research. The extensive notes (10 pages) at the end of this brief work leaves no doubt that this is the case. This book is not a self-help book in the usual sense. But it is an excellent summary of the research which underlies the principles set forth in any contemporary self-help work on divorce, especially in relationship to children experiencing the divorce of parents. The primary readership who would find this book helpful, then, would be educators, mediators, lawyers, legislators, psychologists, etc. whose need to be informed and knowledgeable is essential to their credibility and to their work.

Where To Find/Buy:

Bookstores and libraries.

THE DIVORCE SOURCEBOOK

★★★

Media Type:
Print

Price:
$16.00

Principal Subject:
Legal Issues

Written For:
Adults

ISBN:
1565654749

Author/Editor:
Dawn Bradley Berry, J.D.

Edition Reviewed:
1996

About The Author:
(From Cover Notes)

The author is a lawyer and a writer. According to the cover of her book, she has worked "extensively in the area of civil rights law." She resides in New Mexico.

Publisher:
Lowell House

Internet URL:
N/A

"Christian" Orientation?:
N/A

Focused On Issues For:
N/A

1-4 Stars

Overall Rating	★★★	Sensitive and well informed advice giving guidance on issues of divorce
Design, Ease Of Use	★★★★	Easy to read writing style

Recommended For:
Legal Issues

Description:

This 300+ page book begins with a chapter which traces the development of family law and social attitudes on divorce. The bulk of the remainder of the book concerns the legal and ethical issues which are faced by anyone in American culture who experiences divorce: what to expect in the divorce process, how mediation and litigation work, special legal complications that can arise in any divorce, property settlement issues, family law, and children. The author borrows liberally from other experts, especially mental health experts, in discussing other issues relative to divorce. These include the emotional issues of both adults and children going through the divorce as well as the process of building a new life beyond this experience. An extensive bibliography, list of resources, organizations and state laws conclude the work.

Evaluation:

This work is written by a lawyer and, as we might expect, the majority of the work provides information and advice on the legal issues that any adult and child in this culture must experience, and deal with, as the legal aspects of their divorce begin to unfold. This text can be a very helpful resource for the adult who is experiencing divorce for the first time, and who is intimidated by the legal system, not sure how "litigation" differs from "mediation," or fearful about property settlement or what is best for the children. The book is is not filled with legalese; rather, the author's writing imparts both clarity and sensitivity. Thus, the individual who is suffering the intense emotional trauma of divorce and also stepping into the unfamiliar legal world of lawyers, mediators, judges, accountants, filings of legal documents, parenting plans, and so forth, will find this book a helpful companion.

Where To Find/Buy:
Bookstores and libraries.

BETWEEN LOVE AND HATE
A Guide to Civilized Divorce

★★★

Media Type:
Print

Price:
$13.95

Principal Subject:
All-Inclusive

Written For:
Adults

ISBN:
0452274966

Author/Editor:
Lois Gold, M.S.W.

Edition Reviewed:
1996

About The Author:
(From Cover Notes)
Lois Gold, M.S.W. is past president of the National Academy of Mediators. She is a psychotherapist, specializing in marital therapy and divorce mediation.

Publisher:
Penguin Books (Plume)

Internet URL:
N/A

"Christian" Orientation?:
N/A

Focused On Issues For:
N/A

1-4 Stars

Overall Rating	★★★	A very thorough discussion of handling the divorce
Design, Ease Of Use	★★★	Well organized; small print is hard to read

Description:

The theme of this book, how to respectfully end one's marriage, developed out of the author's work in the field of mediation dating back to the early 1970s. The book consists of five parts. The first part focuses on separation: coping with the intense anger which characterizes so many divorces, establishing mutually acceptable ground rules, and understanding the emotional stages of divorce. The second part addresses the critical issues of helping children cope with divorce and developing sensitive parenting and custody plans. The third par t focuses on how to communicate more effectively with one's former spouse and how to de-escalate angry confrontations. The fourth part consists of the fundamentals of win-win negotiating when developing settlement proposals. The final part covers situations surrounding many divorces: dealing with difficult or hostile former spouses, understanding the nature of postdivorce conflict, and rituals for letting go.

Evaluation:

Divorcing so often involves feeling angry, resentful, or vindictive. This book is one of the more helpful resources available to help couples overwhelmed by the negative emotions of divorce, to divorce in a more "civilized" way. A major theme of the book is that one cannot control one's former mate in making him/her less angry or more cooperative. But, if there is any chance for cooperation and civility, this book can be an invaluable resource in helping couples to work out their divorce agreements more amicably, and for the good of their children. It also is a valuable resource for an adult individual who needs the tools to deal with a difficult, uncooperative partner. In short, it is a resource for creating rationality and civility in the midst of chaos. This chaos is so characteristic of the divorcing process and, oftentimes, can be escalated by the legal system. Another positive feature of this book is the numerous exercises which make it an effective self-help tool.

Where To Find/Buy:

Bookstores and libraries.

ALMOST PAINLESS DIVORCE
What Your Lawyer Won't Tell You

★★★

Media Type:
Print

Price:
$12.95

Principal Subject:
Legal Issues

Written For:
Adults

ISBN:
1879260395

Author/Editor:
Jenny Garden

Edition Reviewed:
1996

About The Author:
(From Cover Notes)
Jenny Garden is an investigative writer and editor who experienced her own personal divorce. She lives and works in Everett, Washington.

Publisher:
Evanston Publishing, Inc.

Internet URL:
N/A

"Christian" Orientation?:
N/A

Focused On Issues For:
N/A

1-4 Stars

Overall Rating   ★★★   Very useful information to consider before hiring legal experts

Design, Ease Of Use   ★★   Quite readable; lacks organization at times

---

Recommended For:
Legal Issues

Also Recommended For:
Mediation

Description:
This book consists of two major parts plus an extensive Appendix. Part One, "How, What, When," consists of five chapters. The first three chapters provide detailed advice concerning the choosing of a divorce lawyer, entering into a working agreement with that lawyer when chosen, and the practical issues involved in working with, and relating to that lawyer during the divorce process. The fourth chapter of this section provides advice on how to represent yourself (Pro Se and Arbitration); the fifth chapter discusses how mediation works and how to determine whether it is a viable alternative. Part Two, "Who, Where, Why," is a collection of "war stories" which the author heard from survivors of divorce. They are true stories of lawyers, the foibles of the legal system, and the disastrous effect many divorces have had on family, careers, finances, and the human spirit. Interspersed throughout the book are checklists and sample documents which helps the reader make wise choices on the use of professionals.

Evaluation:
Clearly, the intent of this author is twofold. First, how to help the reader to enter into the legal divorce process with an understanding of how legal professionals are to be approached and retained. Second, providing guidance on which legal mechanism the divorcing couple should employ—this might be litigation, but could also be self-representation, arbitration, and/or mediation. At the beginning of the legal divorce process, knowledge is power, and the author does a credible job of helping the reader to make informed choices and, if professionals are to be engaged, to set expectations so that the working relationship will be effective. As the title of the book implies, the author has an (informed) bias that couples should choose mediation as their venue, if they have really decided that divorce is the solution to their difficulties. The many checklists, copies of legal documents and antecdotal stories provided can be most helpful for a reader who is considering initiating the legal process of divorce.

Where To Find/Buy:
Bookstores and libraries.

1-4 Stars

Overall Rating ★★★ One of the few books on this topic

Design, Ease Of Use ★★ Readable style

Description:

This 170+ page book is written for individuals who have separated from their mates. Specifically, the book is written for the spouse who wants to be reconciled and "back with" his/her spouse. The first three chapters of the book address positive aspects of separation, the need for detachment, and the dangers of a premature reunion. The next several chapters help the individual examine himself/herself and understand how to be proactive in establishing a plan of action for a reunion. Subjects discussed at length in these chapters are values, priorities, goals, obstacles, and communication. The final chapters help the reader analyze if he/she is really ready to reconcile with his/her spouse, if the couple "as a unit" is ready to reconcile and, once the couple is back together, how to sustain a loving and lasting relationship and avoid the subsequent pitfalls. The book also gives antecdotal examples of couples who have separated and reconciled. It also contains several helpful self directed exercises.

Evaluation:

This book if one of the very few on the topic and, as such, fills a definite need for separated persons yearning to be reconciled with their mates. Certain themes of this book constitute pertinent messages for the reader who would be attracted to the title of this work. The first is that detachment is a necessary first step toward healthy reconciliation. The second is that separation can be an essential ingredient in giving the individual the time and the space to examine one's values, goals, desires, and how he/she contributed to the dysfunction of the relationship. The third is that reunions can be premature and, if so, damaging and destructive to the relationship. Finally, the book gives helpful directions for effective communication in the relationship, as well as other ingredients necessary for its continued growth.

Where To Find/Buy:

Bookstores and libraries.

GETTING BACK TOGETHER

★★★

Media Type:
Print

Price:
$9.95

Principal Subject:
Preventing Divorce

Written For:
Adults

ISBN:
1558508627

Author/Editor:
Bettie Youngs Bilicki, Ph.D,;
Masa Goetz, Ph.D.

Edition Reviewed:
1990

About The Author:
(From Cover Notes)
Bettie Youngs Bilicki is a lecturer, author, counselor, trainer and consultant. Masa Goetz is a clinical psychologist in private practice. Both work in San Diego.

Publisher:
Adams Media Corporation

Internet URL:
N/A

"Christian" Orientation?:
N/A

Focused On Issues For:
N/A

OUR TURN
Women Who Triumph In The Face Of Divorce

★★★

Media Type:
Print

Price:
$12.00

Principal Subject:
All-Inclusive

Written For:
Adults

ISBN:
0671740067

Author/Editor:
C. L. Hayes, Ph.D.,
Deborah Anderson,
Melinda Blau

Edition Reviewed:
1993

About The Author:
(From Cover Notes)
Christopher L. Hayes, Ph.D, "is the director of the National Center for Women and Retirement Research." Deborah Anderson "is the director of research" for the divorce study which resulted in this book. Melinda Blau "is and award-winning journalist and author."

Publisher:
Pocket Books

Internet URL:
N/A

"Christian" Orientation?:
N/A

Focused On Issues For:
Women

		1-4 Stars
Overall Rating	★★★	Powerful, bonding resource for divorcing women
Design, Ease Of Use	★★★	Easy to read writing style but small print is a challenge

Description:

Three authors combine their talents in this 311 page text focusing on surviving divorce for women in midlife. Contents of the book are based on data from the National Center for Women and Retirement Research, (NCWRR), a research and teaching facility. An extensive introduction discusses some of the myths associated with women divorcing in midlife. Using research derived from a NCWRR study, some of the more common myths are identified, shedding light on the true strengths and realities of women. Section 1, "Growing Pains" talks about the ways women have typically viewed themselves and places them into four "Developmental Categories" depending on their way of adjusting to their marriages and their sense of self. In Section 2, "Moving On," again using results of their study, the authors discuss such topics as the importance of friends in healing after divorce, of organizing finances and preparing for retirement. A lengthy questionnaire for the reader wanting to participating in future NCWRR studies is provided.

Evaluation:

This book tells about life after divorce for midlife woman who participated in the NCWRR study. The sample for the study was obtained from the Center's mailing list, through public relations activities, and from other sources. The authors do not identify which percentage of the 352 women (85% were 40-60 years old) come from which source. Without that information, it could be argued that the sample is overly representative of women who are more open than most to healing and establishing a new life. With that in mind, the results of the NCWRR survey, though not entirely positive, illustrate that the women who are sampled are coping and adjusting to living as a single again, and are slowly changing cultural stereotypes about how they should act. The book is filled with anecdotal stories which will touch the female reader. In short, it is a book of hope, representing a group of divorced women whose lives are not over at midlife, but who are "moving on" in many ways that our society does not readily expect.

Where To Find/Buy:

Bookstores and libraries.

DIVORCED KIDS
What You Need To Know To Help Kids Survive A Divorce

★★★

Media Type:
Print

Price:
$5.99

Principal Subject:
Children Of Divorce

Written For:
Adults

ISBN:
0449220761

Author/Editor:
Laurene Johnson &
Georglyn Rosenfeld

Edition Reviewed:
1992

About The Author:
(From Cover Notes)
Laurene Johnson "is a
Certified Reality Therapist
in private practice and is
director of Successful Living
After Divorce in Phoenix,
Arizona". Georglyn
Rosenfeld "is a free-lance
writer living in Scottsdale,
Arizona".

Publisher:
Ballantine Books

Internet URL:
N/A

**"Christian"
Orientation?:**
N/A

Focused On Issues For:
N/A

	1-4 Stars	
Overall Rating	★★★	An insightful resource for parents of children experiencing divorce
Design, Ease Of Use	★★★★	Comfortable, warm writing style. Organization of text facilitates ease of use.

Description:

The Prologue to this 220+ page text describes it as a collaboration of two women who had each been writing a book on children surviving divorce but decided to co-author this book instead. One of the authors is a therapist; the other is a free-lance writer. Both are divorced and mothers of children. Both are teachers and seminar leaders for divorced families. Their collaborative work presents a broad array of guidelines for parents to help their families through crises. The twenty three brief chapters of this book focus on a wide array of topics from effective parenting, to establishing and strengthening self-esteem in one's children, to establishing healthy visitation guidelines, to forming healthy extended families. The final chapter, "Forgiveness: The Ultimate Healer," rounds out the text by discussing how both parents and children can learn to forgive.

Evaluation:

The authors' experience with children of divorce has provided many interesting anecdotal examples, some of them tragic, others truly courageous and hopeful. These real life experiences, no matter how many times we read them, provide insight into the many ways families deal with the trauma of divorce. Such stories may in some way be similar to our own and help us to feel that we are not alone. The authors have included just enough unusual material, presented in an easily readable style, to make this a valuable addition to a parent's library. The focus is not just on surviving divorce, but on quality healing, where parents and children alike take responsibility for their actions. A particularly good chapter called "Protecting and Nurturing Your Child's Self-Esteem" discusses unconditional love, and some of the many ways parents can encourage their child's positive mental growth.

Where To Find/Buy:
Bookstores and libraries.

FRESH START DIVORCE RECOVERY WORKBOOK

★★★

Media Type:
Print

Price:
$14.99

Principal Subject:
All-Inclusive

Written For:
Adults

ISBN:
0840796226

Author/Editor:
Bob Burns & Tom Whiteman

Edition Reviewed:
1992

About The Author:
(From Cover Notes)

Both authors, holding doctorates, are counselors, helping people recover from divorce through their "Fresh Start" seminar approach.

Publisher:
Thomas Nelson Publishers

Internet URL:
N/A

"Christian" Orientation?:
Yes

Focused On Issues For:
N/A

1-4 Stars

Overall Rating	★★★	Illuminating, intensive workbook for surviving divorce
Design, Ease Of Use	★★★	Interesting, eclectic presentation. Easily readable.

Description:

This text is a workbook for the Christian oriented "Fresh Start" seminar program that is a step-by-step recovery guide for all people experiencing separation or divorce. Its 300+ pages are divided into three sections. The main body of text is composed of nine chapters covering such topics as "Stages of Divorce Recovery", "Working Through Bitterness and Learning to Forgive", and "Understanding Your Past for Personal Growth". Several articles written by various authors in the "Fresh Start" family follow, focusing on more specific topics such as finding legal representation or how to form a divorce support group. These sections are followed by a lengthy appendix section where the reader will find an "Anger Inventory" and discussion questions for use in group situations. The authors' strongly recommend that this book be used as a resource for groups. Individuals are encouraged to work with a friend on the material to achieve full benefit of the program.

Evaluation:

This workbook, used as part of a weekly group seminar (as the authors suggest), requires that the participant be emotionally ready to quickly work through the stages of divorce recovery. The reader choosing to work with a close friend, instead of in a group, will have more control over the time they feel is necessary to heal. However it is used, the ability to stick with the workbook's plan requires commitment and a strong sense of responsibility toward one's own healing process. The authors illuminate, in some detail, the workings of the family and the roles we play in our relationships that often lead to unstable marriages. Compared to other divorce workbooks, this one asks the reader to participate a great deal more, with "Make It Your Own" sections scattered heavily throughout the chapters (these ask the reader to answer questions or write at length on various topics). The book includes frequent references to Christian beliefs, as well as a emphasis on examining our pasts as indicators of present and future relationships.

Where To Find/Buy:

Bookstores and libraries.

DIVORCE & NEW BEGINNINGS
Guide To Recovery And Growth, Solo Parenting, And Stepfamilies

★★★

Media Type:
Print

Price:
$19.95

Principal Subject:
Life After Divorce

Written For:
Adults

ISBN:
0471526312

Author/Editor:
Genevieve Clapp, Ph. D

Edition Reviewed:
1992

About The Author:
(From Cover Notes)
The author "has taught both graduate and undergraduate seminars and classes at California State University in Los Angeles, and at Arizona State University. She also has a private consulting firm in San Diego, CA and is a divorce mediator."

Publisher:
John Wiley & Sons, Inc.

Internet URL:
N/A

"Christian" Orientation?:
N/A

Focused On Issues For:
N/A

	1-4 Stars	
Overall Rating	★★★	Comprehensive guide focusing on divorce recovery and parenting thereafter
Design, Ease Of Use	★★★★	Lots of text, but well organized format; helpful table of contents, appendices, and index

Recommended For:
Life After Divorce

Description:
This 377-page text is an intensively researched guide focusing not only on divorce and separation but on establishing healthy relationships after divorce. Data for this book is based upon more recent findings drawn from "more than 400 studies, reports, and books published by experts." The author has organized material into five parts, taking the reader through initial stages of divorce and on into recovery. Parts one and two discuss stages and coping strategies for parents and children experiencing divorce. Part three discusses ways to establish a healthy and happy single life. Advice to readers who may be part-time, non-custodial parents, and suggestions for rebuilding healthy family life through stepfamiliy planning is offered in Parts four and five. The text closes with suggestions for making positive changes in your life and provides a deep relaxation technique to relieve stress. Many case studies and anecdotal examples are intertwined with thoroughly researched data.

Evaluation:
The length of this book should not scare away the reader searching for more immediate help. Its size may be intimidating, but the reader's invested effort and time will be well rewarded. Meant to be read slowly, this text is packed with interesting data, observations, acedotes, and suggestions presented in a very easy to read format. The author has thoughtfully provided bolded subheadings throughout each chapter, allowing readers to quickly make choices about what they want to read (in the same way a person might visit a web page). Although much hard data is presented, the author has maintained a "reader friendly" writing style. A particular strength of this work is the highly organized way the author presents a synthesized and usable summary of key points gathered from some of the best-known and highly respected works on divorce. This resource represents a good investment for those seeking helping themselves, willing to spend the time to carefully read the chapters most relevant to their situation, and disciplined about implementing the many practical suggestions provided. Highly recommended.

Where To Find/Buy:
Bookstores and libraries.

VICKI LANSKY'S DIVORCE BOOK FOR PARENTS

Helping Your Children Cope with Divorce And Its Aftermath

★★★

Media Type:
Print

Price:
$5.99

Principal Subject:
Children Of Divorce

Written For:
Adults

ISBN:
0916773485

Author/Editor:
Vicki Lansky

Edition Reviewed:
1996

About The Author:
(From Cover Notes)
Vicki Lansky has written over thirty books on parenting and household advice, including the bestselling *Feed Me! I'm Yours*, *Games Baby Play*, *Practical Parenting Tips*, and others.

Publisher:
The Book Peddlers

Internet URL:
N/A

"Christian" Orientation?:
N/A

Focused On Issues For:
N/A

1-4 Stars

Overall Rating	★★★	A good overall introduction to a range of issues about children of divorce
Design, Ease Of Use	★★★★	Easy-to-read, approachable style

Description:

The author wrote this book after her own experience with divorce and bringing up children as a single parent. A wide variety of topics pertaining to children and divorce are covered here, with guidelines to follow at each stage of the process, from the decision to separate to living in a restructured family. Chapters 1-4 cover the initial stage of parental separation, including the typical reactions of preschoolers, teens, and young adults, how to talk to your kids sensitively about a departing spouse, and possible communication problems that can arise. Chapters 5-7 provide information on the "technical" aspects of custody and shared parenting, including money matters, options for parenting arrangements, and sole/joint custody issues. The final chapter, "Looking Down the Road," discusses the long-term adjustments of children and parents, and the special difficulties of holidays, dating and remarriage, and children of divorce in the classroom. Suggested readings on selected topics are provided throughout.

Evaluation:

This book provides a good general introduction to the subject of children and divorce. It covers quite a lot of ground, and manages to touch upon just about every issue encountered in helping your kids adjust to divorce and its aftermath. The advice offered here is sound, practical, and even creative, such as in the section describing how to stay connected with children as a long-distance parent, by providing them with self-addressed stamped envelopes or postcards, keeping a special journal, or by sending "coded" messages for younger children to decipher. Other particularly useful sections are those discussing the problems of shared parenting (a.k.a. joint custody) in which the author shares her own experience: specific helpful details are shared here that should make shuttling between homes far smoother. Because this book covers so much ground, it does not delve as deeply as one would like into any one topic, although the author does provide lists of suggested readings on certain topics. However, people in search of an introduction to the the subject of children of divorce and shared parenting will find this a very good place to start.

Where To Find/Buy:
Bookstores and libraries.

WHY ARE WE GETTING A DIVORCE?

★★★

Media Type:
Print

Price:
$16.00

Principal Subject:
Children Of Divorce

Written For:
Children 6-12

ISBN:
0517565277

Author/Editor:
Text by Peter Mayle;
illustrated by Arthur Robins

Edition Reviewed:
1988

About The Author:
(From Cover Notes)
The authors have
collaborated on a number of
books for children and help
for parents, including *Where
Did I Come From?*, *What's
Happening to Me?*, *Sweet
Dreams and Monsters*, and
Baby Taming.

Publisher:
Harmony Books (Crown)

Internet URL:
N/A

**"Christian"
Orientation?:**
N/A

Focused On Issues For:
N/A

	1-4 Stars	
Overall Rating	★★★	A good book for children experiencing divorce to read with parents, or on their own
Design, Ease Of Use	★★	Appropriately geared for children, with sensitive text; illustrations are less attractive

Description:
Written for younger children of divorcing parents, this illustrated book is intended to address some of the issues that children might have to grapple with as they watch their parents separate and their home life change. The book begins with an introduction to the subject of divorce, and then backtracks to "Why Your Parents Got Married," a section describing the reasons why people decide to marry in the first place. In "What Goes Wrong," the book discusses the two kinds of reasons why people get divorced: little things (leaving the top off the toothpaste) and big (falling in love with another person). Towards the end, the book explores how it feels to live with "half your parents" and visit the other half, and the drawbacks and surprise advantages such an "extra life" can have. The book includes lots of color illustrations.

Evaluation:
A book like this can be informative and consoling to younger children who are experiencing the pain and confusion of divorce. It can also be helpful for those parents who are looking for a tool or "prop" to use in explaining divorce to their children—it is a book that can easily be read together, providing a comfortable forum for both children and their parents to share feelings and thoughts they might otherwise keep hidden. The text is sensitive and light-hearted; appropriately geared towards a child's level of understanding. It also seeks to reassure children that their parents love them and that they are not to blame for their parents' divorce: two of the most common fears of children during divorce. The only flaw of this book is that the illustrations are not, unfortunately, up to par with the excellent text.

Where To Find/Buy:
Bookstores and libraries.

INSURING MARRIAGE

25 Proven Ways to Prevent Divorce

★★★

Media Type:

Print

Price:

$5.50

Principal Subject:

Preventing Divorce

Written For:

Adults

ISBN:

0310207401

Author/Editor:

Michael J. McManus

Edition Reviewed:

1st (1994)

About The Author:

(From Cover Notes)

Michael McManus is a syndicated newspaper columnist, a radio commentator, and author of the book Marriage Savers: Helping Your Friends and Family Stay Married. He and his wife oversee marriage preparation at a church in Bethesda, Maryland.

Publisher:

Zondervan Publishing House (Harper Collins)

Internet URL:

N/A

"Christian" Orientation?:

Yes

Focused On Issues For:

N/A

1-4 Stars		
Overall Rating	★★★	Strong Biblically based, Christian orientation
Design, Ease Of Use	★★	Presentation at times is incomplete and choppy

Description:

The theme of Insuring Marriage is that divorce can be prevented. To this end, this 112-page book presents methods for improving marriage, avoiding divorce, and preparing for a strong marriage. It represents a Christian understanding of family and marriage. Consequently, it frequently refers to Biblical passages and standards. It strongly recommends premarital counseling, retreats for married couples, and an overall involvement with religion. It includes 25 chapters spread among seven main topics. The section on "Helping Single Adults and Seriously Dating Couples"concentrates on some of the pitfalls of premarital relations. "Marriage Insurance for Engaged Couples" focuses on premarital counseling. Other topics include: "Helping Couples Strengthen Their Marriage;" "Even Deeply Troubled Marriages Can Be Saved;" "Helping the Separated or Divorced and Step families;"and how to "Be a Marriage Saver."

Evaluation:

This is a fine handbook and a strong guide for those with a strong Christian orientation. Even those who aren't Christian can glean helpful perspectives and suggestions from this work. Because of its Biblical foundation, it frowns gravely upon divorce. On the contrary, it purports to be a blueprint for saving marriages and its message is a strong and positive one. Marriages, it says, can be saved through: effective marriage preparation (e.g. Engaged Ecounter), enrichment of existing marriages (e.g. Marriage Encounter, support groups) and help for the severely troubled (e.g. Retrouvaille). And so the theme of this book is a breadth of fresh air: people can be a community, a community helping and supporting others in the sacred commitment of marriage. The last chapter gives directives regarding establishing a community marriage policy. Statisically, in cities in which policies like this one have been implemented, there has been a significant decrease in the divorce rate.

Where To Find/Buy:

Bookstores and libraries.

LET'S TALK ABOUT IT: DIVORCE

★★★

Media Type:
Print

Price:
$7.95

Principal Subject:
Children Of Divorce

Written For:
Preschool Children

ISBN:
0399228004

Author/Editor:
Fred Rogers

Edition Reviewed:
1st (1996)

About The Author:
(From Cover Notes)
Fred Rogers is better known as Mr. Rogers on the popular children's program Mr. Rogers' Neighborhood. This book is one in a series titled "Let's Talk About . . .".

Publisher:
GP Putnam & Sons

Internet URL:
N/A

"Christian" Orientation?:
N/A

Focused On Issues For:
N/A

1-4 Stars

Overall Rating ★★★ Simple, yet effective, book for young children

Design, Ease Of Use ★★★ Straightforward statements accompanied by colorful pictures

Recommended For:
Children Of Divorce

Description:
This book is written for young children who may be encountering unhappy feelings brought about by their parents' divorce. It seeks to stimulate discussion between child and parent about situations they are experiencing. This is a "picture book" suitable for children of preschool age. Each page contains a statement and a corresponding color photo; for example, the statement "Sometimes you might want to be alone" goes with a large photo of a child off on his own. Different topics addressed are: what a family is, changes that a divorce may bring, feelings and emotions the child might face, the difficulties the parents also have, how the child can address the feelings, and how everything will be all right over time. The book is about 30 pages and includes a short introduction from the author.

Evaluation:
By using a "picture book" format, and by gently introducing sensitive topics of concern to young children, this book should be effective in accomplishing its goal of inspiring conversation between the child and parent. The success of the author's television show, Mr. Rogers' Neighborhood, gives this book added credibility. The flow of the book is cohesive, featuring short, explanatory sentences and paragraphs. The content is easy for the child to comprehend. The colorful pictures should help young children better understand the concrete nature of what is happening to them. Like many children's books, this one can be used over and over again—each time provoking new discussions.

Where To Find/Buy:
Bookstores and libraries.

THE COMPLETE DIVORCE RECOVERY HANDBOOK

★★★

Media Type:
Print

Price:
$9.89

Principal Subject:
All-Inclusive

Written For:
Adults

ISBN:
0310573912

Author/Editor:
John P. Splinter

Edition Reviewed:
1st (1992)

About The Author:
(From Cover Notes)
John P. Splinter, with an M.A. in Christian Education and Counseling Psychology, is currently the director of Single Life Ministries at the Central Presbyterian Church in St. Louis, MO.

Publisher:
Zondervan Publishing House

Internet URL:
N/A

"Christian" Orientation?:
Yes

Focused On Issues For:
N/A

1-4 Stars

Overall Rating	★★★	A spiritually-based guide to divorce/recovery, with good advice/creative activities
Design, Ease Of Use	★★★	Clear writing style & well mapped-out chapters

Best Resource For:
Christian adults looking for guidance during divorce and recovery

Recommended For:
All-Inclusive

Description:
This 250-page book addresses the divorce process, from grieving and anger to forgiveness, healing, and change. Chapters 1-3 present an overview of the grieving process. In chapters 4-6, the author explores the psychological issues inherent in divorce, such as co-dependency, guilt, and "facing forgiveness." Chapter 7 deals with how to help children understand your decision and process their own feelings. Chapter 9, "Getting Your Act Together," describes the path to healing and "wholeness," including self-assessment checklists. Chapter 10 offers Christian-based perspectives on divorce and remarriage. Chapter 11 confronts the issue of dating after divorce, and the last chapter, "Creating Healthy Marriages," ends the book on an inspirational note. At the end of each chapter are questions for reflection, exercises designed to facilitate one's understanding of topics covered, and suggested readings from the Bible. The author created this book out of his experience in running group programs for divorced adults.

Evaluation:
This is an activity-based, non-directive spiritual approach to divorce, useful for support groups and professionals (therapists, pastors) working in the field. The writing style is clear and accessible, and the layout of the book—detailing the progressive stages of divorce—is easy to work through. The author, a practicing minister with experience working with divorced adults, has written the book with two focuses in mind: the "psychological (emotional-relational) and spiritual (God-related) issues inherent in the process of divorce and recovery." As such, it includes much valuable, practical advice and techniques for anyone coping with divorce, but at times limits its appeal to those readers who identify themselves as Christians. This book might not be for everyone—probably not for those whose ideas about spirituality and marriage take radically different forms from the author's. However, for Christians, and for other readers as well, there are a number of valuable insights, questions, and exercises that make this book a useful resource for the reader (or group) who wishes to take a more active role in his/her recovery.

Where To Find/Buy:
Bookstores and libraries.

HOW TO SURVIVE YOUR PARENTS' DIVORCE

★★★

Media Type:
Print

Price:
$7.95

Principal Subject:
Children Of Divorce

Written For:
Children 13+

ISBN:
0531157385

Author/Editor:
Nancy O'Keefe Bolic

Edition Reviewed:
1st (1994)

About The Author:
(From Cover Notes)
Nancy O'Keefe Bolick is the corporate communications manager for an environmental company, and also does environmental consulting. She is a former high school teacher and has previously published works for young adults.

Publisher:
Franklin Watts

Internet URL:
N/A

"Christian" Orientation?:
N/A

Focused On Issues For:
N/A

1-4 Stars

Overall Rating ★★★ A very good first-step resource for teenagers dealing with their parents' divorce

Design, Ease Of Use ★★★★ An accessible, well-structured series of narratives

Recommended For:
Children Of Divorce

Description:
This book is a 126-page compilation of narratives by teenagers for teenagers who have, at some period of their lives, survived the reality of divorce and grown up in a single-parent household. Each chapter introduces us to a different child who proceeds to tell his/her story, describing how he or she handled the divorce and its accompanying fears, anger, and hopes. The stories were chosen with an eye towards illustrating the specific difficulties kids must face: from Chapter 1, "Rob: Losing his Childhood to Divorce," to Chapter 3, "Kristi: Fighting the Isolation," to Chapter 9, "Eduardo: Too Much Abuse." Experiences discussed by these children vary widely, from physical and mental abuse by a parent to extended "step-families" who happily manage to maintain close and loving relations with their children. Chapter 11, "Summing Up & Looking to the Future," offers 7 pages of specific advice culled from the kids' own experiences. The author gathered these stories by traveling to high schools throughout the country; she takes a backseat as these children tell their stories; clarifying and extending on their narratives but allowing them, for the most part, to speak for themselves.

Evaluation:
This is a unique resource, offering a series of "real-life" narratives by children who are struggling to come to terms with the reality of divorce. The author does not try to manipulate what these children are saying; interpretation is kept to a minimum, and for the most part the author simply comments in a non-judgemental way. Most children experiencing divorce first need to realize that they are not alone; others like them have dealt with the kinds of feelings that rise out of the divorce process. For this reason, this work can be of great help and a source of consolation. However, the book offers few "resolutions" or "solutions" to handling divorce. The last chapter describes positive ways of confronting divorce; the advice offered is sound, but scanty. Nevertheless, it is an excellent first-step resource for parents to buy for their children. It opens the door to discussion of sensitive issues and it enables the young reader to see his divorce experiences reflected in the stories of his/her peers.

Where To Find/Buy:
Bookstores and libraries.

DIVORCE DECISIONS WORKBOOK
A Planning And Action Guide

★★★

Media Type:
Print

Price:
$27.95

Principal Subject:
All-Inclusive

Written For:
Adults

ISBN:
0070195714

Author/Editor:
Marjorie L. Angel &
Diana D. Gould

Edition Reviewed:
1st (1992)

About The Author:
(From Cover Notes)

Marjorie L. Angel is
president of Hamilton-
Forbes Associates, "a private
business counseling firm
specializing in the practical
and financial implications of
divorce." Diana D. Gould is
the founder of Daily Bread,
Inc., a not-for-profit center
for career counseling.

Publisher:
McGraw-Hill, Inc.

Internet URL:
N/A

**"Christian"
Orientation?:**
N/A

Focused On Issues For:
N/A

	1-4 Stars	
Overall Rating	★★★	A useful tool to help readers gain control over the more practical issues of divorce
Design, Ease Of Use	★★★★	Well-organized and easy to use

Description:

The Divorce Decisions Workbook is a 166-page book written by two experienced counselors. The various checklists, information forms, reference and resource lists in this book were originally developed for clients, with a focus on understanding and organizing the personal, legal, and business-related aspects of divorce. The book is divided into 8 main sections: the first 3 including an overview of the divorce process, "Understanding the Divorce Process;" and "Pulling Yourself and Your Family Together," which discusses maintaining physical/mental health and other issues of personal concern. Sections 4-7 deal with the "nuts and bolts" of the divorce process: "Financial Value of the Marriage" includes tips on how to become cognizant of your finances and establish financial independence. "Learning About Divorce Law" tells you about the sequence of events from the filing of the complaint/summons to an outline of events at a trial. "Getting Your Legal Decree and a Successful Divorce" discusses how to negotiate a mutually acceptable and affordable agreement with your spouse. The book includes a bibliography, lists of resources, and worksheets intended to be used in conjunction with each section.

Evaluation:

This book's value lies in its unique focus: straightforward information and advice on how to plan, organize, and implement the practical phases of divorce. It enables adults to deal knowledgeably with such issues as personal finances, divorce law, division of property and assets, and child/spouse support. A series of worksheets at the end of the book (FORM-ulas) are particularly useful for gathering information that will be essential in dealing with attorneys and the courts, and in working out a successful, affordable agreement with one's spouse. Although valuable as a whole because of its practical focus, chapters dealing with the personal/emotional issues in divorce seemed cursory and forced, and perhaps are best left to another type of book altogether. In its best sections, however, The Divorce Decisions Workbook offers superb, clear, helpful, no-nonsense information about how to gain command over the financial and legal aspects of divorce.

Where To Find/Buy:

Bookstores and libraries.

	1-4 Stars	
Overall Rating	★★★	A strongly Christian-oriented self-help guide to divorce and remarriage
Design, Ease Of Use	★★	Fairly dense prose; numerous research-oriented references

Description:

Originally written in 1972 as the author's thesis, this 129 page book provides guidance for clergy involved in counseling parishioners who are facing divorce. Part One, "Counseling Perspectives", discusses biblical and societal interpretations of marriage and divorce. Part Two, "Counseling Procedures", provides the reader with a definitive plan for counseling parishioners considering divorce or who would like to remarry. Chapter 1 speaks directly to biblical interpretations of divorce and remarriage. Chapters 2 and 3 review reasons why marriages fail. Chapter 3, "Is Divorce the Answer?" challenges the reader to question divorce as the only solution to an unhappy marriage. "A Model for Pastoral Counseling" suggests techniques drawn from biblical interpretations and other important pastoral counselors, using a "client centered approach". The book also provides the counselor with a set of specific steps through which couples advance in their progression towards divorce, and discussion of options to explore as alternatives to that end.

Evaluation:

This book is directed at the pastor-counselor. As marriage is viewed by the author as a religious experience, Part One provides an historical look at divorce from a broadly painted Christian perspective that examines Old and New Testaments, as well as viewpoints of various Christian churches. Because of the author's religious background, special emphasis is provided from the Mennonite perspective which the reader might well find interesting and enlightening. From Part Two, specific guidelines for the pastor provide insights into what constitutes mature love and expectations for marriage that seek to prevent divorce. Basically, however, this book is the author's thesis which was written in the early seventies. As such, it is a summary of the collected wisdom of Protestant pastoral counseling at that time. Also, as a thesis, it draws heavily on the works of others and not much on the author's experience.

Where To Find/Buy:

Bookstores and libraries.

DIVORCE AND REMARRIAGE
A Perspective For Counseling

★★★

Media Type:
Print

Price:
$6.95

Principal Subject:
Professionals Only

Written For:
Adults

ISBN:
0836117298

Author/Editor:
John R. Martin

Edition Reviewed:
1976

About The Author:
(From Cover Notes)
The author "is Associate Professor of Church Studies at Eastern Mennonite College, Harrisonburg, Virginia. He is currently president of Mennonite Broadcast, Inc. in Harrisonburg, Virginia."

Publisher:
Herald Press

Internet URL:
N/A

"Christian" Orientation?:
Yes

Focused On Issues For:
N/A

CHILDREN OF DIVORCE
Helping Kids When Their Parents Are Apart

★★★

Media Type:
Print

Price:
$10.99

Principal Subject:
Children Of Divorce

Written For:
Adults

ISBN:
0310284713

Author/Editor:
Debbie Barr

Edition Reviewed:
1992

About The Author:
(From Cover Notes)
The author is "a freelance writer and speaker, and has been published in numerous Christian periodicals."

Publisher:
Zondervan Publishing House

Internet URL:
N/A

"Christian" Orientation?:
Yes

Focused On Issues For:
N/A

1-4 Stars

Overall Rating	★★★	Sensitive guide for seeing divorce from a child's point of view
Design, Ease Of Use	★★★	Smooth chapter transitions and easy to read writing style

Description:

This 207-page book (a 2nd edition, originally entitled "Caught in the Crossfire") focuses on helping children survive divorce. Data in the text is drawn from social service specialists , studies on the topic of divorce, and from case histories. A brief introduction discusses some of the reasons for divorce followed by five major sections on coping strategies. Sections explore, from a Christian perspective, the transitional steps for children in divorce. "When The Bough Breaks" deals with physical and emotional losses involved in divorce. Part Two discusses some of the ways children react to divorce and stresses parents' attitudes as having a major impact on how the child adjusts. Part Three further explores the effects of divorce on the child's schoolwork, view of spirituality, and family financial situation. A final section discusses "How Teachers, Friends, and Churches Can Help". The author ends with four short stories followed by discussion questions that track a fictionalized child's journey, through first hearing about his parent's divorce to the break-up of the family.

Evaluation:

The author has created a book from a Christian point of view that is an easy read for parent's in today's fast-paced world. This heavily researched text presents an interesting insights of insights and data on how divorce affects the family, bound together by a thread of caring for children experiencing divorce in their lives. Case histories drawn from a comprehensive 1971 California study on children and divorce add further credibility to the author's research. The result is a plan for parental action based on a sensitivity and respect of the needs of parents and children. The "village" aspect applies to this plan in a recruitment of other relatives, teachers, and clergy who could serve as a source of support to the child. From the words of children interviewed for this book, we experience the feelings of those who were affected most. Excellent guidance for parents, in the form of specific steps to follow, is provided so that a common ground is established with the primary goal of helping children cope.

Where To Find/Buy:
Bookstores and libraries.

DIVORCE: A PRACTICAL GUIDE
What You Need To Know Before, During, And After

★★★

1-4 Stars		
Overall Rating	★★★	Provides general background on the legal and financial issues of divorce
Design, Ease Of Use	★★★	Easy to understand and broken down into 23 easy-to-follow chapters

Media Type:
Print

Price:
$19.95

Principal Subject:
Legal Issues

Written For:
Adults

ISBN:
0964561506

Author/Editor:
Catherine A. Wannamaker, CLA

Edition Reviewed:
1st (1996)

About The Author:
(From Cover Notes)
Catherine A. Wannamaker is the founder of Divorce Equity, Inc., a financial divorce consulting service. She divorced in 1986 and lost everything in the process. She then learned the laws and fought back, winning a judgment against her attorney for malpractice.

Publisher:
Equity Enterprises, Inc.

Internet URL:
N/A

"Christian" Orientation?:
N/A

Focused On Issues For:
N/A

Description:

This guide urges those going through a divorce to take an active role in the process, and it encourages the reader to learn as much as possible about the legal and financial procedures involved in a divorce. The goal is to help the reader get a favorable settlement and avoid being taken advantage of by a spouse, lawyer or the court. The 245-page book contains 23 chapters and a glossary. The topics are wide-ranging and comprehensive; in addition to the early chapters on where to start and general divorce procedures, it covers the many subjects that may come about during the divorce process. There are chapters on records, financial statements, bankruptcy, taxes, and credit. Chapters on attorneys, retainer agreements, representing oneself, mediation and settlement give the reader informed legal options. Several chapters are devoted to distribution of assets, including the home, retirement benefits, child support and alimony. Most chapters include hints and notes that highlight areas one should take particular care to observe along the way. Many chapters have worksheets and checklists to fill out.

Evaluation:

This book, while fundamentally adversarial in tone (and based on an assumption that the divorce will be litigated), nonetheless provides an overview of many legal and financial issues typically encountered during a divorce. Its intent is to support an assertive approach to getting what is "rightfully yours." It is evident from her tone that the author has experienced and witnessed unfair divorce judgments; thus, its basic premise: "Be active—don't be complacent and get taken advantage of by others." It warns of lawyers who may not be acting in the best interest of the client. It discusses the pros and cons of self-representation. It even recommends not mentioning divorce to the spouse until research has taken place and records have been copied and filed away. Chapters on record keeping and finances are quite good, and sections on legal options are thorough. This book will have a special allure to those who anticipate a combative atmosphere throughout the divorce.

Where To Find/Buy:

Bookstores and libraries.

DIFFICULT QUESTIONS KIDS ASK ABOUT DIVORCE

★★★

Media Type:
Print

Price:
$12.00

Principal Subject:
Children Of Divorce

Written For:
Adults

ISBN:
0684814366

Author/Editor:
Meg F. Schneider and Joan Zuckerberg, Ph.D.

Edition Reviewed:
1st (1996)

About The Author:
(From Cover Notes)
Meg F. Schneider is the author of several books, and editorial director of Skylight Press. Joan Zuckerberg, Ph.D., is a clinical psychologist and the supervisor at the National Institute for Psychotherapy.

Publisher:
Fireside (Simon and Schuster)

Internet URL:
N/A

"Christian" Orientation?:
N/A

Focused On Issues For:
N/A

1-4 Stars

Overall Rating	★★★	Useful suggestions for communicating with children about their questions and concerns
Design, Ease Of Use	★★★	Well organized and easily read; could use more discrete subject chapters

Description:

As the title suggests, this book is filled with many questions children ask throughout the stages of divorce, and it attempts to explain and interpret these inquiries. It stresses communication as a key to alleviating troubles common to those experiencing divorce. The book offers suggestions to help parents create an environment conducive to conversation—one which will enable the child to ask questions and express their feelings. It also seeks to help parents understand the inner instincts of their children, and the feelings underneath the surface. Its 225 pages take you through the steady progression of divorce. The book is broken up into two distinct sections: Making Questions Possible and The Questions. Part one describes the psychological complexities of children and the ways they see things, and addresses issues in adult communication, too. Part two covers situations before, during and after the divorce, and the questions that ensue. This includes topics such as dealing with the separation, dating in front of the children, and communicating as the years pass.

Evaluation:

This book comes at the topic of "children of divorce" from a slightly different angle. Many books do try to help parents sort out and decipher children's feelings, but this one does so by focusing on the questions they ask. Its intent is to help parents understand what their children are really asking. The questions raised and their discussion are insightful and can give a parent perspective on how a child is reacting. The authors provide a general discussion of each main area of concern and its possible impact on children ("Dating in Front of the Children"), then provide an analysis of concerns hidden behind the question, and suggestion on addressing those hidden concerns. The authors provide helpful insights and useful recommendations to parents. For example it tells them to truthfully answer what's literally being asked; the children's instincts need to be respected and through this a parent can also see what's beneath the surface. Further, its coverage on how to stimulate discussion and questions from the children is helpful.

Where To Find/Buy:

Bookstores and libraries.

KIDS ARE NON-DIVORCEABLE
A Workbook For Divorced Parents And Their Children

★★★

Media Type:
Print

Price:
$7.95

Principal Subject:
Children Of Divorce

Written For:
Children 6-12

ISBN:
0915388316

Author/Editor:
Sara Bonkowski, Ph.D.

Edition Reviewed:
1987

About The Author:
(From Cover Notes)
The author "is Associate Professor of Social Work at Aurora University in Aurora, Illinois and the founder of the Byrtle Burks Center for Clinical Social Work in Glen Ellyn, Illinois."

Publisher:
ACTA Publications

Internet URL:
N/A

"Christian" Orientation?:
N/A

Focused On Issues For:
N/A

	1-4 Stars	
Overall Rating	★★★	Insightful workbook with exercises for parents and children
Design, Ease Of Use	★★★	Easy to use workbook format; accessible writing style

Description:

As the introduction states, "This is a book about families," a 126 page workbook with a strong focus on healing after divorce, with particular emphasis on helping children from ages six to eleven. From the initial chapter, "Beginning to Rebuild" to the final chapter entitled, "Your Child's Future" the author stresses the importance of a concerted effort, by all those involved in the divorce, to take part in their own healing process. In order to facilitate this, the author has provided exercises for the parent (whether custodial or non-custodial) and the child. Each chapter begins with a summary of the author's views on such topics as understanding the different stages of childhood, dating and remarriage, and future planning. Summaries are followed first by exercises for the parent, then by activities for children ages six to eight, and ending with those for children ages nine to eleven. Activities involve game playing, brainstorming, and creativity exercises.

Evaluation:

This book is a highly usable resource for divorced parent's with children of ages 6-11. The author's work as a clinical social worker and family therapist has allowed her to share, in this text, many real life experiences of those families she has helped survive divorce. Her focus is a positive one that encourages understanding and rebuilding through examination of true feelings, acknowledging those feelings, and working toward establishing healthy relationships. The author's presentation of text and illustrations in short, easy to read chapters makes this a very approachable and practical resource. Organization of chapters works very well in presenting parents' exercises first and children's last. This allows parents to work through their own issues first and to be better prepared to help their children deal with the particular issue involved. While the exercises are really emotional "work" they are also presented in a way which adults and children might consider fun.

Where To Find/Buy:

Bookstores and libraries.

SAILING THROUGH THE STORM
A Child's Journey Through Divorce

★★★

Media Type:
Print

Price:
$8.95

Principal Subject:
Children Of Divorce

Written For:
Preschool Children

ISBN:
0964222302

Author/Editor:
Edie Julik

Edition Reviewed:
1994

About The Author:
(From Cover Notes)

Edie Julik "is a free lance children's creative movement teacher in the Twin Cities. She is also certified in Elementary Education and uses developmental theory to teach younger children how to adjust and grow through divorce."

Publisher:
KIDSAIL

Internet URL:
N/A

"Christian" Orientation?:
N/A

Focused On Issues For:
N/A

1-4 Stars

Overall Rating	★★★	Colorfully illustrated, inviting picture book that encourages child participation
Design, Ease Of Use	★★★	Easy to use resource

Description:

This short, colorfully illustrated picture book was written for preschool aged children to help them understand and heal while experiencing divorce in the family. Intended for a parent to read to the child, it's the story of "a happy little sailboat that runs into a great storm." As a real storm might, it develops slowly and threatens the boat with pelting rain and growing waves. At the height of the storm the little boat is afraid it might be turned topsy turvy. Just as all hope seems to be lost, the storm begins to subside. The sun reappears and the, once again, happy boat is now a new color, signifying change in how it sees the world. The author tells the child, "You sailed through a stormy time and you feel wonderful", but cautions realistically that life is full of smaller or greater storms to be weathered as well. The story is followed by a page where the child can draw their own sailboat picture. This coloring page is followed with several questions a parent might use to discuss feelings and open a pathway to communication with the child about the divorce.

Evaluation:

This book, dedicated to "All children of divorce", can be a useful tool in helping the younger child work through the pain of divorce. Recognizing that, all too often, the child's feelings are often discounted or ignored, it presents the divorce process "in a more concrete way" so that feelings, such as the boat "experiences", will be more easily recognized. By pairing the story's illustrations that focus only on the boat's surviving the storm with text that draws parallels of survival and divorce, the child is gently introduced to this painful topic. The book's organization and colorful illustrations invite reading by the more learned child. For those not yet able to read, the illustrations alone tell the story. After hearing this book read once or twice, the child can "read" the pictures and easily recall the parent's words. Parents should be well prepared when discussing questions the author presents at the close of the book as they go right to the heart of feelings a child may experience in divorce.

Where To Find/Buy:

Bookstores and libraries.

1-4 Stars

Overall Rating ★★★ Useful legal and financial background material for the woman considering divorce

Design, Ease Of Use ★★★ Question/answer format contributes to ease-of-use.

Recommended For:
Financial Issues

Description:
This book provides, in 82 pages, a brief overview of the divorce process as seen through the eyes of a financial planner and attorney. It is intended as a reference book on financial and legal matters for anyone who may be experiencing separation or divorce. It is not intended to be used in place of professional assistance; its information is provided by the authors primarily as background material. Concise text in a question & answer format is presented in 13 chapters, followed by several appendixes, providing checklists for the reader, as well as state-by-state divorce facts and guidelines. The book begins with an introduction that sheds light on some of the financial and legal mistakes commonly made by women divorcing. Chapters that follow are questions and answers that present every aspect of divorce—from initial filing to final decree. Specific issues such as division of property, separation agreements, alimony, child support, debt, insurance, and tax issues are discussed. The book has a companion text titled *Survival Manual For Men In Divorce*.

Evaluation:
The fact that this book is in its third printing is testimony to its popularity and helpfulness for those women experiencing divorce. With an eye towards a fair division of property, this book presents information about subjects most often overlooked by most women going through divorce. Division of cash value insurance policies or sharing of social security benefits after the ex-spouse retires are only two of many mentioned. Chapters are followed with appendixes that provide valuable checklists, e.g. kinds of information to take when you see an attorney (could save you time and money), or what to ask for in your final divorce decree. The authors include a two-page recommended reading list at the book's close. The question/answer format used throughout the text presents an array of some of the most commonly asked questions concerning divorce. The reader can easily bypass those questions not pertaining to them specifically or jot down numbers of those of most interest. This book is a crisp, accessible overview of legal issues women should be aware of.

Where To Find/Buy:
Bookstores and libraries.

SURVIVAL MANUAL FOR WOMEN IN DIVORCE
182 Questions and Answers

★★★

Media Type:
Print

Price:
$10.95

Principal Subject:
Financial Issues

Written For:
Adults

ISBN:
0840397879

Author/Editor:
Carol Ann Wilson & Edwin Schilling III

Edition Reviewed:
1994

About The Author:
(From Cover Notes)
Carol Ann Wilson, CFP, is a pre-divorce financial consultant and founder of the Quantum Institute for Professional Divorce Planning. Edwin C. Schilling III is an attorney and "has served as Director of the USAF Legal Assistance and Preventive Law Programs".

Publisher:
Kendall/Hunt Publishing Company

Internet URL:
N/A

"Christian" Orientation?:
N/A

Focused On Issues For:
Women

JOINT CUSTODY & SHARED PARENTING

★★★

Media Type:
Print

Price:
$21.95

Principal Subject:
Professionals Only

Written For:
Adults,

ISBN:
0898624819

Author/Editor:
Jay Folberg, Editor

Edition Reviewed:
1991 (2nd)

About The Author:
(From Cover Notes)
Jay Folberg is "Dean and Professor of Law at the University of San Francisco School of Law, was President of the Academy of Family Mediations and a past President of the Association of Family and Conciliation courts."

Publisher:
The Guilford Press

Internet URL:
N/A

"Christian" Orientation?:
N/A

Focused On Issues For:
N/A

1-4 Stars

Overall Rating	★★★	Thoughtful, focused study on joint custody by many expert contributors
Design, Ease Of Use	★★★	Very small print, periodical style, self contained chapters

Recommended For:
Professionals Only

Description:
This updated 380-page text, focuses on joint custody of children, how this concept historically came into being as a option for divorcing parents, and how it is successful as a method of helping children adjust to life changes after divorce. Text is presented in four parts that discuss, historical considerations, why parents and courts choose joint custody, current research available on the subject, and related law. Experts in the field who are therapists, lawyers, economists, and researchers have each contributed chapters to the text in which they discuss current trends in the law, with a focus on finding the best method of helping the child adjust to divorce. A chapter entitled "Joint Custody Is Not for Everyone", written by child psychiatrist, Richard A. Gardner, M.D., explains when this kind of custody should and should not be used, its inherent requirement for cooperation and communication between both parents, coupled with affection for the child. This comprehensive resource is directly primarily at professionals.

Evaluation:
Concern for the "best interests of the child" is apparent in this text. It is both refreshing and reassuring to realize this caring aspect for children is part of our system of law. The ways our custody laws have been shaped by cultural, economic and research studies is interestingly developed in this book. The fact that we are currently in a period in which our culture currently views joint custody as one of the best routes to take, and how we got to this point, is intelligently discussed. Focusing in on this single topic and devoting so many pages to its development, instead of broadly discussing all divorce law, ensures that the reader will be able to make more informed choices, and provide well-researched advice, when it comes to custody questions. Writing styles vary from chapter to chapter as authors change and some are more easily read than others. Not meant to be read in one sitting, this book's many authors provide chapters that are interesting enough to stand on their own. Recommended for professional reference libraries and for divorcing adults who want a comprehensive treatment of the subject.

Where To Find/Buy:
Bookstores and libraries.

TWO HOMES TO LIVE IN
A Child's-Eye View of Divorce

★★★

Media Type:
Print

Price:
$10.95

Principal Subject:
Children Of Divorce

Written For:
Children 6-12

ISBN:
0898851734

Author/Editor:
Barbara Shook Hazen

Edition Reviewed:
1983

About The Author:
(From Cover Notes)
Barbara Shook Hazen is author of several children's books including, *Very Shy*, and *It's A Shame About The Rain—The Bright Side of Disappointment*.

Publisher:
Human Sciences Press, Inc.

Internet URL:
N/A

"Christian" Orientation?:
N/A

Focused On Issues For:
N/A

	1-4 Stars	
Overall Rating	★★★	Informative and helpful story should be helpful to children
Design, Ease Of Use	★★★	Illustrations and text invite reading by children

Description:

This 35-page book, illustrated by Peggy Luks, was written for the grade school-aged child whose parent's are experiencing divorce. It is meant either to be read to the child by the parents or for the child to read alone. Dedicated to the author's son, who experienced his parent's divorce, this book presents a short scenario of the divorce process. The story is told by a young child, (drawn so that it could be either a boy or girl), named "Niki". The story begins with Niki reassuring the young reader that even though parents divorce, "they are still your parents and will always love you". The developing storyline tells about the gradual break up of Niki's parents and the realization that things would never be the same again. The child's feelings surrounding these ideas are developed as Niki gradually learns that his parents love for him will remain even though they do not live together anymore. Niki soon learns that some of the things he used to do with each parent separately while they were married, he can continue to do with each while they are apart.

Evaluation:

Colorful, interesting illustrations coupled with short, easily readable text makes this child's storybook about divorce a helpful resource. The illustrations contribute to development of the story line by conveying the idea of loving, reassuring parents. Page one presents a survivor role model for children to follow as Niki opens "his" story about his parent's divorce. The illustration shows a happy child playing with his toys, beginning to tell the story of what he and his parents went through and how other children could survive as well. Issues dealt with in this book are common to children of divorce, such as dealing with feelings of anxiety, anger, and depression. Some reasons why parents divorce are given but there is no real attempt to explain why "grownups just can't get along". For children of this age-group this is probably enough. The explanation that "grownups sometimes fall out of love" is coupled with the idea that even though this happens, "they never fall out of love with their children". Recommended.

Where To Find/Buy:

Bookstores and libraries.

FIVE MINUTE LAWYER'S GUIDE TO DIVORCE

★★★

Media Type:
Print

Price:
$4.99

Principal Subject:
Legal Issues

Written For:
Adults

ISBN:
044021761X

Author/Editor:
Michael Allan Cane

Edition Reviewed:
1995

About The Author:
(From Cover Notes)

The author is the president and CEO of Tele-Lawyer, Inc., teaches law at Western State University School of Law in Irvine, CA., and is the author of three other books in the "Five-Minute Lawyer" series.

Publisher:
Dell Publishing (Bantam Doubleday Dell)

Internet URL:
N/A

"Christian" Orientation?:
N/A

Focused On Issues For:
N/A

1-4 Stars		
Overall Rating	★★★	Good basic coverage of many of the legal issues in divorce
Design, Ease Of Use	★★★	Easy to read, question & answer format

Description:

This 271-page guide focuses on the most commonly-asked questions about legal issues in divorce. The author is the founder of the "Tele-Lawyer" service (which allows people to talk directly by phone to experienced lawyers without paying high fees) and has written this book using the real-life situations and questions that he has most frequently encountered when dealing with the public about the legal aspects of divorce. Each of ten sections begins with a brief description of the issue at hand (e.g. how to find a good divorce attorney, costs, property division, alimony, custody, etc.) and then proceeds to ask and answer common questions about each issue. The author intersperses stories and anecdotes gathered from his legal experience and through "Tele-Lawyer." The book contains six appendices listing various divorce laws and information from state to state, including a helpful listing of "Self-Help Divorce Books By State."

Evaluation:

This is one of a growing number of resources designed to help the general public educate itself and gain power over the legal process of divorce. As legal costs rise, more people are turning away from the hostile (and potentially expensive) litigated divorce and gaining the basic knowledge necessary to draw up divorce papers themselves or with the help of a mediator or independent paralegal. Surely this is a welcome trend. The author (himself a lawyer) spends a good deal of his time warning the reader away from divorce attorneys, most of whom, he says, are out for money, not equitable divorces: "Having a divorce attorney . . . is sort of like letting Charles Manson take care of your kids." Keeping in mind that a single consultation with a divorce attorney about any one of the questions in this book could run you up hundreds of dollars, it is probably worth the book's price to answer some of these ahead of time. However, as the author himself points out, the questions in this book are not "substitutes for careful, professional analysis of a legal problem or question."

Where To Find/Buy:
Bookstores and libraries.

1-4 Stars

Overall Rating	★★★	Extensively researched resource most useful to practitioners in the field
Design, Ease Of Use	★★★★	Well-written and organized

Recommended For:
Professionals Only

Description:
Based on extensive research, this 272-page book offers a new approach to child custody. After fifteen years of observing mother-custody and father-custody families through the Texas Custody Research Project, the author came to the conclusion that "raising children should not be the exclusive prerogative of women any more than work outside the home should be the exclusive domain of men." The bulk of this book consists in debunking the myth of the mother as primary caregiver, and re-establishing the importance of the father in the development of children. Part 1 describes the history of child custody and the gradual switch to mothers as preferred custodians of children. Parts 2-3 describe two radically different kinds of custody decisions made today (by fathers who assume sole custody, and mothers who give it up) and the ensuing effects on children. Part 4, "The Custody Revolution," explores the various types of joint custody and the author's belief that joint custody should replace the current favoring of sole mother custody in court decisions as the healthiest solution for children of divorce.

Evaluation:
This book uses extensive research to support its assertion that fathers make just as good caretakers for their children as mothers. This flies in the face of contemporary sentiment about mothers (what the author calls "the Motherhood Mystique") and the current practice of granting sole custody to mothers except in cases of neglect or abuse. The author makes the claim that fathers should not be discriminated against in the custody process, and should have every right to be considered as responsible and caring as mothers. This book overturns some long-upheld cultural beliefs and points the way to the possible future of the custody process—perhaps one day men will be on equal footing with women in the custody court. For some, the question will remain, *should* they? Is there something more to motherhood than just mystique, something essential to the upbringing of children? This is a question crucial for those involved in the custody process (judges, child psychologists, evaluators, etc.) to weigh and consider. Others—real parents making custody decisions—may find this book too theoretical to meet their individual needs.

Where To Find/Buy:
Bookstores and libraries.

CUSTODY REVOLUTION
The Father Factor And The Motherhood Mystique

★★★

Media Type:

Print

Price:

$21.00

Principal Subject:

Child Custody

Written For:

Adults

ISBN:

0671746944

Author/Editor:

Richard A. Warshak, Ph.D.

Edition Reviewed:

1992

About The Author:

(From Cover Notes)

The author is a Clinical Associate Professor at the University of Texas Southwestern Medical Center. Reviews of his work have appeared in such magazines as *Time, Omni, Psychology Today,* and *The New York Times Magazine,* among others.

Publisher:

Poseidon Press (Simon & Schuster)

Internet URL:

N/A

"Christian" Orientation?:

N/A

Focused On Issues For:

N/A

DON'T SETTLE FOR LESS
A Woman's Guide To Getting A Fair Divorce

★★★

Media Type:

Print

Price:

$12.95

Principal Subject:

Legal Issues

Written For:

Adults

ISBN:

0385482116

Author/Editor:

Beverly Pekala

Edition Reviewed:

1996

About The Author:

(From Cover Notes)

The author is a practicing divorce lawyer.

Publisher:

Main Street Books
(Doubleday)

Internet URL:

N/A

"Christian" Orientation?:

N/A

Focused On Issues For:

Women

1-4 Stars

Overall Rating	★★★	A fair, no-nonsense, helpful guide to the legalities of divorce for women
Design, Ease Of Use	★★★	Clear, concise writing throughout; well-ordered structure

Description:

This 272-page book opens with an introduction by the author, in which she explains her belief that the legal system of divorce is unjust towards women: it does not seek to address the inequalities that exist between men and women in the larger framework of society. Thus, she has written this book to allow women to get "an advantage in a system that isn't always fair." She divides her book into two major sections: the first devoting itself to "pre-divorce" issues and strategies, including the warning signs that your husband is considering leaving you, and what to do to protect yourself if divorce seems probable; choosing and maintaining a working relationship with your lawyer; and what to do in the case of domestic violence. Section II gets down to the nitty-gritty of property division, the "discovery" process and depositions, child support and custody; and successfully negotiating the final settlement (including how to get alimony, which, as the author points out, women actually receive in less than 15% of all divorce cases). The last chapters focus on the special issues of prenuptial agreements, mediation as "the future of family law," and other topics. The book also contains appendices listing women's bar associations and battered women's shelters.

Evaluation:

The author makes some important remarks in her introduction about the nature of the legal system, stating that the laws themselves are not unfair but simply the application of them in a world where great inequalities still exist between men and women. This book aims at righting this imbalance by giving women the knowledge necessary to protect their interests while navigating the troubled waters of divorce settlements. The basics of divorce law are explained clearly here, and the preventative measures to take to avoid falling into the common (and often unseen) pitfalls for women. This is a sound, thorough overview of the legal side of divorce for women, without a "take him for all he's worth" mentality. However, alternatives such as mediation are not mentioned at all here, except at the very end as part of "the future of family law." With this limitation in mind, this book should stand as a helpful aide to the legal divorce system for women.

Where To Find/Buy:

Bookstores and libraries.

WHEN MOM AND DAD SEPARATE
Children Can Learn To Cope With Grief From Divorce

★★★

Media Type:
Print

Price:
$6.95

Principal Subject:
Children Of Divorce

Written For:
Children 6-12

ISBN:
0962050229

Author/Editor:
Marge Heegaard

Edition Reviewed:
1991

About The Author:
(From Cover Notes)
Marge Heegaard, MA, ATR, LICSW, is a "licensed Clinical Social Worker, registered Art Therapist, and certified Grief Counselor" in Minneapolis, MN. She works with both children and adults using art as a means for expressing grief.

Publisher:
Woodland Press

Internet URL:
N/A

"Christian" Orientation?:
N/A

Focused On Issues For:
N/A

1-4 Stars

Overall Rating	★★★	An unusual workbook for children
Design, Ease Of Use	★★	Format and layout could become tedious

Description:

This is a 32-page workbook/coloring book designed "to teach children some concepts about divorce and to recognize and express feelings of grief from family change." The author, an art therapist, believes that the process of expressing ideas and feelings through the drawings in this book will help children come to grips with their own reactions to divorce. The book is divided into six parts: "Change is Part of Life," "Understanding Divorce," "Feelings About Divorce," "Expressing Feelings," "Living With Divorced Parents," and "Living Well in a Changing World." Each part includes drawing and writing activities to help a child explore the concepts in terms of his/her own experience. The author also includes advice for parents and their children about how best to use this book and "make it special."

Evaluation:

The idea behind this book is to get children to actively participate in the discovery and expression of their own feelings through creating art. It presents aspects of the process of grief in a clear, simple format which invites a child's involvement. It would best be used by a child in conjunction with an adult who would provide support, interest and focus. After exploring concepts presented in the first nine pages, the child might want to pick and choose, according to his/her needs, drawing on pages which deal with his/her feelings throughout the midsection of the book. The last section on communication and living with change can be helpful for the child in dealing with issues which may have surfaced. A danger of this book, however, is that this whole process many become quite tedious, because the visual format lacks variation. If that happens, the adult might well turn to other mediums which might be more exciting and provocative for that child, e.g. parables, stories, fairy tales, or other applied art resources.

Where To Find/Buy:

Bookstores and libraries.

WOMEN AND DIVORCE, MEN AND DIVORCE

Gender Differences In Separation, Divorce, And Remarriage

★★★

Media Type:
Print

Price:
$19.95

Principal Subject:
Professionals Only

Written For:
Adults

ISBN:
1560241144

Author/Editor:
Sandra S. Volgy, Ph.D.

Edition Reviewed:
1991

About The Author:
(From Cover Notes)
Sandra Volgy Ph.D. is a clinical psychologist and family therapist who has specialized in the area of divorce and families. She is also on the faculty of the Arizona Institute of Family Therapy.

Publisher:
The Haworth Press

Internet URL:
N/A

"Christian" Orientation?:
N/A

Focused On Issues For:
N/A

1-4 Stars

Overall Rating	★★★	A collection of research in the field
Design, Ease Of Use	★	Solely a collection of articles; no index

Recommended For:
Professionals Only

Description:
This book is a collection of twelve research articles which are arranged under three headings: "Comparison of Gender Differences," "Men and Divorce," and "Women and Divorce." Under "Comparison of Gender Differences," three articles appear. The authors of these studies report their findings in "self-other orientation" and "sex-role orientation" of men and women who remarry; gender differences in divorce adjustment; and gender differences in college students' attitudes toward divorce and their willingness to marry. Under "Men and Divorce," four articles appear. Again, the authors of these studies report their findings which range from divorced fathers describing their former wives, to adjustment to stepfatherhood, to child support compliance and noncompliance. Under "Women and Divorce," five articles are listed. Their authors report their findings in studies which range from women's adjustment during separation and divorce, to the economic consequences of divorce for women, to the effectiveness of child rearing by divorced mothers. This section also includes two cross cultural studies.

Evaluation:
If the reader is looking for a single volume collection of research studies conducted primarily in the mid to late eighties concerning gender differences of men and women who divorce, this book is it. It is nothing more and nothing less. The editor (collector?) presents a very terse introduction to the book . There is no index; there are no editorial comments or editorial notes. The value of the work is that the reader can find a collection of these studies in one volume for his/her perusal and that of his/her students. The same work, by the way, has also been published as Journal of Divorce and Remarriage, Volume, 14, Numbers 3/4, 1991.

Where To Find/Buy:
Bookstores and libraries.

1-4 Stars

Overall Rating	★★★	A work written by the masters; needs some updating
Design, Ease Of Use	★★★★	Easy to read text; comprehensive index

Description:

This rather lengthy (400+ pages) self-help book is addressed to adult men and women. Its purpose is to "help you keep the breakup of your marriage from becoming a legal nightmare or an emotional catastrophe." The fourteen chapters of the book follow this theme. After the principal authors, Belli and Krantzler, describe their own divorces in the first chapter, subsequent chapters address financial/legal issues of divorce (e.g. "how to take skillful charge of your legal divorce") and the emotional trauma involved (e.g. "bridging the divorce communication gap between you and your children"). The last four chapters of the book focus on the four stages of establishing a new relationship following the divorce. Woven into the text of each chapter are anecdotal accounts of persons experiencing divorce. A unique chapter in this book is Chapter 5 which describes divorce among the rich and the famous. The book also contains a helpful bibliography (although dated) and an index.

Evaluation:

The principal authors of this book are universally renowned and respected. Melvin Belli, Sr. is a prolific writer and has had center stage in numerous high profile divorce cases in this country. Mel Krantzler gained national notoriety by becoming one of the first full time divorce counselors in this country and his book, Creative Divorce, was a first in the field. One might expect that a collaborative effort by these two men would result in a superior book; Belli and Krantzler fulfill these expectations. Not only is their work given credibility by their having "walked the walk," but their advice concerning the legal, financial, and emotional aspects of divorce reflect years of experience with clients. Of special interest are the chapters dealing with children, especially from a father's point of view. Krantzler's chapters on the stages of the process of finding a new and lasting love—a task which seems so many times impossible for one whose life has been shattered by divorce—is especially helpful. Unfortunately, the bibliography and text do not reflect scientific studies and self-help literature that has been published in the past ten years.

Where To Find/Buy:

Bookstores and libraries.

DIVORCING
The Complete Guide For Men And Women Divorcing

★★★

Media Type:

Print

Price:

$15.95

Principal Subject:

All-Inclusive

Written For:

Adults

ISBN:

031201760X

Author/Editor:

Melvin Belli; Mel Krantzler, Ph.D.; Christopher Taylor

Edition Reviewed:

1988

About The Author:

(From Cover Notes)

Melvin Belli, Sr. is one of the world's foremost trial attorneys. Mel Krantzler, Ph.D. is an internationally recognized authority on the psychology of divorce. Christopher Taylor is a divorce attorney.

Publisher:

St. Martin's Press

Internet URL:

N/A

"Christian" Orientation?:

N/A

Focused On Issues For:

N/A

MOM AND DAD DON'T LIVE TOGETHER ANYMORE

★★★

Media Type:
Print

Price:
$4.95

Principal Subject:
Children Of Divorce

Written For:
Preschool Children

ISBN:
0920236871

Author/Editor:
Kathy Stinson; Nancy Reynolds (Illustrator)

Edition Reviewed:
1984

About The Author:
(From Cover Notes)

The author "is the mother of two children and has worked as an elementary school teacher and in preschool programs." She is the author of two other children's books.

Publisher:
Annick Press Ltd.

Internet URL:
N/A

"Christian" Orientation?:
N/A

Focused On Issues For:
N/A

1-4 Stars		
Overall Rating	★★★	Quality of illustration and text facilitates this book's use as a helping resource
Design, Ease Of Use	★★★★	Easy to read and use by young children; beautiful illustrations

Best Resource For:
Parents who need to introduce and discuss the subject of divorce with their preschoolers

Recommended For:
Children Of Divorce

Description:
This 23+ page storybook (in its tenth printing) was written as a result of the author's experience in teaching elementary school children and out of her own life experiences. Dedicating this book to her own two children, she has written in a style easily understood by younger children, with text focusing on helping youngsters adjust to a divorce that has already happened. The main character in the book is a young girl about six years old whose comments about how she feels about her new life make up the story. These comments focus on how she likes being with and doing things with each parent, but still wishes they weren't apart. Illustrations are by Nancy Lou Reynolds (a painter and graphic artist) compliment the text in helping to show feelings associated with the words.

Evaluation:
This author's choosing not to focus broadly on all aspects of divorce but instead to deal only with one phase of adjustment is a good choice for younger readers. This focus results in a positive, non-threatening book, one in which divorce isn't even mentioned in the title, for a child to pick up and read or have read to them. The author's writing style is appropriate for the main character whose easily understood short statements relay feelings about her likes and dislikes, her frustrations, and questions she has about the divorce. These comments should provide, for parents, a path to more open communication with their own children. Illustrations, particularly of the main character, are especially well done in that they convey a broad range of feelings. Interest is stimulated by the illustrator's eclectic use of color pages mixed with black and white.

Where To Find/Buy:
Bookstores and libraries.

THE DIVORCED PARENT
Success Strategies For Raising Your Children After Separation

★★★

Media Type:
Print

Price:
$10.00

Principal Subject:
Children Of Divorce

Written For:
Adults

ISBN:
0671511289

Author/Editor:
Stephanie Marston

Edition Reviewed:
1994

About The Author:
(From Cover Notes)
Stephanie Marston is a licensed marriage, family, and child counselor, president of Raising Miracles Educational Seminars, and the author of a previously published book on children and self-esteem.

Publisher:
Pocket Books (Simon & Schuster, Inc.)

Internet URL:
N/A

"Christian" Orientation?:
N/A

Focused On Issues For:
N/A

1-4 Stars

Overall Rating	★★★	A comprehensive, sensible guide to helping yourself and your children through divorce
Design, Ease Of Use	★★★	Straightforward, uncluttered style

Description:

This 348-page book was written for divorced parents who wish to create stable, healthy, and loving environments for their children. It covers a wide span of topics related to child rearing and the unique problems of being a divorced parent. The author, not a believer in the "scarred-for-life" theory about children after divorce, thinks instead that children are basically resilient beings, able to recover from the trauma of divorce if it results in a positive, functioning life for the children. This book shows the reader how to create such a "functional divorce" and a stable home life for children. Topics covered in this book include how to tell your children about the divorce, the types of unhealthy games parents can play with one another through their children, how to "emotionally" separate from your spouse and create a non-adversarial, cooperative relationship, keeping both parents involved in the task of child-rearing, legal and financial issues, and how to build your life anew after divorce and "reclaim your identity."

Evaluation:

This is a comprehensive treatment of many issues related to being a divorced parent. A chapter of particular merit discusses how to keep both parents involved in their children's upbringing, often involving active steps on the part of the primary parent to change his or her own behavior towards an "ex" to facilitate frequent contact with a child—not an easy thing to do if emotions are still running high, but of utmost importance to the child. Another chapter of particular interest suggests how to rebuild your life anew as a divorced parent, making life more fruitful and pleasant for yourself by not giving in to parental guilt or trying to become a "supermom." These two chapters confront issues that are not often discussed. This book takes a unique perspective on its subject by looking at aspects of child-rearing from the standpoint of being a *parent*; many focus only on the child's perspective, and while this is certainly important, can lead to parents neglecting their own growth and health. This never works—and in fact the overall message here seems to be that in order to raise healthy, happy children, parents must first help themselves to become healthy, happy people.

Where To Find/Buy:

Bookstores and libraries.

DEAR CLIENT
A Complete Handbook For Understanding And Surviving Your Legal Divorce Process

★★★

Media Type:

Print

Price:

$24.95

Principal Subject:

Legal Issues

Written For:

Adults

ISBN:

0936417447

Author/Editor:

Ellen D. Ostman

Edition Reviewed:

1996

About The Author:

(From Cover Notes)

The author is "Board Certified by the Florida Bar in Marital and Family Law, and has handled more than 4,000 cases in her nearly 20 years of practice." She is also a Certified Family Law Mediator.

Publisher:

Axelrod Publishing

Internet URL:

N/A

"Christian" Orientation?:

N/A

Focused On Issues For:

Women

	1-4 Stars	
Overall Rating	★★★	A useful, informative, and entertaining look at the legal side of divorce
Design, Ease Of Use	★★★	Dense legal issues presented clearly in an unusual narrative style

Description:

This thick, 525-page book is an in-depth look at "the process by which information is gathered and presented to resolve the legal issues involved in obtaining a divorce." Creating the figure of "Hazel," the author's portrait of a typical client, the author proceeds to tell the story of divorce to her (and to us), beginning with a mini-history of romantic love and a description of how the left and right brain hemispheres function and interact, and how this affects people's behavior during a divorce. This is followed by chapters outlining the stages of a litigated divorce and its legal issues, a questionnaire to help you compile most of the essential information that you (and your lawyer) will need to try your case, and a chapter about child custody with its own information questionnaire. Other chapters present three true-life stories of other clients in their own voices, actual transcripts from court trials, and information and sample documents for various litigation procedures such as court injunctions, the discovery process, and depositions. The last chapters focus on mediation and negotiation, and how to prepare for a trial.

Evaluation:

This resource is an interesting blend of history, anecdote, and workbook-type questionnaires, as well as a detailed foray into the legal forest of divorce. What holds it all together is the figure of Hazel, whom the author deploys as a sort of stand-in listener, so that the book takes on an "Ancient Mariner" feel as we listen along to the "tale" told by the author about divorce. This ploy is wholly successful: books on this subject can often run a little on the dry side, but this one makes a surprisingly easy read. And when you emerge, blinking, at the end, you find you've actually learned quite a lot about the legalities of divorce. It is unusual to find a book that blends the emotional and the legal sides of divorce, but this book manages to do it: we hear people's histories of their marriages, and listen in on how such marriages are legally dissolved in the courtroom through trial transcripts. At times the sections are long-winded (do we really need to see *all* those documents?). Overall, though, this book makes for a pleasant and practical read.

Where To Find/Buy:

Bookstores and libraries.

LOVE IS NEVER ENOUGH
How Couples Can . . . Solve Relationship Problems Through Cognitive Therapy

★★★

Media Type:
Print

Price:
$13.50

Principal Subject:
Preventing Divorce

Written For:
Adults

ISBN:
0060916044

Author/Editor:
Aaron T. Beck, M.D.

Edition Reviewed:
1988

About The Author:
(From Cover Notes)
The author "is the father of cognitive therapy and University Professor of Psychiatry at the University of Pennsylvania. He is also Director of the Center For Cognitive Therapy at that university."

Publisher:
Harper Perennial

Internet URL:
N/A

"Christian" Orientation?:
N/A

Focused On Issues For:
N/A

	1-4 Stars	
Overall Rating	★★★	Highly instructive guide for positive change in communication patterns for couples
Design, Ease Of Use	★★★	Two part division facilitates use; interesting, easy to read writing style

Description:

Based upon theories of cognitive therapy, this 415 page book is a self help guide for couples experiencing problems in their relationships. This book focuses on changing ineffective ways of communicating and understanding how our actions affect others. From the author's many years as a therapist and researcher, he is able to base his work on the anecdotal experiences of former patients as well as recent studies by other noted researchers in the field. A brief Introduction opens the book and familiarizes the reader with the basic premises of cognitive therapy. Chapters One through Nine discuss the many ways couples err in communicating with each other, causing problems in relationships to escalate unnecessarily. Negative thinking, "mind reading," and holding certain expectations are a few examples of problems examined. Chapters Ten through Eighteen discuss and analyze suggestions for improving communications (and your relationship) with your spouse.

Evaluation:

This text provides a detailed examination of the ways people communicate, providing an insightful and occasionally humorous look at ourselves and the ways we interact with one another. Using the myriad experiences of his patients over the years, the author engagingly and clearly describes patterns of miscommunication and the resulting problems this causes in relationships. Although the author does an excellent job of describing cognitive techniques, success in using this kind of therapy relies heavily on a couple's wanting to get along and willingness to make changes in the way they talk to each other as well as in some of their expectations. It also relies on an ability of the individual to see the way they interact with others in a new light, contrary to old patterns of behaving. The author suggests methods to change communications styles, including eliminating negative thinking patterns, and learning to tolerate differences in personalities and attitudes. Mastering the art of conversation, particularly between spouses, is a lifelong challenge. This book will be a help in meeting that challenge.

Where To Find/Buy:

Bookstores and libraries.

UNCOUPLING
Turning Points in Intimate Relationships

★★★

Media Type:
Print

Price:
$13.00

Principal Subject:
Preventing Divorce

Written For:
Adults

ISBN:
0679730028

Author/Editor:
Diane Vaughan

Edition Reviewed:
1990

About The Author:
(From Cover Notes)

The author completed most of the fieldwork for this book at Yale University as a post-doctoral fellow. She continued her research at Wellesley College Center for Research on Women, and began writing the book while teaching at Boston College.

Publisher:
Vintage Books (Random House, Inc.)

Internet URL:
N/A

"Christian" Orientation?:
N/A

Focused On Issues For:
N/A

1-4 Stars		
Overall Rating	★★★	An intelligent, in-depth look at an unusual subject
Design, Ease Of Use	★★★	Well written and structured, though scholarly language may make it "tough going"

Description:

This 250-page book was written by a scholar/researcher in the field of sociology who herself experienced the ending of a 20-year marriage, which led to her initial interest in "how people make transitions out of intimate relationships." Drawn from interviews with a wide variety of couples (divorced, cohabitating, younger, older, homosexual), this book seeks to uncover the often mysterious ways by which people end relationships. The results of her research proved that this process takes an orderly, patterned form, and takes place both in the realm of the private (between partners) and the public (the larger sphere of friends, relatives, and associates). Although this book does not offer specific advice about how to avoid uncoupling, it is the author's belief that "possessing information is a first step" toward reversing or halting the process. Chapters reflect the patterned stages couples go through during uncoupling, including "The Display of Discontent" to "The Breakdown of Cover-Up," "Trying," "Going Public," and finally, "Uncoupling" (10 stages in all). The last two chapters focus on other "transition rituals" we go through during a lifetime, as well as a description of the methodology used in the author's research.

Evaluation:

This book might be put to better use by professionals working in the field of relationships and divorce than by individual couples seeking a resource that will give them specific "self-help"-type advice. This is a scholar's book—and has some of the benefits and the drawbacks of this kind of book for the general reader. It does not look at the process of uncoupling in terms of offering couples hope and advice, but tries instead to uncover the patterns of behavior we all follow when leaving a relationship. As such, it offers a scrupulously-researched, fascinating glimpse at a subject that is not often looked at closely. This book is not about salvaging relationships; its attitude can be coldly realistic: "A couple is working against insurmountable odds" when trying to save a relationship after uncoupling has already begun, and "trying usually results in cosmetic changes that do not alter the fundamental social changes" that have already taken place. These are bitter, but oftentimes necessary, pills for us to swallow; but the author does light up a brief candle of hope at the very end, when she suggests that "with early revelation of secrets . . . two people may try—and succeed."

Where To Find/Buy:
Bookstores and libraries.

MARRIAGE, DIVORCE, REMARRIAGE
Social Trends In The United States

★★★

Media Type:
Print

Price:
$14.95

Principal Subject:
Professionals Only

Written For:
Adults

ISBN:
067455082X

Author/Editor:
Andrew J. Cherlin

Edition Reviewed:
1992

About The Author:
(From Cover Notes)
The author "is Professor of Sociology at John Hopkins University. He is the coauthor of *Divided Families: What Happens to Children When Parents Part* and *The New American Grandparent: A Place in the Family, A Life Apart.*"

Publisher:
Harvard University Press

Internet URL:
N/A

"Christian" Orientation?:
N/A

Focused On Issues For:
N/A

	1-4 Stars	
Overall Rating	★★★	Thought provoking essay on past, present and future state of marriage and divorce
Design, Ease Of Use	★★★	Readable, although heavily researched

Description:
This 178 page study of marriage, divorce and remarriage is a second edition text originally written in 1981, that has been heavily revised and updated, incorporating results of demographic studies and new research in this field. Its focus is on trends in marriage, divorce, and family relationships beginning in the years immediately following World War II to the present. The Introduction explains the authors presentation of the data and analysis and scope of this project involving cohort and historical, over time, comparisons. Chapters One and Two discuss "Demographic Trends" and "Explanations" of those trends. Chapter Three discusses "Consequences" of trends resulting from economic and societal influences backed up with extensive data from recent data. Chapter Four speaks about "Race and Poverty" including many statistics relating to African American experiences in marriage and divorce and how these are influenced by the American culture and economy. Chapter Five makes predictions about the "State of Our Unions".

Evaluation:
This book should thoroughly satisfy the reader who is looking for an up-to-date, highly researched but readable, discussion of the state of marriage and divorce. Written in the form of a long essay, it breaks down the years following WW II into separate time frames with an analysis of the influences of major historical and economic events on the institutions of marriage, divorce, and remarriage. Readers should be able to discover their own generation's trends and what motivated them, or continues to motivate them, when choosing or leaving a mate. A final, thought provoking chapter, "State of Our Unions," reveals the costs and benefits our changing views of marriage and divorce have brought. Here the author discusses some of the benefits that include growing trends toward equality and autonomy for women and lower birth rates. Many of the negative impacts of these trends pertain directly to children, and the author provides ideas for major changes as remedies.

Where To Find/Buy:
Bookstores and libraries.

COMPLETE IDIOT'S GUIDE TO SURVIVING DIVORCE

★★

Media Type:
Print

Price:
$16.95

Principal Subject:
All-Inclusive

Written For:
Adults

ISBN:
0028611012

Author/Editor:
Pamela Weintraub and Terry Hillman

Edition Reviewed:
1996

About The Author:
(From Cover Notes)

Pamela Wintraub and Terry Hillman are co-founders of Divorce Central, an online service on divorce.

Publisher:
Alpha Books

Internet URL:
N/A

"Christian" Orientation?:
N/A

Focused On Issues For:
N/A

1-4 Stars		
Overall Rating	★★	Helpful listing of information; emotional impact not given due attention
Design, Ease Of Use	★★★★	Clear layout; comprehensive index, lists of resources

Description:

This 300+ page book consists of six parts. The overall purpose of the book is to present the reader with as much information as possible on the trauma of divorce and all issues which must be dealt with by a couple embarking on the divorce process. The first major part of the work addresses the question of whether or not the marriage can be saved. Then, if divorce is to happen, it examines "emotional divorce," the ritual of separation and deciding to "end it." Part 2 concerns legal issues: how to hire a lawyer, legal fees, mediation, and settlement agreements. Part 3 addresses financial matters which include division of assets, maintainence, support and solo management of money. Part 4 concerns children and addresses questions of custody, communicating the reality of the divorce to them, visitation, transitions for children, single parenting, and the bi-nuclear family. Part 5 focuses on re-creating one's life. Part 6 is an extensive listing of organizations, printed, and internet resources.

Evaluation:

Divorce has two aspects: there is the emotional trauma and recovery for all persons concerned, and there are the legal, financial and custodial decisions which must be made. This book does an excellent job of addressing the second aspect. In introducing those concerns, it presumes that the reader has no knowledge and/or expertise. As a result, he/she will not be intimidated by the information as presented, and the book can become a "user friendly" companion for a oftentimes arduous journey. And if he/she gets confused or forgetful, there is an excellent glossary of terms and a comprehensive index to get back on track. Emotional trauma, however, is less well addressed, While there are lists focused on the emotional aspects, the author's approach addresses more the "head" than the "heart." A significant strength of this book is the listing of other resources, especially websites, which other books often ignore or are ignorant of.

Where To Find/Buy:

Bookstores and libraries, or direct from the publisher at 1-800-428-5331.

1-4 Stars		
Overall Rating	★★	Useful firsthand accounts and introspective written exercises
Design, Ease Of Use	★★	Left pages have lessons, right pages have exercises and worksheets

Description:

This 150+ page resource is for parents who not only want to make the divorce better for the children, but for themselves as well. Its thrust is to have the parents move on with their lives by taking an active role. Each left handed page is a lesson; each right handed page an exercise or worksheet designed to help adults make changes so they can better handle the emotional trauma of divorce. These written exercises range from quick (identifying similar feelings) to time consuming (in-depth responses to anger). The first three chapters focus on moving on with life, managing stress and getting over destructive feelings. Chapters 4–6 address more concrete issues such as resolving conflict with the other parent, helping children cope with divorce at different stages, and ensuring positive relationships with children. The final chapter wraps up the book with the broad goal of "creating a happy new life for you and your children."

Evaluation:

The intent of the authors of this book is to encourage readers to take a proactive role in improving their mind set and approach to divorce, both for themselves and their children. To accomplish this, the authors present the reader with a brief lesson and then encourage him/her to complete the worksheet which accompanies each lesson, worksheets they have developed in their work of counseling individuals, couples and families. If the reader invests time in this approach, this book will likely bear fruit. However, the reader will often be challenged. The lessons cover a wide array of topics and, as such, can suffer from the brevity of one page of text. Also, the exercises (by their original design) are best used in a therapeutic setting; thus, there is no mechanism for the reader to process his/her completion of these exercises. Nevertheless, for the reader who wants to interact with the text and to subsequently have a "diary" of impressions, feelings, ideas and strategies concerning his/her divorce, this book can be a helpful tool.

Where To Find/Buy:

Bookstores and libraries.

DIVORCE IS THE PITS, SO STOP DIGGING
Success Strategies For Parents

★★

Media Type:
Print

Price:
$19.95

Principal Subject:
All-Inclusive

Written For:
Adults

ISBN:
0964733420

Author/Editor:
Thomas Muha, Ph.D. and Maureen Vernon, Ph.D.

Edition Reviewed:
1st (1996)

About The Author:
(From Cover Notes)
The authors are both clinical psychologists who have experience working with the repercussions of divorce. Thomas Muha is also a newspaper columnist, while Maureen Vernon has been a radio and television talk show host.

Publisher:
Looking Glass Productions

Internet URL:
N/A

"Christian" Orientation?:
N/A

Focused On Issues For:
N/A

DIVORCE RECOVERY
Putting Yourself Back Together Again

★★

Media Type:
Print

Price:
$5.39

Principal Subject:
All-Inclusive

Written For:
Adults

ISBN:
0310573513

Author/Editor:
Randy Reynolds &
David Lynn

Edition Reviewed:
1st

About The Author:
(From Cover Notes)
Randy Reynolds is the
founder and executive
director of Renewal
Counseling. David Lynn is
the co-founder and program
director of an adolescent
and family treatment center.

Publisher:
Zondervan Publishing House

Internet URL:
N/A

**"Christian"
Orientation?:**
Yes

Focused On Issues For:
N/A

1-4 Stars

Overall Rating	★★	A brief, generalized overview of some divorce issues, best for groups and workshops
Design, Ease Of Use	★★★	Easy to work through, structured format

Description:

Divorce Recovery is a Christian-based, 96-page pamphlet written by two experienced counselors who are also founders and directors of counseling/ treatment centers in Arizona. It contains 11 brief chapters, each divided into 5 sections: a "Recovery Focus" box outlining the specific issues to be detailed in the chapter, "Recovery Information" which explains the issues, "Recovery Probers," or questions intended to aid the reader in applying each chapter's focus to his/her own life, a "Recovery Guide" which explores the issues from a Christian perspective, and finally, at the end of each chapter, a series of "Recovery Goals" or brief questions intended to help guide the reader in setting his/her own personal recovery goals. Issues contained in each chapter are followed in a chronological fashion to take you step-by-step through divorce, from "Facing Your Grief" to "Letting Go" to "Learning to Live with Loneliness," and finally "Reconciling With Those Who Let You Down." This book also includes a "Leader's Guide," guidelines intended to help a workshop leader plan and create a divorce recovery group with this book as its focus.

Evaluation:

This pamphlet, because of its slim size and focus on group questions, references to the Bible, and goal-setting activities, as much as actual treatment/ explanation of divorce issues, seems more suited for use by groups and workshops than by individuals. The authors do state in the introduction that readers should "discuss insights and feelings with someone—ideally with a small group that will study this workbook together." Whether used by groups or by individuals, this resource nevertheless does not seem to go beyond the rote: treatment of such issues of grief, loneliness, and helping children cope with divorce seems not only brief but routine, and the focus questions and exercises seem too vague to be of much help (e.g. "How are you going to fill the empty spots in your life without getting into a relationship that will lead to more pain and loss?") However, for Christian-based recovery groups this book could serve as a starting-off point for discussion and activities.

Where To Find/Buy:

Bookstores and libraries.

1-4 Stars

Overall Rating	★★	Useful, practical advice with a specific focus on tax issues in divorce
Design, Ease Of Use	★★	Some technical language and difficult material

Recommended For:

Financial Issues

Description:

This 224-page manual includes twelve chapters, each of which addresses a single tax issue for divorcing spouses, including a summary of points covered, and charts and tables for use in organizing your own and/or your spouse's taxes. Issues covered in this book range from successfully negotiating the taxes involved in child support and alimony payments, property settlements, capital gains and losses, house payments, deductions and credits, dependency exemptions, and many others. Chapters 1-2 discuss how to deal with the "warning signals" of a spouse's tax filings, and how to prepare yourself for the worst by safeguarding your interests. Chapters 3-4 examine your marital status for tax purposes, and whether it is in your best interest to file jointly or separately. Child dependency exemptions, property disclosure, settlements, and transferals, and alimony payments are all examined in chapters 5-9. Audit issues and IRS scrutiny are discussed in chapter 11, and chapter 12 discusses the advantages of a prenuptial agreement and the dangers of "too-hasty" commingling of spousal assets.

Evaluation:

This book contains much valuable tax information for divorcing spouses—information that may be difficult to locate anywhere else, and which could potentially save a lot of turmoil. The author's advice takes a distinctly self-protective stance: one must protect oneself from the potential cunning and misdeeds of one's spouse as well as the IRS, which, in the author's own words, "is not the industrious, impartial, and competent federal agency that its official public imaging would have us believe." (For instance, if a separating spouse does not hasten to file a separate return by April 15th, the IRS can declare him or her responsible for the other spouse's tax due and seize any and all assets.) A drawback to this book is that it is fairly tough read: people unversed in the basics of tax law and finances may have difficulty wading through some of this material (or could use this guide in conjunction with advice from an attorney or accountant). However, readers willing to invest some time into working through their taxes with the aid of this book would be well-served for their efforts, and possibly save themselves from potential tax disaster.

Where To Find/Buy:

Bookstores and libraries.

RESOLVING DIVORCE ISSUES
Heed "Warning Signals" And The Misdeeds Of Spouse

★★

Media Type:
Print

Price:
$18.95

Principal Subject:
Financial Issues

Written For:
Adults

ISBN:
0944817262

Author/Editor:
Holmes F. Crouch

Edition Reviewed:
1996

About The Author:
(From Cover Notes)
The author is a licensed private tax practitioner with his own tax preparation and counseling business. He has prepared over 9000 federal tax returns, and represented many people on their IRS audits. This book is part of a series written for the taxpayer.

Publisher:
Allyear Tax Guides

Internet URL:
N/A

"Christian" Orientation?:
N/A

Focused On Issues For:
N/A

MONEY-SMART DIVORCE

What Women Need To Know About Money And Divorce

★★

Media Type:
Print

Price:
$22.00

Principal Subject:
Financial Issues

Written For:
Adults

ISBN:
0684811650

Author/Editor:
Esther M. Berger

Edition Reviewed:
1996

About The Author:
(From Cover Notes)

The author is a certified financial planner, and an "expert and frequent speaker on the subject of women and money." She has been interviewed by CNN, The New York Times, Los Angeles Times, Forbes, and many other periodicals.

Publisher:
Simon & Schuster

Internet URL:
N/A

"Christian" Orientation?:
N/A

Focused On Issues For:
Women

1-4 Stars

Overall Rating	★★	Helpful financial advice, limited to women litigating for a divorce
Design, Ease Of Use	★★	Somewhat incoherent shuffling of issues within chapters, lack of graphic aids

Description:

Written by an expert on women and finances, this newly-published, 236-page resource is intended to be read by women to help them become "moneysmart" before, during, and after divorce. The book consists of five major sections, which follow the divorce process in a chronological fashion. Part I, "Making the Divorce Decision," includes information on what questions to ask during an initial consultation with a lawyer, gathering a divorce "A-Team," whether or not to move out of the house, and how to handle joint accounts. Part II, "The Planning Period," discusses managing your own finances for the present and planning for the future, and how to begin gathering information for the divorce: financial documents, statements, tax returns, etc. Part III, "The Big Picture," takes a look at the documents put together before the negotiating a settlement: putting a value on assets, dealing with alimony and child support, and filing taxes. Part IV, "Resolution," discusses the final settlement, and investments you can make. Part V, "Reentry," discusses post-settlement issues: budgeting, supporting children, and prenuptial agreements.

Evaluation:

This book contains some helpful financial advice and information, designed to allow women to take control of their finances before and after divorce. Particularly useful sections were those about how to gather financial information before a divorce, and how and where to invest your savings after divorce. The author is a strong believer in the rights of women to assert themselves financially, and is herself an example of a "moneysmart" woman: a certified financial planner, a vice president of PaineWebber Inc., and popular speaker. However, at times a patronizing tone intrudes when she jokingly echoes some women's passive attitudes: "Don't call a lawyer . . . you're sure to be rescued as soon as the village maidens finish braiding the flower buds. . . ." At other times the book was cluttered by a chatty, "prime-time" mentality as if desperate to keep us entertained. Another drawback is that this book focuses on the antagonistic, pricey, litigated divorce, and only briefly mentions and then discounts mediation as a potential solution. However, women undergoing litigation for a divorce will find this a practical source of good advice.

Where To Find/Buy:

Bookstores and libraries.

TALKING ABOUT DIVORCE AND SEPARATION
A Dialogue Between Parent and Child

★★

Media Type:
Print

Price:
$9.95

Principal Subject:
Children Of Divorce

Written For:
Children 6-12

ISBN:
0807023752

Author/Editor:
Earl A. Grollman

Edition Reviewed:
1975

About The Author:
(From Cover Notes)
The author "is a rabbi in Belmont, Massachusetts, a lecturer on family-related issues, and author of numerous guidance books for children and adults."

Publisher:
Beacon Press

Internet URL:
N/A

"Christian" Orientation?:
N/A

Focused On Issues For:
N/A

1-4 Stars

Overall Rating ★★ Useful parent/child workbook also includes community resource suggestions

Design, Ease Of Use ★★★ Well organized, short easy to read text passages for child and parent

Description:

This 87 page book focuses on different ways parents can help their children survive divorce. The text begins with an introduction that explains how to use the text as a resource in helping children. A 54-page, simply illustrated picture book follows. Text in this section is intended for parents to read with the child, discussing the progression of separation and divorce in words the child can understand. Parents are instructed to first read the "discussion guide" (found in the second half of this book) in preparation for reading the book with their child. Specific topics introduced in the read-together section focus on the parents' inability to get along, expression of feelings, and parent's reassurance of their love for the child. The parent's guide explores the ideas presented in the children's section in more detail, presenting ways to discuss the text with the child. A short chapter entitled "Some Final Thoughts" covering some do's and don'ts for parents, rounds out the text portion.

Evaluation:

Even though first glance gives the impression that this book is a children's book because of its illustrations and simplistic text, the reader soon discovers that it's really more of a workbook/resource text for the parent to use to help their child. Its primary value, then, is that it is a tool which can enable parents to discuss their divorce with their child in a way that child can understand. Certain topics for discussion are clearly presented through the illustrations and/or the "Parents' Guide" text of the book, i.e. conflict between the parents, negative feelings, physical separation, etc. Other topics which one might well expect would be a part of a workbook/resource text to stimulate these types of discussions are lacking, e.g. the concreteness of a divorcing family so important to the child: where his/her bed will be, will he/she change shcools, what will friends think, will friends have to be left or lossed, which parent will have the puppy, etc.

Where To Find/Buy:
Bookstores and libraries.

GUIDE TO DIVORCE MEDIATION

How To Reach A Fair, Legal Settlement At A Fraction Of The Cost

★★

Media Type:
Print

Price:
$12.95

Principal Subject:
Mediation

Written For:
Adults

ISBN:
1563052458

Author/Editor:
Gary J. Friedman, J.D.

Edition Reviewed:
1993

About The Author:
(From Cover Notes)

The author "is an experienced attorney/ mediator and is founder and director of the Center for Mediation and Law."

Publisher:
Workman Publishing

Internet URL:
N/A

"Christian" Orientation?:
N/A

Focused On Issues For:
N/A

	1-4 Stars	
Overall Rating	★★	Useful introduction to mediation as an alternative in divorce
Design, Ease Of Use	★★★	Book is largely mediation dialogues, interspersed with authors' observations

Description:

Formerly a trial lawyer, the author of this book turned to mediating out of a need to see couples seek more amicable divorce solutions. Through this 376+ page book, he provides a detailed introduction to the process of mediation and offers it as an alternative to traditional alternatives involving divorce lawyers. Part One describes the mediation process, inviting the reader to consider for themselves whether or not the process is appropriate for their own situation. It also provides an in-depth look at all steps taken in the process, and prepares the reader to choose their own mediator. Part Two explores case histories of twelve couples, taken from the author's experience as a mediator, and discusses how they were able to reach a settlement both could agree upon. Although mediation provides an alternative that could be used for any kind of conflict resolution, the targeted audience of this text is anyone considering separation or divorce; a secondary audience would be those considering a career as a divorce mediator.

Evaluation:

One of the many benefits of using mediation is that those who are involved in the dispute have control over the process. As described by the author, willingness to take control but at the same time be guided by a third person who works for both parties best interests, is what mediation is all about. Amicable resolution is the main goal. The author's thorough discussion and explanation of mediation in Part One is an enlightening trip into conflict resolution with focus on respect for the individual. Part Two helps clarify the process by quoting and discussing case histories that used mediation. This resource will be helpful for those planning separation or divorce who want to remain on favorable terms with each other and want to learn about mediation as an alternative. The extensive use of actual examples of mediated dialogues, interspersed with the author's comments and observations, is more appropriate to teaching mediation than using it, and potentially confusing to divorcing adults using this resource.

Where To Find/Buy:

Bookstores and libraries.

DIVORCE HANGOVER
A Step-by-Step Prescription For Creating A Bright New Future After Your Marriage Ends

★★

Media Type:
Print

Price:
$5.50

Principal Subject:
Life After Divorce

Written For:
Adults

ISBN:
0671703323

Author/Editor:
Anne N. Walther, M.S.

Edition Reviewed:
1991

About The Author:
(From Cover Notes)
Anne N. Walther heads a career development firm in San Francisco, where she "conducts workshops, gives presentations, and works with individuals on their divorce hangovers and career transitions."

Publisher:
Pocket Books (Simon & Schuster, Inc.)

Internet URL:
N/A

"Christian" Orientation?:
N/A

Focused On Issues For:
N/A

1-4 Stars

Overall Rating	★★	A generally useful, sensible book on a seldom explored issue
Design, Ease Of Use	★★	Fairly cramped but structured pages; comprehensive table of contents

Description:

This book addresses the issues of overcoming "post-divorce" feelings of dependency, guilt, obsession, and anger and moving towards financial and emotional independence. The book contains twelve chapters, each including a summary and workbook exercises. Part One (chapters 1-4) introduces the concept of a "divorce hangover," including how to identify one through the fifteen most common symptoms; a discussion of the ways a divorce hangover can negatively affect your life; and "10 Steps to Healing the Hangover," or specific techniques to use to "cure" one. Part Two (chapters 5-12) discuss "post-hangover" issues such as maintaining your "cure" and keeping the hangover at bay; learning to effectively wield power in the areas of finances, child rearing, and social life; and dealing with children's own "hangovers." Chapters 7-8 discuss the more practical issues of creating successful settlements, the legal process of divorce, and dealing with lawyers. Chapters 9-12 explore how to handle your ex-spouse's own "hangover," and new and evolving relationships after divorce.

Evaluation:

This book concentrates solely on the aftermath of divorce, and is intended to be read by those for whom this aftermath has become more of a "hangover" (when the self-destructive feelings and behaviors that normally attend the breaking up of a marriage hang around for too long, affecting your ability to create a new life). This is an important issue sometimes overlooked in other books that concentrate on divorce's immediate effects and less on the long-term effects that can be far more insidious and destructive. The advice offered here is generally sound and useful, particularly when the book is dealing with issues of control and power (as in chapters 4-5) which may be of particular use to women, for whom divorce can be turned into an opportunity to become a more assertive, self-reliant person. The book's weaknesses are found when advice becomes generic or over-generalized, or when the author glosses over issues that may deserve longer treatment (sections about children or new relationships). However, readers in search of a resource that will provide a helpful overview of the long-term effects of divorce and how to confront them will find this book a good place to start.

Where To Find/Buy:

Bookstores and libraries.

REBUILDING WHEN YOUR RELATIONSHIP ENDS

★★

Media Type:
Print

Price:
$11.95

Principal Subject:
Life After Divorce

Written For:
Adults

ISBN:
091516695X

Author/Editor:
Bruce Fisher

Edition Reviewed:
2nd (1992)

About The Author:
(From Cover Notes)
Bruce Fisher, Ed.D., is a divorce therapist, author, and teacher, as well as a clinical member of the American Association of Marriage and Family Therapists, and the founder of the Family Relations Learning Center.

Publisher:
Impact Publishers

Internet URL:
N/A

"Christian" Orientation?:
N/A

Focused On Issues For:
N/A

1-4 Stars

Overall Rating	★★	A broad, somewhat simplistic, rendering of the divorce recovery process
Design, Ease Of Use	★★★	Easy to work through, some helpful graphics and illustrations

Description:
The author, a practicing divorce therapist, has written this 324-page book from his experience running divorce process seminars. This 2nd edition reflects some additions and changes from his continuing work in the field. The book is designed as a series of nineteen "rebuilding blocks" towards full recovery from divorce or the end of a relationship, each with a description of the issue, anecdotes, advice, and checklist exercises to work on in a journal. The "building blocks" are followed in the sequence in which you may experience them when recovering from a divorce, from denial, fear, loneliness, grief, and anger to self-worth, openness, trust, sexuality, and freedom. Four appendices are included: a "Workshop for Children of Divorce;" an outline of a divorce alternative, "The Healing Separation;" a contract for such a separation; and an outline of programs at the author's Family Relations Learning Center in Boulder, CO. The book contains a bibliography and an index.

Evaluation:
This book's structure is clear, graphic, and easy to work through: chapters followed in a chronological fashion reflect the series of steps one goes through in recovery from a past relationship/divorce, for a total of nineteen "rebuilding blocks," at the end of which, the author suggests, one will have "reached the top of the mountain" and achieved full recovery. However, the ease and simplicity with which this process can be followed also points to its major flaw: there's a certain slickness to the advice offered here that does not allow any one issue to be discussed in very much depth. The writing style can also be off-putting: authorial encouragement is of the cheerleader variety, and the language employed can sometimes degenerate into terms like "healing your love wound," filling your "life bucket," and the two parties in every failed marriage, the "dumper" and the "dumpee." While this may be entertaining within a workshop/class setting, in a book the language feels inappropriate. In fact, this book would be more suited for use by groups and workshops who could use its clear structure to build upon.

Where To Find/Buy:
Bookstores and libraries.

BOYS AND GIRLS BOOK ABOUT DIVORCE

★★

Media Type:
Print

Price:
$5.50

Principal Subject:
Children Of Divorce

Written For:
Children 6-12

ISBN:
0553276190

Author/Editor:
Richard A. Gardner, M.D.

Edition Reviewed:
1971

About The Author:
(From Cover Notes)
The author is an experienced child psychiatrist/psychoanalyst. He is a member of Columbia University's College of Physicians and Surgeons and the William A. White Psychoanalytic Institute, and has authored over twenty-five books.

Publisher:
Bantam Books

Internet URL:
N/A

"Christian" Orientation?:
N/A

Focused On Issues For:
N/A

1-4 Stars

Overall Rating	★★	An honest discussion of divorce that may not, however, truly appeal to children
Design, Ease Of Use	★★★	Simple, readable prose style and clear division of issues into short chapters

Description:

Written by an experienced child psychiatrist and psychoanalyst, this 157-page book is intended to be read by children of divorcing parents. The book contains two introductions, one for children and one for their parents, and twelve short chapters, each of which confront a single issue such as blame, anger, loneliness, fear, and relationships with each parent and with stepparents. It is the author's belief that parents must learn to be more honest with their children, and many of the chapters reflect this straightforward, truth-telling approach to some of the most painful issues for children, such as whether or not a parent or stepparent truly loves them, parental flaws and characteristics, and the likely pleasant (and unpleasant) outcomes of growing up as a child of divorced parents. The book is written in a simple, readable prose style suitable for children within a wide age range (centered around ages 8-14).

Evaluation:

This is a well-known resource, one of the first of its kind (first penned in 1970). The author has taken pains to write in a manner suitable for children, while still seeking to encompass many complex and painful issues. However, the question must be asked: Would a child really read this book? Undoubtedly, it contains information that would be of great help to any child experiencing divorce. Yet it is hard to imagine a child picking up this book willingly and walking away from it with practical, usable tools and techniques as a grown-up would. This kind of information is best presented to children in a fictional or other creative form, which engages their hearts and imaginations as well as their minds. But these resources were not available in 1970. And they are available today only because such pioneers like this author helped us to notice the children of divorce and to identify their feelings. This book can still be effectively used through the intervention of an adult, who can help present some of the more sensitive information in a more palatable form, or connect it more readily to each child's life and individual set of circumstances.

Where To Find/Buy:

Bookstores and libraries.

KIDS' BOOK OF DIVORCE
By, For & About Kids

★★

Media Type:
Print

Price:
$10.00

Principal Subject:
Children Of Divorce

Written For:
Children 13+

ISBN:
0394710185

Author/Editor:
Fayerweather Street School
(edited by Eric E. Rofes)

Edition Reviewed:
1982

About The Author:
(From Cover Notes)

The authors of this book
are 20 children, ages 11-14,
at an open school in
Cambridge, Mass. Eric Rofes
was their teacher, who
directed these children's
2-year project on divorce,
resulting in the publication
of this book.

Publisher:
Vintage Books (Random
House)

Internet URL:
N/A

**"Christian"
Orientation?:**
N/A

Focused On Issues For:
N/A

1-4 Stars

Overall Rating	★★	An honest but somewhat dated look at children's concerns about divorce
Design, Ease Of Use	★★★	Very readable, with wonderful drawings and stories told by the kids themselves

Description:

This book grew out of discussion groups on divorce organized by a teacher at an open school in Cambridge, Mass., that eventually turned into a 2-year project that took the 20 children, ranging in age from 11-14 years, through the process of writing, editing, and publishing a book about divorce intended to be read by other children. The book begins with a preface by the children and another by their teacher, Eric Rofes, in which he explains his belief that schools "play an important role in helping children understand the divorce process and deal with their feelings." There are ten chapters, each of which deal with a single issue related to kids and divorce, which follow a roughly chronological order from "War in the Household" and "The Decision to Separate" to "The First Legal Day of Divorce" and "Stepparents and Other People." Throughout the chapters, the children intersperse their own stories, personal accounts and reactions, and drawings. At the end of the book is a list of other resources—fiction and nonfiction—that have been written for kids about divorce, which the children rate and review themselves.

Evaluation:

The inspiration behind this book is the idea that children themselves are best suited to tell other children about divorce, and according to this book, do not need to gloss over some of the more painful realities in the process. The students could not find a book that discussed divorce issues in a non-condescending manner; indeed, the best part of this book is its honest and straightforward tone. The stories they tell feel real and full of believable detail, unlike other books on the subject in which the anecdotes feel tailor-made. This book seeks to address issues that other books skip over or neglect in the mistaken belief that children may find them too upsetting: issues such as how poor people divorce, the "legalese" of custody, and loving a gay parent. This book's major drawback is that its information dates back to the early 1980's, so that there is somewhat less information about such "modern" issues as mediation and living in blended families. It is easy to guess that a similar group of children writing a similar book today might have different concerns, although this book could still be generally useful for children to read alone or with a parent.

Where To Find/Buy:
Bookstores and libraries.

1-4 Stars

Overall Rating	★★	Insightful advice section, but the story itself lacks vivid appeal
Design, Ease Of Use	★★	Effective format

Description:

This is a slim, 74-page storybook with a light Christian focus, intended to be "read aloud" by parents to children who are experiencing the pain of divorce. Aimed primarily at 4-8 year old children, it tells the story of "Mandie" and how she and her two young brothers react to their parents' separation, and her gradual understanding and acceptance of her own feelings and those of her family. The book contains a number of pages at the end addressed "To the Care giver," in which the authors suggest helpful ways to use the story to discuss their children's own concerns and feelings, as well as some general advice about communicating sensitively and effectively with the younger child.

Evaluation:

The intention behind this book is well-meaning, with a helpful format (a story, followed by advice for the care giver/storyteller). Children often find it easier to express their feelings, especially about events as confusing and upsetting as divorce, when approached through fiction and stories. This book shows how adults can use this story to gently and sensitively open lines of communication with real children. The book contains other good advice, such as the need for young children to make decisions on their own during traumatic times, and the importance of maintaining routine in the midst of chaos. However, the integral part of this book—the story itself—is marred by clichéd expression and situations. Even a 6-year old may find this a dull read. There is no juicy, absorbing description of people or places, and little evocative language to enliven the story: just flat, stereotypical characters responding to divorce in flat, stereotypical ways. This is unfortunate, as it fails to expand children's ideas of what divorce is: without imagination, such a story is no better than a book of rules.

Where To Find/Buy:

Bookstores and libraries.

OUR FAMILY IS DIVORCING
A Read-Aloud Book For Families Experiencing Divorce

★★

Media Type:
Print

Price:
$11.95

Principal Subject:
Children Of Divorce

Written For:
Children 6-12

ISBN:
0893903914

Author/Editor:
Patricia Polin Johnson and Donna Reilly Williams

Edition Reviewed:
1996

About The Author:
(From Cover Notes)
This is the authors' second collaboration in the "Helping Children Who Hurt" series. Patricia Johnson helps prepare couples for marriage through her work in the Catholic Archdiocese of Los Angeles. Donna Williams has a private counseling practice, and also works as a "grief consultant to institutions and faith communities."

Publisher:
Resource Publications, Inc.

Internet URL:
N/A

"Christian" Orientation?:
Yes

Focused On Issues For:
N/A

CREATIVE DIVORCE
A New Opportunity For Personal Growth

★★

Media Type:
Print

Price:
$22.00

Principal Subject:
Life After Divorce

Written For:
Adults

ISBN:
0871311311

Author/Editor:
Mel Krantzler

Edition Reviewed:
1974

About The Author:
(From Cover Notes)

The author is "a divorce therapist whose specialty was motivated by the break-up of his own twenty-four year marriage." He runs university-based seminars for divorced adults.

Publisher:
M. Evans and Company

Internet URL:
N/A

"Christian" Orientation?:
N/A

Focused On Issues For:
N/A

	1-4 Stars	
Overall Rating	★★	A dated, but still useful, exploration of the "creative" side of divorce
Design, Ease Of Use	★★★	Some anachronistic language and terms but generally well-written

Description:

First published in 1973, this book explains the steps to achieving the "creative divorce," which can become, in the author's words, "the beginning of a journey of self-discovery and development." The author opens with an introduction describing the hardships of his own life as a single person after the demise of his marriage, and his coming to terms with that period of his life as an opportunity for self-growth. The first four chapters discuss how to face the aftershock of divorce and the end of your marriage, and adjusting to the single life. Chapters 5-6 confront the "new realities" of life after divorce, including how to draw on "unsuspected inner resources," rethinking your values, making new choices in the realm of work, and learning how to relate to others in fresh and healthy ways. Chapter 7 introduces the topic of children of divorce and how to acknowledge their own need to "mourn" the end of the marriage while helping them cope with their feelings. Chapter 8 asks the question, "was my divorce creative?," and discusses how to use your changed sense of identity to achieve intimacy in a new relationship.

Evaluation:

This book is a first in the entire field of self help books whose focus is on becoming a whole, healthy person after the end of a marriage. Its author, Mel Krantzler, is a pioneer in this field and established a theme that divorce can be the beginning of good things for the individual, a theme that other good self help books have emulated during the past twenty five years. For this, the book receives the highest of ratings. Its main drawback, however, is that it *was* written twenty five years ago. Without revision, it is beginning to show signs of age: the author manifests a distinctly early 1970's new-found appreciation for "the women's liberation movement," joking now and then about his "male chauvinist piggism" and his struggles with shopping, cooking, and laundry as a single man. Many men today would not have such a hard time in the kitchen, although much of what the author says about loneliness and the sense of disconnection as a newly-single person certainly still holds true. There is also advice here that can still be useful today, from searching for a more fulfilling job to mastering the art of stocking a fridge.

Where To Find/Buy:
Bookstores and libraries.

THE DIVORCE BOOK
For Men and Women

★★

Media Type:
Print

Price:
$10.00

Principal Subject:
Legal Issues

Written For:
Adults

ISBN:
0380758296

Author/Editor:
Harriet Newman Cohen,
Ralph Gardner, Jr.

Edition Reviewed:
1994

About The Author:
(From Cover Notes)
Harriet Newman Cohen is
an experienced divorce
attorney.

Publisher:
Avon Books

Internet URL:
N/A

"Christian" Orientation?:
N/A

Focused On Issues For:
N/A

1-4 Stars

Overall Rating	★★	Quite litigious in tone
Design, Ease Of Use	★★★	Easy reading

Description:

This 170+ page book has as its focus the legal issues surrounding divorce. It consists of seventeen chapters. The first three chapters are the author's suggestions concerning the initiation of the divorce, i.e. choosing an attorney, meeting with that attorney, and initiating the divorce process. Chapter 4 is a discussion of mediation (which the author vehemently opposes). Chapters 5 and 6 address paying the lawyer and providing him/her with all the information that can be useful. Chapters 7 and 8 address the client's life during the divorcing process (can one date, or not?) and who "gets" the kids and who is going to pay for them. Chapters 9 and 10 outline how a settlement might best be negotiated by the lawyer and his/her client. Chapter 11 focuses on suing or being sued by one's spouse. Chapter 12 discusses the divorce decree, and modifications and appeals to that decree. The final chapter addresses other divorce topics, including various special situations, court orders, prenuptial agreements, and life after divorce.

Evaluation:

The author's intent in the book is to educate the reader about the legal aspects of the divorce process. As the "disclaimer" at the beginning of the book states, however, the family laws of various states are different from one another and frequently change. That fact constitutes the primary weakness of this book, for the principal author is practicing law in a state in which one of the spouses can "fault" the other (proving infidelity or cruelty or abandonment, etc.) in order to obtain a divorce. In many states (California, Washington, many others) neither the husband or the wife can officially "blame" the other for the divorce, for they are "no-fault" states. Also, there are so many directives in the book which, while possibly valid legal strategies, can help destroy the emotional, psychological, and spiritual fabric of the person and the family (e.g. a lawyer advising his/her client to keep their meetings confidential from the other spouse and to immediately begin to gather information which will strengthen the position of the initiator of the divorce). Perhaps the most revealing chapter in the book is entitled "Paying;" such a litigious approach to divorce can be quite costly to one's spirit and one's pocketbook.

Where To Find/Buy:
Bookstores and libraries.

MARITAL SEPARATION
Coping With The End Of A Marriage And The Transition To Being Single Again

★★

Media Type:
Print

Price:
$20.00

Principal Subject:
All-Inclusive

Written For:
Adults

ISBN:
0465097235

Author/Editor:
Robert S. Weiss Ph.D.

Edition Reviewed:
1975

About The Author:
(From Cover Notes)
Robert S. Weiss is Chairman of the Department of Sociology at the University of Massachusetts.

Publisher:
Harper Collins (Basic Books)

Internet URL:
N/A

"Christian" Orientation?:
N/A

Focused On Issues For:
N/A

1-4 Stars		
Overall Rating	★★	Landmark book, but dated
Design, Ease Of Use	★★★	Comprehensive index, easy to read text

Description:
This book (300+pages) is authored by a sociologist who has not only researched marital separation as a scientist, but has also experienced it in his own life. As the author himself notes, much of his book is theoretical in nature, especially Chapter 3, on the role of attachment in love and marriage; Chapter 5, on the impact of separation on identity; and Chapter 11 on strategies of recovery. Other chapters represent a sociologist's report and observations of the phenomenon of separation and divorce twenty years ago in American society. The materials of the book are presented in the order in which they might become concerns for someone trying to grasp the phenomena of marital separation: why separations take place, the emotional impact of separation, the various aspects of relationship between the separating spouses, the problems likely to arise in their relationship to their children, and establishing a new life.

Evaluation:
This book is an interesting book in many ways. It is written by a sociologist who has extensively researched the societal aspects of marital separation. Second, it is written by a person who has established close collaborative and healing relationships with separated persons, as evidenced through his association with Parents Without Partners and Seminars for the Separated (which he helped design and present and which are reported on the the Appendix of his book). Also, his book is saturated with quotations of separated persons which he has collected. However, the book is a photograph of separation and divorce in our society over twenty years ago, and the reader cannot fail to notice how "things" have profoundly changed. The Index of the book, for example, does not even list the word "mediation;" joint custody receives a footnote, and the father being the primary custodial parent is unheard of. While of interest, the book's copyright date may well be a block to present day readers seeking contemporary self-help resources.

Where To Find/Buy:
Bookstores and libraries.

MY MOMMY AND DADDY DIDN'T DIVORCE ME!

★★

Media Type:
Print

Price:
$6.95

Principal Subject:
Children Of Divorce

Written For:
Preschool Children

ISBN:
0964617315

Author/Editor:
Richard Esterman

Edition Reviewed:
1996

About The Author:
(From Cover Notes)

This book was written and published by Richard Esterman, and illustrated by his son and daughter, Jonathan and Sarah.

Publisher:
Richard Esterman

Internet URL:
N/A

"Christian" Orientation?:
N/A

Focused On Issues For:
N/A

1-4 Stars

Overall Rating	★★	The drawings are far superior to the actual text
Design, Ease Of Use	★★★	Evocative, striking artwork by the author's son and daughter

Description:

This is a slim illustrated storybook for young children about how it feels to live with divorced parents in separate houses. Illustrated by the author's son and daughter, this book tells what happens in the two separate houses where their mother and father live, what special things take place at each house, and the different activities they pursue with each parent, in order to show children that "Mommy and Daddy didn't divorce them."

Evaluation:

The best thing about this book is definitely the wonderful and colorful drawings by the author's children. Extremely evocative, they tell a story perhaps more complex and less stridently cheerful than the actual text, whose only message seems to be "we received two times the love which made us feel like very special little people." The drawings tell the real story, and are, in themselves, almost worth the price of this book. In fact, a book with simply the drawings and their captions would have told a subtler, richer, and truer tale of how young children feel about divorce. Readers with young children of their own might consider buying this as a model for a similar book their own children could make about how divorce feels and looks to them.

Where To Find/Buy:

Bookstores and libraries.

A CHANGE OF HEART

Words Of Experience And Hope For The Journey Through Divorce

★★

Media Type:
Print

Price:
$12.50

Principal Subject:
Life After Divorce

Written For:
Adults

ISBN:
0060951052

Author/Editor:
Julia Thorne

Edition Reviewed:
1996

About The Author:
(From Cover Notes)

Julia Thorne is a public speaker, poet, and the author of *You Are Not Alone,* a national bestseller about depression. She lives in Wyoming.

Publisher:
HarperPerennial

Internet URL:
N/A

"Christian" Orientation?:
N/A

Focused On Issues For:
N/A

	1-4 Stars	
Overall Rating	★★	A potential source of comfort and companionship, but short on real help
Design, Ease Of Use	★★★	Very nicely arranged series of "testimonies;" very readable

Description:

The anecdotes of people who have survived divorce are gathered together here in this book, which represents a wide variety of voices and experiences, from young children to single mothers, older divorcing wives, fathers, and the author herself, divorced from her husband of many years (a one-time member of the U.S. Senate). The author begins by telling us, in her introduction to the book, her own story of marriage and divorce, and her reasons for writing this book: "to offer you the hope, understanding, acceptance, empathy, and support you may not currently have." The book is divided into seven sections, the first five of which reflect the emotional stages of divorce, from "Falling Apart," "Separating," and "Trying to Cope," to "Coming to Terms" and "Moving On." The last two sections include similar anecdote-style advice from various professionals (therapists, lawyers, mediators) and a guide to divorce-related support services.

Evaluation:

As one struggles through an emotional upheaval of any sort, it is always a comfort to know that one is not alone—that other people have had similar struggles, and have emerged out the other side. This is the author's chief aim: to gather together a variety of voices whose overwhelming effect is that peculiar solace to be found when you realize, after all, that what you are experiencing is part of the human condition. In this goal the book succeeds. However, the book does not go beyond this immediate "solace." It cannot—the testimonies themselves are too short to allow us to sink into any one in much depth, and the voices themselves, though drawn from a variety of sources, are more like divorce "sound bytes" than true revelations of people's experiences. Interspersed among these are the author's own, which are set apart from the others in italics, with their own title and special graphic. The effect of this is to set her narratives apart from anyone else's, and yet they don't seem especially thoughtful or insightful. All in all, this book does not give much direction to the practical, legal, or even the emotional journeys of divorce, but it can offer some companionship along the way.

Where To Find/Buy:

Bookstores and libraries.

I-4 Stars

Overall Rating   ★   A unique workbook resource

Design, Ease Of Use   ★★★   Simple, easy to comprehend worksheets

Description:

This 147+ page books consists essentially of worksheets. The intent of the author is that these worksheets will empower the reader to make good choices during the divorce process. These good choices consists primarily in selecting the appropriate professionals who will walk with her/him through the divorce process, learning to deal with the spouse, as well as to help focus self care for oneself and one's children. The book is also an organizational tool for helping the reader prepare the information needed (especially financial) for the legal processing of the divorce.

Evaluation:

In his Introduction, the author states that this book presents a fresh approach to managing divorce and maximizing personal recovery. His materials as presented in this work certainly have the potential to do this, for they enable the reader to take a proactive role in the oftentimes chaotic divorce process. His worksheets and checklists enable the reader to avoid pitfalls he/she never knew existed, to ask questions that might never be thought of, to remember to care for oneself and loved ones in the midst of the turmoil which so often characterizes a divorce. The book is exactly what it claims to be, a workbook. Consequently, it does not contain a great deal of information and/or antecdotal material concerning the emotional and psychological process of divorce. Rather it is an interactive tool for best handling the countless decisions and practicalities regarding any divorce. Published in 1995, it is largely up-to-date with current laws and processes.

Where To Find/Buy:

Bookstores and libraries.

MY DIVORCE WORKBOOK
Your Self Empowerment Guide

★

Media Type:
Print

Price:
$19.95

Principal Subject:
All-Inclusive

Written For:
Adults

ISBN:
0964658119

Author/Editor:
Godwin O. Igein

Edition Reviewed:
1995

About The Author:
(From Cover Notes)
The author has worked as a child support enforcement field investigator and as a crisis intervention management counselor.

Publisher:
Destiny Publications

Internet URL:
N/A

"Christian" Orientation?:
N/A

Focused On Issues For:
N/A

THE BEST IS YET TO COME
Coping With Divorce And Enjoying Life Again

★

Media Type:
Print

Price:
$12.00

Principal Subject:
All-Inclusive

Written For:
Adults

ISBN:
0671865692

Author/Editor:
Ivana Trump

Edition Reviewed:
1995

About The Author:
(From Cover Notes)
Ivana Trump is a novelist, a designer, and a mother of three children. Her divorce from Donald Trump was one of America's more publicized divorces.

Publisher:
Pocket Books

Internet URL:
N/A

"Christian" Orientation?:
N/A

Focused On Issues For:
Women

1-4 Stars		
Overall Rating	★	Lacks depth other sources provide
Design, Ease Of Use	★★★	Easy to read, informal style

Description:

This book is divided into five parts. Part 1 is "The Beginning of the End." It prepares the reader to watch for the warning signs of the end and how to prepare for the breakup. Part 2 addresses the actual breakup which involves the "explosion," lawyers, personal coping strategies, and helping your children adjust to the breakup. Part 3 is "On Your Way to a New Life." In this part the author discusses learning new ways to manage one emotional life and financial life. Part 4, "On Your Own," concerns the "body beautiful," social life and romance. Part 5 restates the title of the book, "The Best Is Yet To Come." It includes the author's suggestions for raising children following the divorce, and how one's postdivorce life will be better than one's predivorce life. Each chapter is usually sprinkled with quotations from other women who contacted her and/or wrote to her while this author was going through her own divorce.

Evaluation:

The author of this book has experienced personal losses of those near and dear to her, whether those losses came through premature death or divorce. Her book reflects on these losses. At the same time, it is a "gossipy," antedotal commentary on how the "rich and the famous" experience infidelities and divorce. Also, the book is superficial as it addresses the divorce process. The principal theme of the book—"the best is yet to come"—is a strong, hopeful message for women who feel left and abused by their husbands. But the process of surviving divorce in fact is, and must be, deeper and more substantive than positive self talk, a new relationship, or a body beautiful. Rather, there must be a healing of the spirit which takes an extended period of time and focused energy. Otherwise, as the more perceptive self-help books tell us, so much unresolved "baggage" is carried into the future.

Where To Find/Buy:

Bookstores and libraries.

1-4 Stars

Overall Rating	★	May provide a short lift, but neither informative nor constructive in purpose
Design, Ease Of Use	★★	Charming illustrations

Description:

This small, illustrated humor book traces one woman's path from anger and loneliness to "freedom," showing scenes of her husband leaving, reading self-help books in bed, starching his underwear, cutting his belongings in two, eating chocolate chip cookies, going to bed alone in an ugly flannel nightgown, and other behaviors a woman may fall prey to after separation from a spouse.

Evaluation:

This self-described "good-bye, good riddance, and get-on-with-your-life guide" is intended to be read by women whose husbands have left them. Somehow, a comic book on this subject seems somewhat depressing, surely not the effect the author intended. Why? There is a kind of humor that heals what it touches, but this isn't it. All the old cliches of an unloved woman taking petty household revenge on an estranged husband are pulled out here; they are, in reality, offensive, trivializing both women and their pain. It is hard to imagine any potential buyer of this book, unless it be an angry husband sending it as a revenge on his ex-wife who cut his favorite cashmere sweater in two. Not recommended for anyone.

Where To Find/Buy:

Bookstores and libraries.

BREAKING UP
From Heartache To Happiness In 48 Pages

★

Media Type:
Print

Price:
$3.95

Principal Subject:
Life After Divorce

Written For:
Adults

ISBN:
0894808397

Author/Editor:
Yolanda Nave

Edition Reviewed:
1985

About The Author:
(From Cover Notes)

Publisher:
Workman Publishing Company, Inc.

Internet URL:
N/A

"Christian" Orientation?:
N/A

Focused On Issues For:
Women

I ONLY SEE MY DAD ON WEEKENDS

Kids Tell Their Stories About Divorce

★

Media Type:
Print

Price:
$4.49

Principal Subject:
Children Of Divorce

Written For:
Children 6-12

ISBN:
0781401100

Author/Editor:
Beth Matthews and Andrew Adams with Karen Dockrey

Edition Reviewed:
1st (1994)

About The Author:
(From Cover Notes)

Beth Matthews and Andrew Adams are pen-names for two young Christian students in 11th and 10th grade, who have created the characters in this book .
This book was written with the help of Karen Dockrey, a youth minister and writer, and the author of 20+ books.

Publisher:
Chariot Books (David C. Cook Publishing Co.)

Internet URL:
N/A

"Christian" Orientation?:
Yes

Focused On Issues For:
N/A

	1-4 Stars	
Overall Rating	★	A rather limited resource for children facing the pain of divorce
Design, Ease Of Use	★★★	Easy-to-read, "child-size" booklet

Description:

This 42-page book is part of the "Kids Helping Kids" series, books with a Christian focus written by children, and intended to be read by children. The authors of this book are two young Christian students, who have created various characters who tell their stories and share experiences about living through divorce or in "blended" families in each of the six brief chapters. Each chapter ends with a list of questions on the issue at hand, such as "Memories and Feelings," "Sad Times," "Happy Times," "God Then, Now, And In My Future," "Our Advice to You," and "Other Friends Who Can Help" (a short list of resources for kids).

Evaluation:

Although the idea behind this book is interesting (having children tell their stories of divorce and step-families the way they see them), the "characters" speaking all the way through are fictitious and the book has an unsettlingly contrived quality. The manner in which these imaginary children speak is forced and artificial, even though some of the issues raised seem valuable and real enough. The overall effect is to cheapen children's experiences of the real suffering inherent in divorce and its aftermath. This book has an explicitly Christian focus—many of the chapters' discussions are of how these children turned to their religion as a source of consolation. A book with this focus would have a lot more value if it allowed real children to speak in its pages and bring up those issues that are truly and uniquely important to them, and not to the well-meaning grown-ups around them.

Where To Find/Buy:

Bookstores and libraries.

THE CASE AGAINST DIVORCE

★

Media Type:
Print

Price:
$5.99

Principal Subject:
Preventing Divorce

Written For:
Adults

ISBN:
0804106339

Author/Editor:
Diane Medved

Edition Reviewed:
1989

About The Author:
(From Cover Notes)
The author has ten years' experience as a psychologist, conducting workshops and publishing books on "major life choices."

Publisher:
Ivy Books (Ballantine)

Internet URL:
N/A

"Christian" Orientation?:
N/A

Focused On Issues For:
N/A

1-4 Stars

Overall Rating	★	An intelligent but anachronistic rationale for marriage-saving
Design, Ease Of Use	★★	Fairly dense pages and crowded type

Description:

The author, an expert psychologist, had originally done research for a "morally neutral book" about divorce as a life choice, but instead found that those individuals who had chosen to divorce had emerged emotionally and psychologically battered. This 258-page book was written as a result, which builds up a "case" against divorce using the results of that research. There are three main sections, which move from a discussion of the recent cultural devaluation of marriage as an institution, to overturning the ten most common "exit lines" from a marriage (e.g. "We're not well-matched," "We've grown apart," "I need to be appreciated"), and finally, reinstating some of the "seven good reasons to stay together that have gotten a bum rap" ("We should stay together for the sake of the children," "I want to stick it out," "We should stay together because our friends and families would be devastated."). The emotional and financial costs of divorce are explored in the last section; included as well is a discussion of the social, moral, and personal benefits of staying married.

Evaluation:

This book contains some sound, sobering advice about the dangers of divorce and the high toll it can exact on people's lives, as compared to the spiritual and emotional benefits of remaining in a marriage. The author presents a penetrating critique of today's "disposable" culture, pointing out that the current ethic of "getting the most out of life" is disastrous for marriage. Her dismantling of such myths as the mid-life crisis, the lure of the single life, and pursuing opportunities to the detriment of one's marital responsibilities is interesting and valid. The main problem with this book is its assumption that it is *possible* to turn back the clock, throw over current society's "cheap values," sacrifice personal ambition, and view marriage as "the ultimate setting for fulfilling life's purpose." This book is best for those who feel able to reinstate past mores and values in their marriages, but others may require a book that presents valid alternatives to marriage or some practical redefinitions of marriage itself.

Where To Find/Buy:

Bookstores and libraries.

LIVING & LOVING AFTER DIVORCE

★

Media Type:
Print

Price:
$4.99

Principal Subject:
Life After Divorce

Written For:
Adults

ISBN:
0451149882

Author/Editor:
Catherine Napolitane &
Victoria Pellegrino

Edition Reviewed:
1978

About The Author:
(From Cover Notes)

Catherine Napolitane is the
founder of Nexus, "the first
self-help organization for
the divorced woman." She
lectures on divorce and the
single life. Victoria Pellegrino
is a journalist and author,
and the director of a career
counseling firm for women.

Publisher:
Signet (Penguin Books)

Internet URL:
N/A

**"Christian"
Orientation?:**
N/A

Focused On Issues For:
Women

1-4 Stars		
Overall Rating	★	A warm, personable, but limited look at some of the issues in "post-divorce" life
Design, Ease Of Use	★★	Extremely cramped pages, little breathing room

Description:

The author wrote this 241-page book out of her experience running the Nexus support groups for divorced women, and out of her own personal experience with divorce. The book covers a range of women's issues related to life after divorce, based primarily on a personal insights and anecdotes gathered from friends, associates, and members of Nexus. Part One is a discussion of such post-divorce issues as bringing up children as a single parent, dating, the job world, personal finances, dealing with your ex's new wife, holidays, and traveling as a single woman. Part Two delves into the more personal/ psychological effects of divorce and living "newly-single," with a description of the eight separate stages a woman may go through from "active bleeding" to "euphoria" to "all work, no play" to the final "search for the real me." The book contains a list of women's support organizations, as well as a list for further reading.

Evaluation:

The major part of this book's appeal lies in its personable, down-to-earth tone and friendly advice for women in the throes of the single life. The author intersperses her own trials and tribulations as a divorced woman throughout, as well as stories gathered from friends and associates. The advice offered by the author is warm and almost motherly, such as when she suggests you drink a glass of warm milk to get to sleep on those lonely nights, or ways to avoid being picked up by the wrong type in a single's bar: a welcome change from the more abstract, theoretical approach of most self-help books. Although this book stands as a kind of "hurrah" for the single life, there are places in which some words of warning are conspicuously absent, such as in the chapter discussing the morality of one-night stands ("You are bound to feel 100% better the next day") or dating married men ("this man is interested and they're needy. It's that basic and simple.") The author also discusses the "reality" of multiple sexual partners, with no mention of the "reality" of AIDS. Women looking for a serious, in-depth manual to single life issues will not find much help here.

Where To Find/Buy:

Bookstores and libraries.

DIVORCE
A Woman's Guide to Getting a Fair Share

★

Media Type:
Print

Price:
$14.95

Principal Subject:
Financial Issues

Written For:
Adults

ISBN:
0028603443

Author/Editor:
Patricia Phillips and George Mair

Edition Reviewed:
1995

About The Author:
(From Cover Notes)
Patricia Phillips is a lawyer, Fellow of the Academy of Matrimonial Lawyers, and a certified Family Law Specialist. George Mair is a nationally-syndicated columnist at the *Los Angeles Times*.

Publisher:
Macmillan (Simon & Schuster Macmillan Co.)

Internet URL:
N/A

"Christian" Orientation?:
N/A

Focused On Issues For:
Women

	1-4 Stars	
Overall Rating	★	Overall, an uneven resource showing women how to play "hardball" in divorce
Design, Ease Of Use	★★★	An organized, carefully-executed book

Description:

This 243-page book is aimed at helping women about to undergo divorce gain the knowledge necessary to get their "fair share" in an upcoming settlement. Coauthored by a lawyer and an extensively published writer, this book confronts the various stages and issues in divorce from a woman's standpoint. Chapters 1-3 explore what to do before you marry (prenuptial agreements), and what to do when your marriage is "dying" (advantages and disadvantages of walking out vs. staying, legal separation, and avoiding behaviors that may be used against you). Chapters 4-6 include information about finding a good attorney and "crafting a strategy" for divorce, costs, and how to take control of the process. Children's issues and custody are reviewed in chapter 7. Chapter 8 explains the "tricks and unsavory truths" by which your husband may be hiding assets from you, and how to find them. Chapters 9-13 take you step-by-step through the divorce process, from terms and language used by lawyers and the courts, to how to prepare mentally and physically for a deposition or court trial. Five appendices are included.

Evaluation:

This is a highly uneven resource with a rather nasty agenda. To be fair, it pulls no punches and does not pretend to be anything other than it is: early in the book the authors state "When it becomes clear divorce in unavoidable, you should know how to play one of the most vicious, unfair, hardball games in our American culture." And indeed, the purpose of this book is to arm women and teach them strategies to fight and win what can become an ugly battle. At several points in the book, the authors urge their readers to use unseemly tactics such as pawing through their husband's diaries and receipts in search of incriminating evidence, and hiring a private investigator to find secret assets he may be hiding. The odd thing about this book is that at times it lifts itself above such pettiness, as in the chapter discussing children, and becomes surprisingly insightful and sensitive. The world could well use a book written for specifically for women about how to take control over the various aspects of divorce. However, a book like this, instead of empowering women, throws them back 100 years to the stereotype of the wily, devious, grasping harper whose only means of power lies in the manipulation of men.

Where To Find/Buy:

Bookstores and libraries.

THERE'S HOPE AFTER DIVORCE

★

Media Type:
Print

Price:
$5.99

Principal Subject:
All-Inclusive

Written For:
Adults

ISBN:
0800786343

Author/Editor:
Jeenie Gordon

Edition Reviewed:
1996

About The Author:
(From Cover Notes)

The author, herself a survivor of divorce, currently works as a family therapist and seminar leader.

Publisher:
Spire

Internet URL:
N/A

"Christian" Orientation?:
Yes

Focused On Issues For:
Women

1-4 Stars		
Overall Rating	★	A look at divorce as an opportunity for self-growth and change
Design, Ease Of Use	★★	Readable and accessible

Description:

The author, a family therapist who has suffered through her own painful divorce, decided to write this book to help others recover from emotional devastation by building their lives anew. This book seems primarily addressed to women (although could probably be used by men) and has a Christian perspective. The first few chapters explore the stages of the healing process from a life trauma, as well as "choosing to let go" of a marriage and making a "clean break" from your spouse while learning to communicate with him in a healthy, productive manner. Chapters 4-6 discuss how to get on with your life, goal-setting, and dealing with fears of failure, as well as issues of self-esteem and assertiveness. Effective parenting techniques for single parents, stress, and new relationships are all included in chapters 7-9, and a more Christian-based exploration of the issues is approached in the last two chapters. The author highlights her discussion of the issues with personal anecdotes and stories gathered from her experience as a therapist; "growth" questions round out each chapter's close.

Evaluation:

The more intimate, psychological aspects of divorce are explored here in this book, which looks at a variety of issues through the lens of self-growth. This focus explains the rather bewildering array of topics that convene in these pages, any one of which could arguably merit a book in itself. The author uses a wide assortment of sources to bolster her discussion of the issues, drawing liberally on others' more in-depth work in the field as well as highlights from her personal history as a divorce survivor. Throughout the book, she grounds her discussion in a Christian perspective. The most useful section by far is the one in which she talks about how to raise children as a single parent; she gives some intelligent and sensitive advice about how to effectively set limits for your kids without "punishing" or "rescuing" them. The majority of this book, alas, is not half so useful—consisting of a fairly general and overly-broad treatment of the post-divorce blues.

Where To Find/Buy:

Bookstores and libraries.

1-4 Stars

Overall Rating	★	Unscrupulous tactics outlined in a thoroughly unattractive picture of divorce
Design, Ease Of Use	★★★	Clear strategies in an organized format

Description:

This 224-page book explains how to get the most out of your divorce from your spouse, including the "50 Strategies Every Woman Needs to Know to Win." The book is divided into "pre-divorce" and "actual divorce" sections, and includes many familiar and some less known strategies for winning the divorce war. Topics covered in the first section include finding the best divorce lawyer your money can buy, investigating your husbands income and assets, accumulating money and purchasing goods (that cannot be taken away from you later), how to become "unemployed" prior to divorce (and thus able to receive more alimony), ways to get custody of your children, and ways "to convince your husband to divorce you." Part Two, "Are You Ready For Battle?," uncovers such divorce strategies as claiming a "marital tort" against your husband, tape-recording incriminating evidence, hiring a private investigator, and testifying effectively in court, as well as a bevy of "post-divorce" strategies.

Evaluation:

Consisting of war-like "strategies" and a vengeful sensibility, the motto of this book is summed up early in the first chapter: "Well, you may be the sweetest woman in the world—but are you going to let him take your soul, pull it out, and stomp on it until your feelings are dead?" Although a portion of this book contains basic common-sense advice to women about protecting their rightful interests, most of it outlines the shadier tactics of the divorce battle that your lawyer (or best friend) may not tell you, the worst of which (and the subject of an entire chapter) is "how to prove marital torts against your husband" on the slightest pretext of abuse. There should be no need to say how such an abuse of the "tort" system could ultimately backfire on those women who, unhappily, have genuine claims to being abused by their husbands. In short, this is a mean-spirited and unscrupulous guide for women who believe they would have nothing to lose and everything to gain by approaching divorce with their husbands as if they were their bitterest enemies.

Where To Find/Buy:

Bookstores and libraries.

DIVORCE WAR!
50 Strategies Every Woman Needs To Know To Win

★

Media Type:
Print

Price:
$12.00

Principal Subject:
Financial Issues

Written For:
Adults

ISBN:
1558506004

Author/Editor:
Bradley A. Pistotnik

Edition Reviewed:
1996

About The Author:
(From Cover Notes)
The author runs a domestic law and trial practice in Wichita, Kansas.

Publisher:
Adams Media Corporation

Internet URL:
N/A

"Christian" Orientation?:
N/A

Focused On Issues For:
Women

DIVORCE IS NOT THE ANSWER
A Change of Heart Will Save Your Marriage

★

Media Type:
Print

Price:
$12.95

Principal Subject:
Preventing Divorce

Written For:
Adults

ISBN:
0830635831

Author/Editor:
George S. Pransky, Ph.D.

Edition Reviewed:
1990

About The Author:
(From Cover Notes)
The author has over fifteen years' experience as a licensed marriage and family counselor. He is a clinical member of the American Association of Marriage and Family Counselors.

Publisher:
TAB Books (McGraw-Hill)

Internet URL:
N/A

"Christian" Orientation?:
N/A

Focused On Issues For:
N/A

1-4 Stars

Overall Rating	★	A basically appealing philosophy that is taken too far to be useful
Design, Ease Of Use	★★	Clear, readable

Description:
This book is a guide to finding "an easy, satisfying relationship" through understanding and acceptance of one's mate. This book rejects 13 of the most prevalent myths about marriage and relationships, based on a philosophy that is a complete reversal of contemporary theories about relationships. The author believes that couples do not need to "work" on a relationship in order for it to be successful: all couples need is a "change of heart" to create dramatic healing changes in their relationships. Each chapter of the book presents a commonly-held "myth" about relationships and then provides ways to easily and painlessly resolve areas of conflict through a new way of thinking about one's partner and the relationship based on understanding. Issues covered in the chapters include compatibility, communication, emotions, dealing with problems, intimacy, and commitment.

Evaluation:
There is an certain appeal to this book's philosophy. It would be a much happier world if everyone sought to transcend pettiness and conflict through the simple act of understanding others. The author states at one point that couples with satisfying marriages don't "cope with" and "work on their marriages," and that bringing up areas of conflict in a relationship "makes things look worse than they really are." Instead, couples should, in a sense, "transcend" their problems. The philosophy of this book is based on similar beliefs: compatibility, bad moods, and dissatisfaction in relationships are really just states of mind, and thus, not fully real. You can, therefore, either choose to ignore them or transform them into more positive feelings. However, such an approach could be a precursor to a life of denial, as potentially damaging to families as continued marital discord. There is some value to this book, but the extremes to which this philosophy is taken are simply illogical, especially when one considers that negative emotions are at least as real, if not as pleasant, as positive emotions.

Where To Find/Buy:
Bookstores and libraries.

DIVORCE ONLINE

★★★

Media Type:
Internet

Principal Subject:
All-Inclusive

Written For:
Adults

Publisher:
The American Divorce Information Network

Internet URL:
http://www.divorce-online.com

"Christian" Orientation?:
N/A

Focused On Issues For:
N/A

1-4 Stars

Overall Rating	★★★	A useful site, particularly for its articles on divorce and its discussion forums
Design, Ease Of Use	★★★	Crisp, professional design, easily navigable, forums work well

Description:

One of the "older" divorce-centered websites (and a Netguide "Gold" award winner), the site receives over 5,000 visitors/week (according to their response to our email inquiry). A variety of "channels" are offered: a number of short articles on various divorce topics, some written by sponsors of the site, all searchable by keyword; a forum for exchanging questions and ideas called "He Said . . . She Said" (registration for a password is required); a "Professionals" directory where you can find professional resources listed by discipline (financial, legal, etc.); a "Bookstore" containing a directory of books on divorce, arranged by subject (an earlier visit found this listing; a recent visit found this section under construction as they build in a purchasing link to Amazon.com Books); and "Your 2 Cents," a solicitation for your vote and written input on a current issue in divorces. The site publisher is a "group of professionals who believe in an interdisciplinary approach for dealing with divorce and family law. We are members not only of the legal system, but also therapists, accountants, financial planners, educational planners and other consultants."

Evaluation:

This is a useful place to visit, principally for its searchable articles on divorce topics and its informative (and entertaining) threaded mail forum. The articles, while short, offer useful insight into a variety of topics, and the keyword search engine provided really helps speed a search for articles on specific topics of interest. This site is a lively place, full of messages from folks concerned about their divorce (or spouse, ex-spouse, etc.). Their listing of books is thorough, although they don't rate the books shown or offer much information about them; the planned link to Amazon.com Books will support online purchases of books listed. Most of the professional listings (sponsors who pay $100/month for the privilege) seem concentrated in Michigan, with few other states represented (the search engine for finding professional resources will be of limited utility until they enlarge their database). A well-designed site, useful to adults concerned about divorce, that should grow in value as more professionals add their listings to the site's database.

Where To Find/Buy:

On the Internet's World Wide Web, at the URL: http://www.divorce-online.com.

THE DIVORCE PAGE
A Support Page For Those In Divorce . . .

★★★

Media Type:
Internet

Principal Subject:
All-Inclusive

Written For:
Adults

About The Author:
(From Cover Notes)

From "About Dean Hughson": "Dean . . . is a consultant in the . . . food processing industry, a Net journalist, a human rights (divorce) activist . . . He speaks widely on divorce issues in the press. . . ." Dean lives in Las Vegas with his second wife.

Publisher:
Dean Hughson

Internet URL:
http://hughson.com

"Christian" Orientation?:
N/A

Focused On Issues For:
Men

	1-4 Stars	
Overall Rating	★★★	A wonderful gift from an concerned individual, rife with links and personal opinion
Design, Ease Of Use	★★★	Easy to use (good organization and cross-referencing); many "dead links"

Description:

The author/publisher of this website is a divorced father of three kids (now remarried) who participates in their parenting long distance. He has created this website ". . . as a public service to give people links and referrals." The site includes a huge variety of links to other resources, organized into more than a dozen categories. The links and referrals include, in many cases, his editorial comments and observations about the resources linked to or described. Important categories include lists and links for legal resources, resources for men (and women), and resources for parenting and children's issues. An annotated bibliography of books on Divorce & Custody is provided. More personal aspects of the site include the author's essay on the divorce process and the implications of joint custody ("Welcome To The Back Of The Bus"), as well as his suggested "Steps Towards Recovery." Each channel on the site includes extensive cross-referencing to other resource lists on the site. An index lists all resource links alphabetically (150+).

Evaluation:

This website is an example of the wonderful gift that the Internet has brought to us all: the selfless sharing of ideas and experiences by concerned individuals. Dean Hughson has obviously invested an extraordinary amount of time in developing his ideas and sharing his resources and experiences through this media, and for that gift he deserves many kudos. Unique to this site and unusual among resources on divorce is the author's concern about, and suggested resources for, men experiencing divorce, and in particular, men who have unwillingly been divorced and forced into a long-distance, shared-parenting relationship with their children. Like many sites that are maintained on a limited budget by individuals, the quality of content is variable and reflects the strong bias of its author. Some (perhaps many) of the links Dean has created will seem of limited relevance to some visitors; some (too many) links are "dead" (no longer refer to a live web page). But this doesn't really matter. If you're thirsty for information on divorce, we'd say give this site a try; be prepared to spend several hours exploring all it offers.

Where To Find/Buy:
Find on the Internet, using the URL: http://hughson.com.

DIVORCENET
★★★

Media Type:
Internet

Principal Subject:
All-Inclusive

Written For:
Adults

Publisher:
LawTek Media Group, LLC

Internet URL:
http://www.divorcenet.com

**"Christian"
Orientation?:**
N/A

Focused On Issues For:
N/A

	1-4 Stars	
Overall Rating	★★★	The best bulletin boards and chat rooms we've found; huge array of newsletter articles
Design, Ease Of Use	★★	OK design and navigation; few graphics; OK response times

Description:
This website was created in 1995 to showcase the law offices of Sharyn T. Sooho (Newton, Mass.), and to disseminate their Family Law Advisor newsletter; it has grown in scope (and awards) since then to encompass more content and more law firms specializing in family law. The site includes a state-by-state resource center (currently, for 18 states), which typically include one or more sponsoring law firms, with FAQs written by members of those firms, and other state resources. A comprehensive index to 2+ years' of newsletters is provided; 100+ articles address issues from abuse to stepfamilies. A variety of bulletin boards (threaded email) are supported, on 10+ topics ranging from financial issues to parental abduction. A chat room is also supported, providing visitors with the option of "talking" to other visitors to the site in real time. A "Reading Room & Library" includes more FAQs, an annotated divorce law dictionary, and book reviews (a sentence or two on roughly 20 books) on a variety of subjects.

Evaluation:
This site, although supported by "sponsors" (other law firms specializing in family law), has a unique twist in that it requires its sponsors to create content (state-specific articles). Like all sponsor-supported sites of this nature, two caveats dominate: very few firms are represented, and no attempt is made to rank such firms by quality or experience. On the positive side, this site's bulletin boards (threaded email) are among the most comprehensive and active we've found; the site is alone (so far) in providing live chat rooms for visitors who want to "talk" to others about their questions in real time. Less useful: links provided are very limited and are focused principally on law-oriented sites. Also, answers provided for frequently asked questions seemed uniformly brief; they don't provide a comprehensive treatment of subjects covered. The huge variety of articles made available from their newsletter make for interesting reading on a wide variety of topics. Our feeling that this site is worth a visit, particularly for these articles and its bulletin boards and chat rooms. It state-oriented features are, at this point, of less value.

Where To Find/Buy:
On the Internet at the URL: http://www.divorcenet.com.

MARITALSTATUS
The Comprehensive On-Line Resource for Divorce And Remarriage

★★

Media Type:
Internet

Principal Subject:
All-Inclusive

Written For:
Adults

Publisher:
Adler Group

Internet URL:
http://
www.maritalstatus.com

"Christian" Orientation?:
N/A

Focused On Issues For:
N/A

1-4 Stars

Overall Rating	★★	Still largely "under construction"
Design, Ease Of Use	★★	Still largely "under construction"

Description:

Set for full release in July of 1997, the intent of this web site is to provide a place of information and interaction for adults contemplating or experiencing divorce. Currently this site is focused on the states of Virginia and Maryland, with the developers stating they anticipate a broader geographical audience in the future. The site consists primarily of a resource directory in which lawyers, accountants, and therapists have advertised. A second section, Legal Help, is a resource on family law in the State of Maryland. Another facet of the site is "Talk About It," a threaded discussion facility with areas such as "Ask the Experts," "Money Talk," "Hearts & Flowers" and "Kid's Love." The site will also include a Marital Status Associations section which will include links to local nonprofit organizations focusing on legal services, child custody, counseling, and financial support. Marital Status writers and professionals will also be providing information regarding the impact of divorce on children, the costs of divorce, hiring a lawyer, and other topics.

Evaluation:

This site is difficult to evaluate because of its current state of development, like standing at the beginning construction of a building with blueprints in hand. We can see the foundation and the prints tell us much about the intended construction, but we can only imagine the finished work. At the present time, the focus is primarily on the states of Maryland and Virginia. Naturally, the developers of this site will want to broaden that focus if the site is to have national appeal. This website appears to have strong potential to helpfully address the needs of adults who are experiencing divorce when complete.

DIVORCE MAGAZINE

★★

Media Type:
Internet

Principal Subject:
All-Inclusive

Written For:
Adults

Publisher:
Dan Couvrette, Publisher

Internet URL:
http://www.divorcemag.com

"Christian" Orientation?:
N/A

Focused On Issues For:
N/A

	1-4 Stars	
Overall Rating	★★	Unique, timely resource
Design, Ease Of Use	★★	Site still under development

Description:

According to information found on this website, this magazine is currently published in four cities/areas: Chicago, New York/New Jersey, Southern California, and Toronto. This website is an introduction to the magazine. It lists the table of contents for the magazines, to be published four times a year. It also contains excerpts from the magazine (currently only the Winter '96/'97 Chicago Divorce Magazine is shown). For each of the cities/areas in which Divorce Magazine is published, the site provides a listing of professional divorce-related services; services who have chosen to advertise through Divorce Magazine can be accessed as well. The site also contains information about subscribing ($10.95/year on the online form), obtaining back issues of the Magazine, and an email address for comments and/or suggestions. This website is still under construction and not all links are complete, so one may get a "not found" error when exploring.

Evaluation:

As the reader peruses this web site, he/she is going to be caught up in the enthusiasm of the designers of the site and the product it advertises, Divorce Magazine. The site boasts that it has had "more hits than a hall of famer!" This site and the magazine have the potential to fulfill an important need. The adult (and the child) experiencing divorce oftentimes feels so isolated, so alone. It is reassuring for him/her to be able to peruse this site and discover a friendly source of information and advice to help him/her survive the divorce. A useful contribution this magazine and site can provide is a listing of local resources, from lawyers to therapists, entertainment to insurance, accountants to employment agencies, and so forth. We hope publications for additional cities/areas will continue to be added.

Where To Find/Buy:

Internet, at the URL http://www.divorcemag.com, or where magazines are sold.

DIVORCE CENTRAL

★★

Media Type:
Internet

Principal Subject:
All-Inclusive

Written For:
Adults

Author/Editor:
Pam Weintraub, Terry Hillman (Editors)

About The Author:
(From Cover Notes)

Editors and Webmasters are Pam Weintraub and Terry Hillman, authors of *The Complete Idiot's Guide To Surviving Divorce.*

Publisher:
Online Concepts, Inc.

Internet URL:
http://
www.divorcecentral.com

"Christian" Orientation?:
N/A

Focused On Issues For:
N/A

1-4 Stars		
Overall Rating	★★	Broad mission, not yet matched with consistently good coverage; flippant tone
Design, Ease Of Use	★★	No distinguishing design elements; better layouts and graphics would help

Description:

The "About Divorce Central" page states: "The Divorce Central team has developed this service to offer help, support, and some guidance from experts, and to give you the opportunity to communicate with others. . . ." The primary focus of the site is found in features which support communication between adults wrestling with their divorce and its aftermath. Bulletin boards (threaded email) are focused on the subjects of Lifeline, Finance, Legal, and Parenting, with the usual assortment of "serial conversations." FAQs (frequently asked questions) for the same topics are offered; questions number in the dozens, and short answers are provided by various experts. Also included on the site are a "Legal Center" and a number (roughly 20) of annotated links to other websites, organized by topic. A particularly unique section is titled "Divorce Experts Online;" this link takes you to transcripts of online interviews with experts on a variety of topics (mediation, singles services, etc.). The site also includes a bookstore (hosted by Booksite.Com) which offers a collection of books on divorce; a separate section makes book recommendations within several categories. Finally, they offer a "Personals" listing for those who want to try again.

Evaluation:

While we appreciate any effort to help adults experiencing the trauma of divorce, this website is, on balance, pretty lightweight. Maybe that's the intent of its authors and editors, but we'd argue that this serious a topic deserves a consistently mature treatment. While there are aspects of this site that are truly useful—the bulletin board discussion threads, the online interview transcripts, and the FAQs—much of the rest of the site seems conflicted in tone, at times inappropriately flippant. The site's limited recommendations for books seem both incomplete and inconsistent to us (they recommend Ivana Trump's book; we think it's a waste of money). We don't particularly applaud an essay in the legal section titled "20 Winning Strategies For Coming Out Ahead," nor do we think a link to a web page called "Bob Dole's Divorce" is particularly enlightening. All this, and personal ads too (". . . I'm looking for a single woman, in excellent shape . . .")! For those adults who are looking for understanding and healing , perhaps other websites and print resources would better match their seriousness of purpose.

Where To Find/Buy:

On the Internet, at the URL: http://www.divorcecentral.com.

DIVORCE SOURCE

★★

Media Type:
Internet

Principal Subject:
All-Inclusive

Written For:
Adults

Publisher:
Divorce Source, Inc.

Internet URL:
http://
www.divorcesource.com

**"Christian"
Orientation?:**
N/A

Focused On Issues For:
N/A

1-4 Stars

Overall Rating	★★	An advertiser-supported database of divorce services, by state
Design, Ease Of Use	★★★	Good graphic and navigation design; ad banners intrude a bit

Description:

This is a relatively new (Feb '97), but very ambitious website focused on divorce, with a strong emphasis on providing advertiser-supported, state-by-state listings of information and professional service providers. You can select your state, then your county, then a variety of articles of state-specific information and resources, and/or lists of service providers (attorneys, counselors, mediators, financial consultants, appraisers, etc.). A variety of short articles (including answers to frequently asked questions) are provided, organized by topic. A "Publications" section is similarly organized, with a simple listing of titles (with contact/ordering information). The "Family Law Links" consists of a wide variety of links, organized by topic (from saving your marriage to child abduction); some links are to on-site books and articles, some take you off-site. Chat rooms (currently limited to scheduled times) are provided as well, as are a variety of Bulletin Boards (threaded email messages, organized by topic). A bibliography of divorce terms is provided, too.

Evaluation:

This is an interesting site, founded by a 25-year old with a BA degree, graphic design training, and a strong business sense (they "own"—for banner advertising purposes—the search term "divorce" on Yahoo, for example). The site facilitates state-by-state listings (advertisements) by individuals and companies interested in providing services to adults facing divorce. We've looked at their pricing (tiered by county/state and options) and think their costs are quite reasonable and should eventually result in a comprehensive offering of services. Many of the site's reference articles are written by the site's advertisers, who may or may not be qualified to provide advice and counsel. The site's publications index is simply a title/author listing by subject (with an order form for some); no information on content is provided. We found the "Family Law Links" one of the more comprehensive collection of links on the subject of divorce. Our overall impression: since much of the information and referrals on this site are provided by advertisers, they should be used with a strong "buyers beware" attitude. But, visit the site to see for yourself.

Where To Find/Buy:

On the Internet, at the URL: http://www.divorcesource.com. You can also call them direct at 610-820-8120, or email them at divorce@divorcesource.com.

DIVORCE-WITHOUT-WAR

★★

Media Type:

Internet

Principal Subject:

Mediation

Written For:

Adults

Author/Editor:

Gerald S. Deutsch

About The Author:

(From Cover Notes)

Mr. Deutsch "has been a practicing member of the Florida Bar for 37 years and a Florida Supreme Court certified family mediator. He appears frequently on radio and television to discuss divorce mediations and the need for legislative reform."

Publisher:

Divorce Mediation Services, Inc.

Internet URL:

http://www.divorce-without-war.com

"Christian" Orientation?:

N/A

Focused On Issues For:

N/A

	1-4 Stars	
Overall Rating	★★	A site focused on those interested in mediation; unfortunately, many database gaps
Design, Ease Of Use	★★★	A clean design

Description:

This is a website focused solely on mediation as the best option for divorcing couples, and is maintained by a Mediation Services firm located in Ft. Lauderdale, Florida. Principal features of the site include a short essays on "Facing Divorce" (a discussion of problems leading to divorce and the practice of "No-Fault" divorce), and "Avoiding The War" (condemning the adversarial divorce process and explaining the option of mediation). Search engines are provided for searching their database of mediators (by City, State, ZIP), and State statutes. The section of "Links To Relevant Sites" was under construction when we visited. A "Professional Corner" contains links that allow mediators to "subscribe" (advertise), offers logos to use in promoting their site in mediator's ads, discusses the benefits of pre-suit mediation, and provides an events schedule for mediators.

Evaluation:

In addition to the link-page being under construction, the principal disappointment of this site is the paucity of information contained in its searchable databases. It appears that the database contains only mediators who have paid a "subscription;" this means (as is does in most cases where websites are trying to support themselves with advertisers) that very few mediators are listed (only ONE mediator in Chicago?), and no clues are provided on how well qualified the listed mediator might be. Also disappointing is the fact that most links to "State Statutes" is just a link to the state's legislative page, with no apparent clue on how to find applicable state laws; other divorce-oriented sites provide this service much better. The site generally has a flavor that tilts toward the commercialization of the site (mediator listings and advertising), not towards divorcing adults seeking help learning about and finding mediators; until they correct this and provide more complete databases, we can't recommend the site.

Where To Find/Buy:

On the Internet, at the URL: http://www.divorce-without-war.com.

Commercial Online Service Resources

DIVORCE & SEPARATION COMMUNITY (AMERICA ONLINE)

★★

Media Type:
Online Service

Principal Subject:
All-Inclusive

Written For:
Adults

Publisher:
Health ResponseAbility
Systems

Internet URL:
AOL Keyword: "Better
Health" ("PEN" for broader
health topics)

**"Christian"
Orientation?:**
N/A

Focused On Issues For:
N/A

1-4 Stars

Overall Rating	★★	A very small component of a large online community; little depth available
Design, Ease Of Use	★★	The AOL interface is awkward and non-intuitive at times

Description:
Health ResponseAbility Systems has developed and published many medical-related information databases and communities on America Online. Using the keyword "PEN" takes you to their main site, which then branches into a huge variety of medical and health-related topics. One branch, which uses the keyword "Better Health," brings you to a "Relationships" community, with a "Divorce & Separation Forum" one among a dozen choices. Within this forum, books on divorce are offered for sale, along with message boards and chat rooms to facilitate online interaction and sharing of concerns and ideas among those visiting the site. A number of website links are also provided.

Evaluation:
The network of health-related communities supported by this publisher on AOL is huge, and provides a broad variety of helpful information and facilities to contact others with common interests. However, its offerings focused solely on divorce are pretty slim, particularly when compared to divorce-oriented sites on the Internet. The bookstore's titles on the topics of divorce are limited (30 when we visited), and only very brief descriptions are provided. Message boards (threaded email) include a broad variety of topics, with a just a few focused specifically on divorce issues. Chat room choices do NOT include any focused on divorce (when we visited), a major disappointment (the most-valued aspect of AOL's services have been its chat rooms). Only a few of the divorce websites we've reviewed are linked from their site. A much higher level of investment will be required before this AOL community provides much value to divorcing adults.

Where To Find/Buy:
On America Online, using the Keyword "Better Health".

CHILDREN IN THE MIDDLE

★★★

Media Type:
Videotape

Price:
$358.00

Principal Subject:
Children Of Divorce

Written For:
Adults

Author/Editor:
Jack Arbuthnot, Ph.D.;
Donald A. Gordon, Ph.D.

About The Author:
(From Cover Notes)

Jack Arbuthnot, Ph.D. is a
Professor of Psychology at
Ohio University, with a
focus on the effects of
divorce upon children.
Donald Gordon, Ph.D. is
a Professor of Psychology
at Ohio University. He
conducts research on
factors that help children
adapt to divorce.

Publisher:
The Center for Divorce
Education

Internet URL:
N/A

**"Christian"
Orientation?:**
N/A

Focused On Issues For:
N/A

1-4 Stars		
Overall Rating	★★★	One of the few video resources available
Design, Ease Of Use	★★	Amateur acting hinders credibility

Description:

This video program, in its second edition, consists of two videos, a Parents' version (37 minutes) and a Children's version (30 minutes). The Parents' video features realistic scenes portrayed by actual families of divorce, a presentation of issues, clinical advice from a husband/wife team, and cued discussion points for use in group interaction. Its intent is to teach skills needed to avoid putting children in the middle of their parents' conflicts. The Children's version presents information that children of divorced parents need to understand: replacing common myths about divorce with truths, helping clarify and normalize children's feelings and reactions to divorce, helping them to get out of the middle of parents' conflicts, teaching them to change their thoughts, and encouraging them to get on with their lives. Clearly its intent is to help them understand and deal with their reactions to divorce. Workbook and discussion guides for both videos are available for children, parents and teachers.

Evaluation:

If a picture is worth a thousand words, then a moving picture is worth even more. In groups comprised of children or parents, this resource can be quite helpful. Conflictual parents can catch children in the middle in so many ways, with devastating results. Research has shown that two-thirds of children from families of divorce suffer enduring problems, ranging form low self-esteem to severe depression. Thus, this visual tool can be an effective catalyst for reflection and group discussions by parents and children. The accompanying discussion workbooks for parents and for children appear to be well thought out and helpful. Two weaknesses, however, are present in the videos. First, the visual content is often presented too succinctly, with a cue for discussion then immediately presented without sufficient time to assimilate the information before they are asked to discuss it. Second, the actors in the videos are actual members of divorced families. While this is intended to give credibility to the videos, the producers of these videos must remember that they are competing with seasoned actors from the TV and cinema world; this obviously amateur acting might be a turnoff.

Where To Find/Buy:

Direct from the Publisher, by calling 614-593-1065 or 614-593-1074.

Audiotape Resources

ADULT CHILD OF DIVORCE
A Recovery Handbook

★★

Media Type:
Audiotape

Price:
$12.99

Principal Subject:
Life After Divorce

Written For:
Adults

ISBN:
0840799861

Author/Editor:
Bob Burns and
Michael J. Brissett, Jr., Ph.D.

Edition Reviewed:
1992

About The Author:
(From Cover Notes)
Bob Burns is the author
of *Through the Whirlwind*, a
book on divorce recovery,
and the founder of Fresh
Start Seminars for people
undergoing divorce.
Michael J. Brissett, Jr. has
twenty years' experience
as a clinical psychologist.

Publisher:
Thomas Nelson Publishers

Internet URL:
N/A

**"Christian"
Orientation?:**
Yes

Focused On Issues For:
N/A

1-4 Stars

Overall Rating	★★	An overly broad treatment of an often neglected subject
Design, Ease Of Use	★★	At times difficult to listen to due to monotony of reading tone & presentation

Description:
Devoted to a Christian based interpretation of the issues, these two cassettes comprise "a recovery handbook" for adult children of divorce. Through these tapes you'll learn, in the authors' words, "how your life has been impacted by divorce, how emotional healing can take place, and how forgiveness plays a part in the recovery process." Tape 1 opens with a general discussion of the characteristics of functional and dysfunctional families, and the unique issues that adult children of divorce must face because of their past history with divorce. Noting that these adults often become "stuck" on early issues that they seem unable to move beyond, the discussion shifts to "survival methods" they learned to employ as children, and how these become incompatible with healthy adult life. A section on "handling old baggage" follows, which talks about various unhealthy coping patterns. "Defusing the time bomb," or learning how to deal with past traumas and take responsibility for your present and future, comes next. Tape 2 includes a discussion of "the process of forgiveness" in which adult children learn to reconcile broken family relationships, make positive changes for self-growth, and break old cycles of dysfunction through healthy interaction with others.

Evaluation:
These tapes confront some important issues in an oft-neglected subject: how adult children of divorce can learn to deal with their past history in order to set up healthier, happier modes of being for themselves and for their own children. The information presented here serves as an adequate introduction to the subject, but treatment of the issues is rather broad and diffuse, making it difficult to figure out how it all actually translates into everyday life. Another potential drawback to this resource is the manner in which the information is presented: the voice reading here is somewhat monotonous, making listening a chore. Additionally, an inside sleeve listing the topics and the order in which they will be presented would have helped pre-organize listeners to the material, and aided in giving a sense of coherence to the whole. Although the most of the discussion on these tapes is straightforward, most people would be better served using a more in-depth resource on this subject.

Where To Find/Buy:
Bookstores and libraries.

INDEXES

VI

TITLE INDEX

AUTHOR INDEX

PUBLISHER INDEX

SUBJECT INDEXES

APPENDICES

VII

RESOURCE PATHWAYS, INC.

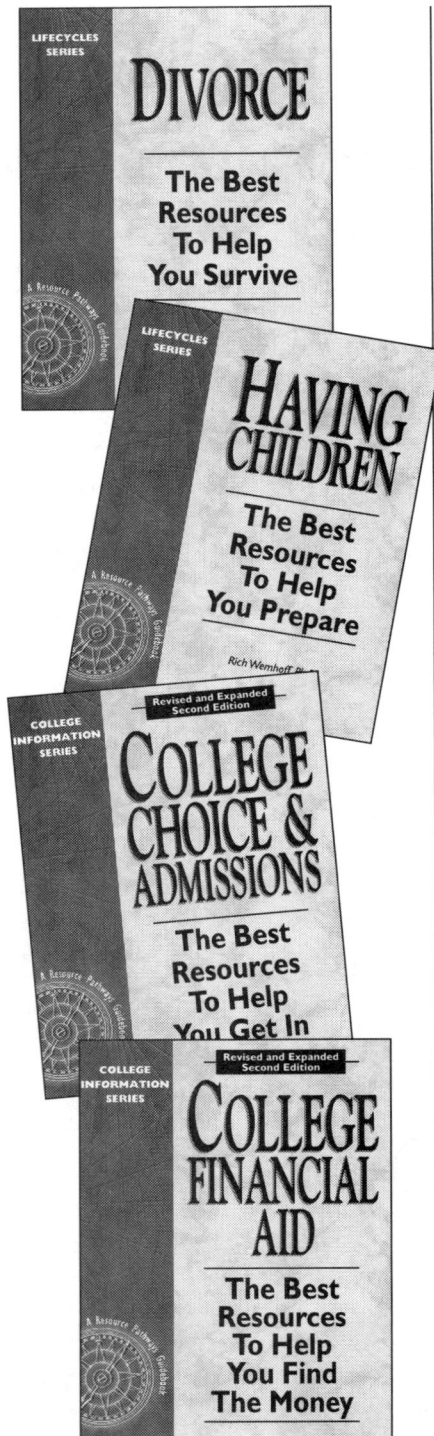

For every important issue we face in our lives, there are resources that offer suggestions and help available to us. Unfortunately, we don't always know where to find these sources of information. Often, we don't know very much about their quality, value, or relevance. In addition, we often don't know much about the issue we've encountered, and as a result don't really know where to begin our learning process.

Resource Pathways guidebooks help those doing research on important decisions or facing a challenging life-event by helping them find the information they need to understand the issues they face and make necessary decisions with confidence. Every guidebook we publish includes these important values:

- We review and rate **virtually all quality resources** available in any media (print, the Internet, CD-ROMs, software, and more).

- We define and **explain the different issues** that are typically encountered in dealing with each subject, and **classify each resource** we review according to its primary focus.

- We make a reasoned judgment about the quality of each resource, give it a **rating**, and decide whether or not a resource should be **recommended**. We select only the best as "Recommended" (roughly 1 in 4).

- We provide information on **where to buy or how to access** each resource, including ISBN numbers for print media and URL "addresses" for Internet websites.

- We publish a **new edition of each guidebook annually**, with updated reviews and recommendations.

Those who turn to Resource Pathways guidebooks will be able to locate the resource they need, saving time, money, and frustration as they research decisions and events having an important impact on their lives.

Mike Osborn, President
Resource Pathways, Inc.
mosborn@sourcepath.com

HOW TO SEND YOUR SUGGESTIONS TO RESOURCE PATHWAYS

We want to hear from you! Your feedback is an important factor in improving the quality of our existing guidebooks, and helps us create new products to meet your needs!

So, please tear out (or copy) the form below and fill it out with your comments and suggestions. Fax it to us at the number below or mail it to us by folding and using the self-mailing information on the reverse side.

My feedback or suggestion is:

_____

_____

_____

_____

_____

_____

_____

_____

Fax us at: (206) 727-6771

Mail this form to us at this address:
   Resource Pathways, Inc.
   22525 S.E. 64th Place, Suite 253
   Issaquah, WA 98027

You can also send us email at:
   info@sourcepath.com

Thanks, in advance, from Resource Pathways!

PLACE

STAMP

HERE

Resource Pathways, Inc.

22525 SE 64th Place, Suite 253

Issaquah, WA 98027

ORDER FORM

Order by phone: (800) 247-6553

Order by fax: (419) 281-6883

Order by mail: **Complete order form and mail to:**
Bookmasters, PO Box 388 (Dept. D), Ashland, OH 44805

Please send me:

Divorce: The Best Resources To Help You Survive _____ copies at $24.95 = _____
(ISBN 0-9653424-2-5)

Having Children: The Best Resources To Help You Prepare _____ copies at $24.95 = _____
(ISBN 0-9653424-3-3)

College Choice & Admissions: The Best Resources To Help You Get In _____ copies at $24.95 = _____
(ISBN 0-9653424-4-1)

College Financial Aid: The Best Resources To Help You Find The Money _____ copies at $24.95 = _____
(ISBN 0-9653424-5-X)

Shipping = $4.00

Total = _____

Payment enclosed ☐ Check (Make payable to Resource Pathways)
Charge my credit card ☐ Visa ☐ MasterCard ☐ AMEX

Account Number _____ Exp Date _____

Signature _____

Name (please print) _____

Organization _____ Title _____

Address _____

City _____ State _____ Zip _____

☞ We now offer Subscription Programs for libraries and professionals!

Call 1-800-247-6553 to join and each year receive a new updated edition of *Divorce: The Best Resources to Help You Survive*. Members receive a special discount on all new editions, a free quarterly newsletter, and other exciting benefits.

☐ Check here to receive more information on the benefits of our Subscription Program for **Libraries**.

☐ Check here to receive more information on the benefits of our Subscription Program for **Professionals**.

Please be sure to include your name, organization and address above.

PLACE

STAMP

HERE

Resource Pathways, Inc.

c/o Bookmasters

P.O. Box 388 (Dept. D)

Ashland, OH 44805

ABOUT THE EDITOR

Rich Wemhoff, Ph.D. is a clinical psychologist, licensed to practice in the State of Washington. He is a member of the Washington State Psychological Association as well as the American Psychological Association. He is past director of the M.A. Psychology Program, Antioch University, Seattle and has been an adjunct member of the faculties at the University of Idaho, Seattle University and Chapman College. His career in counseling (25+years) has been situated in the secondary, university and private practice setting. In 1986 he founded and has since directed Emmaus Counseling Center, Redmond, Washington, providing individual, couple, and family therapy. His special interest and that of the Center is helping individuals and families move through the various stages of the life cycle successfully.